Bilingual Education

 A Reference Handbook

Other Titles in
ABC-CLIO's
CONTEMPORARY EDUCATION ISSUES
Series

African American Education, Cynthia L. Jackson
Charter Schools, Danny Weil
School Vouchers and Privatization, Danny Weil
Special Education, Arlene Sacks
Student Rights, Patricia H. Hinchey
Migrant Education, Judith A. Gouwens

FORTHCOMING

Educational Leadership, Pat Williams-Boyd

CONTEMPORARY EDUCATION ISSUES

Bilingual Education

A REFERENCE HANDBOOK

Rosa Castro Feinberg

A B C CLIO

Santa Barbara, California • Denver, Colorado • Oxford, England

© 2002 by Rosa Castro Feinberg

Library of Congress Cataloging-in-Publication Data
Feinberg, Rosa Castro.
  Bilingual education : a reference handbook / Rosa Castro Feinberg.
    p. cm. — (Contemporary education issues)
  Includes bibliographical references and index.
  ISBN 1-57607-125-1 (alk. paper)
  1. Education, Bilingual—United States—Handbooks, manuals, etc. 2. Education and state—United States—Handbooks, manuals, etc. I. Title.
II. Series.
LC3731.F45 2002
370.11'75'0973—dc21

                                      2001008424

This book is also available on the World Wide Web as an e-book.
Visit www.abc-clio.com for details.

07 06 05 04 03 02 01   10 9 8 7 6 5 4 3 2 1

ABC-CLIO, Inc.
130 Cremona Drive, P.O. Box 1911
Santa Barbara, California 93116-1911

This book is printed on acid-free paper ∞.
Manufactured in the United States of America

*This book is dedicated to Diana Castro
and Lincoln Jones, and to others who joined us
where only loved ones may enter.*

⦿ Contents

❧ Series Editor's Preface

The Contemporary Education Issues series is dedicated to providing readers with an up-to-date exploration of the central issues in education today. Books in the series will examine such controversial topics as home schooling, charter schools, privatization of public schools, Native American education, African American education, literacy, curriculum development, and many others. The series is national in scope and is intended to encourage research by anyone interested in the field.

Because education is undergoing radical if not revolutionary change, the series is particularly concerned with how contemporary controversies in education affect both the organization of schools and the content and delivery of curriculum. Authors will endeavor to provide a balanced understanding of the issues and their effects on teachers, students, parents, administrators, and policymakers. The aim of the Contemporary Education Issues series is to publish excellent research on today's educational concerns by some of the finest scholar/practitioners in the field while pointing to new directions. The series promises to offer important analyses of some of the most controversial issues facing society today.

Danny Weil
Series Editor

❧ Preface and Acknowledgments

This text is intended as an introduction to bilingual education. It describes the evolution of bilingual education in the United States with an emphasis on its relationship to educational and civil rights reform. Federal, state, and district policies affecting the implementation of bilingual programs are identified, along with related legal, political, demographic, and economic factors and controversies. International comparisons of bilingual education programs illustrate additional types of language education and policies that incorporate diverse groups into mainstream society.

In Chapter 1, curricular components for immigrant, language minority, and language majority students are identified. A chronology of events in Chapter 2 provides the historical context for current issues. Descriptions of district and state educational systems and curricula (Chapters 3 and 4) contribute to an understanding of contemporary programs in second- and foreign-language education, heritage-language education, and bilingual education. A summary of federal law and legislation related to bilingual education is presented in Chapter 5.

Chapter 6 summarizes recurring political issues in debates on immigration, language rights, and language legislation, and identifies related research findings. Media coverage of these issues is reviewed as a factor affecting the formation of public opinion about language matters and contributing to the myths about bilingual education. School finance and district governance considerations that affect the selection of bilingual education components are also outlined in this chapter.

Several resources are incorporated into the text to help the reader reach conclusions about the matters in dispute. Chapter 7 is a directory of organizations associated with bilingual education, immigration, and language minority groups; Chapters 8 and 9 include annotated bibliographies of print and nonprint resources. To aid further research, whenever possible, resources accessible online have been identified in these chapters.

I acknowledge with appreciation the valuable information and insights on drafts of this work provided by J. E. Alatis, J. M. Aybar,

M. Bert, B. Cypress, E. Dwyer, J. A. Fleming, M. Escotet, R. V. Farrell, M. Fernández-Zayas, D. García, P. Hansen, D. Hasson, L. H. Jones, P. Killian, J. Kwok, J. R. Llanes, W. Lyshkov, T. L. Moore, K. Oshima, L. Okalik, M. Pederson, Q. A. Cao, R. R. Prust, R. L. Rice, S. H. Rothfarb, P. Roos, C. A. Ryan, T. J. Summers, N. Willows, and N. Zelasko.

Chapter One

⬦ Introduction: What Is Bilingual Education?

Bilingual education in the United States is the use of English and another language for instructional purposes. Although instruction in more than one language has been part of the education of the elite since at least the times of classical Greek civilization (and is part of the curriculum for all students in many parts of the world), in the United States, the term *bilingual education* is often used to refer to programs designed for language minority students. According to Krashen (1996), this variety of bilingual education should include instruction in and through English (i.e., instruction designed to teach English and instruction delivered in English designed to teach other subjects), literacy instruction in the home and second languages of the students, and instruction in content areas provided through the home language. In popular use, *bilingual education* has become an umbrella term applied to various forms of language instruction that may include diverse combinations of components, first- or second-language use, models, subjects, and goals, and is imprecisely applied even to programs that may be monolingual. This extension of the meaning of the term *bilingual education* mirrors the ways in which the basic idea of education through two languages has been adapted to meet the requirements of each school community.

VARIABLES

These conditions may vary to reflect the historic, demographic, economic, and political factors unique to each locality. Within the framework established by those factors, the precise configuration of bilingual education components included in any given program varies along certain dimensions. Examples of those variables include student, language, and teacher characteristics; reform and accountability attributes; governance and community participation features; and logistics. Each of these dimensions may be defined by its characteristics.

Student Characteristics:

- ⟶ The ages and grades of participating students
- ⟶ The native language of the participating students and the extent of similarity or difference between the home and target language
- ⟶ The extent to which participating students speak third languages
- ⟶ The extent to which each language group (including students whose native tongue is English) in the school is represented in the program
- ⟶ The extent to which all children in the community are eligible to participate
- ⟶ The amount of time in the school day that language minority and majority students are together in the same instructional setting
- ⟶ The prior schooling and literacy levels of the students and their parents
- ⟶ The extent to which language learners' attitudes toward school are influenced by the norms of their peer group
- ⟶ The achievement and high school completion status of the language minority group
- ⟶ The national origin, race, and ethnicity of the participating language groups
- ⟶ The social and economic status of the participating language groups
- ⟶ The extent to which the families of participating students are recent immigrants
- ⟶ The extent to which participating students are refugees from political and other traumatic situations
- ⟶ The extent of mobility among the program participants
- ⟶ The extent to which the ethnic communities of the participating students are long-term residents of the country and locality
- ⟶ The official government categorization of immigrant groups that include participating students
- ⟶ The treatment by the receiving community accorded to immigrant groups that include participating students
- ⟶ The number and severity of risk factors affecting the participating students

Language Characteristics:

- ⟶ The extent of similarity or difference between the academic version of the target language and the variety of that language used in the students' neighborhoods

↝ The language of initial literacy instruction

↝ The literacy traditions of the participating language groups

↝ The extent to which the students have opportunities to communicate with native speakers of the target language in and out of school settings

↝ The extent to which participating students come from linguistically isolated households

↝ The extent to which bilingual role models are present in the language learners' school and community environments

↝ The extent to which the target languages are used by the local media and supported in other community institutions

↝ The extent to which bilingualism is an asset in the local economy

Teacher Characteristics:

↝ The availability of appropriately trained and credentialed teachers

↝ The availability of teachers with schooled levels of competence in the program languages

↝ The subject areas in which bilingual teachers hold teaching credentials

↝ The extent to which teachers have access to instructional materials in program languages

↝ The extent to which the faculty is familiar with the language and culture of the students participating in the program

↝ The extent to which native speakers of the language are represented in the program's faculty

Characteristics of Reform and Accountability:

↝ The extent to which the schools participate in school reform efforts

↝ The degree of influence teachers and parents of students in bilingual programs have on the school's reform planning process

↝ The languages in which student evaluations are conducted and reported

↝ The availability of standardized tests, testing accommodations for English-language learners, and state assessments in the target languages

↝ The schools' standing on public accountability measures

Governance and Community Participation Features:

↝ The extent of community dissension related to language or immigration issues

→ The adequacy of resources allocated to the program

→ The type or source of authority for appointed or elected district policymakers (public, charter, private, religious)

→ The extent to which the parents of participating children are involved in the election of board members

→ The extent to which parents are actively involved with the program

→ The extent to which community-based organizations are involved with the program

→ The extent of support for biliteracy goals provided by the business sector

→ The extent of support for biliteracy goals provided by the state's constitution or legislation

→ The overall purposes of schooling served by the program (academic, social, economic, political)

→ The extent to which school districts' policies and procedures support the acculturation and cultural pluralism goals of additive bilingualism, or the assimilation goals of replacement of English for the home language and culture

Logistical Arrangements:

→ The amount of time in the school day devoted to each language and to literacy instruction in each language for each language group

→ The number of years of program duration

→ The grade placement of the program

→ The extent to which a sequence of program courses throughout the levels of the pre-K–12 grade span and beyond is offered

→ The extent to which all students in the school participate in the program

→ The prestige associated with the physical location of the program

→ The availability of instructional material and equipment

→ The extent to which school and public library collections include books and periodicals in languages other than English

→ The allocation of language of instruction to various subject areas

Intergroup Relations and Cross-Cultural Communications:

→ The extent to which cross-cultural communication and intergroup relations goals are part of the program

→ The extent to which goals related to instruction in the history

and traditions associated with the participating language groups are part of the program
➥ The extent to which self-concept development goals are part of the program

The term *local conditions* means a set of interrelated factors and dimensions, such as those listed above, that form the unique background of circumstances for bilingual programs. Pedagogical decisions regarding curriculum and instruction are made within the context of these mutually interacting circumstances.

With so many variables to consider, it is no easier to describe bilingual education than it would be to portray monolingual education. The task is complicated by the assumptions held by observers of a specific bilingual program (and widely shared, in the case of media reports) that its characteristics are common to all varieties of that program. To understand the field, an awareness of its fundamental elements is helpful. Any or all major program components and characteristics may be part of the curriculum at grades pre-K through 12, at adult education levels, or at the college level. Additional information on program availability and participation levels is presented in Chapter 4.

Components of Bilingual Education Programs

Bilingual education programs may be designed to serve national origin minority students or language majority students, or those programs may be combined to serve the first- and second-language development needs of both sets of students simultaneously. For language majority students in the United States, the home language is English, and the target language is one other than English. For language minority students, the home language is the native, first-acquired language, and the target language is English. The major building blocks of programs for both sets of students include instruction designed to teach the target language; instruction in various subjects that uses the target or the home language, or both languages, as the media of instruction; and opportunities for the continued development of home-language skills.

Language Minority Students

Students whose home languages are not English are national origin minority students whether they are immigrant or native born. Of this group, a student who has not learned English is referred to as an English-language learner (ELL), a linguistically and culturally diverse learner

(LCDL), or a limited English proficient (LEP) student. Programs for these students include instruction in the English language, often through courses in English as a Second Language (ESL), also known as English for Speakers of Other Languages (ESOL) or as English Language Development (ELD). The National Board for Professional Teaching Standards (NBPTS) refers to the field as English as a New Language (ENL).

ENGLISH-LANGUAGE INSTRUCTION

An ESL course, like a foreign-language course, provides instruction in a language that is foreign to students: English. The goal of an ESL course is to help students learn English. An ESL program is composed of an articulated set of ESL courses, each concentrating on different aspects of second-language learning. The curriculum may be organized, for example, according to levels of language acquisition (beginners, intermediate, advanced), the skills involved in language acquisition (listening, speaking, reading, writing), or the anticipated use of the second language (English for Academic Purposes, English for Vocational Purposes). Learning materials and experiences may be organized around the structure of the language, or grammar; the functions of language (such as obtaining information or offering an apology); or the situations in which language will be used (such as shopping or registering for school). School is one of the most meaningful situations in the lives of schoolchildren. One approach to teaching language, therefore, is to provide comprehensible instruction in the content areas of the school curriculum, thereby teaching the target language indirectly; still, the goal of content-based language learning is primarily to master a language.

Some states establish one set of guidelines for instruction in English-language arts that encompass those of the ESL curriculum. Other states establish separate content standards in ESL to reflect differences in objectives, timelines, methods, materials, and teacher preparation requirements for the two distinct subject areas. In either case, ESL course objectives correlate with those of the English-language arts program and lead to accomplishing the English-language arts standards set by the district or state. Student groups from different language backgrounds may be scheduled into the same ESL class because instruction is presented in English. In most districts, the ESL teacher may be a monolingual English speaker.

ACADEMIC LANGUAGE

Many ESL programs consider helping students to use English for academic purposes a second major goal. Using a second language as a tool for learning in all the subject areas requires students to command a far more complicated set of skills than is required for social communication, survival purposes, or playground English. Consider the degree of difficulty you might have in expressing "Good morning," "I need a doctor," "I'm hungry," or "Give me the ball" in a language foreign to you. These simple expressions about concrete situations are fairly easily mastered, but are just the beginning. Compare that with the greater difficulty you would face if you were required to understand and apply in that foreign language the Pythagorean theorem (i.e., the square of the hypotenuse of a right triangle is equal to the sum of the squares of the other two sides). Yet that is exactly what English-language learners in the elementary and middle school years are expected to do. The curriculum standards published by the National Council of Teachers of Math (NCTM) state that in grades 6 through 8, all students should create and critique inductive and deductive arguments concerning geometric ideas and relationships such as congruence, similarity, and the Pythagorean relationship. To be successful in school, then, students must be able to work with abstract concepts. The language used under these conditions is known as "academic language." See the NCTM site for additional information on the recommended grade placement of mathematics standards at http://standards.nctm.org/document/chapter6/geom.htm#TOP.

The complexity of academic language is also easily appreciated in relation to the secondary-level English-language arts curriculum, which traditionally includes the study of Shakespeare's *Julius Caesar, Macbeth,* or *Romeo and Juliet.* ThinkQuest is a global network of students, teachers, parents, and technologists dedicated to exploring youth-centered learning on the Internet. The following questions, taken from the "Shakespeare with Will" section of ThinkQuest's Web site at http://library.thinkquest.org/19539/works.htm, http://library.thinkquest.org/19539/macbeth.htm#qng, and http://library.thinkquest.org/19539/randj.htm), give examples of the knowledge students are expected to gain and be able to express in writing after reading those classics:

- Explain the line "Fair is foul, and foul is fair" that the witches chant. What role does this statement play in *Macbeth?*
- What role is played by fate and by the characters' choices in *Romeo and Juliet?*

➥ Choose one of *Macbeth's* soliloquies and discuss and explain the moral condition of Macbeth at the time.

To answer these questions, English-language learners must have acquired a high level of academic reading and writing skills, as well as a specialized vocabulary, such as *wherefore* (meaning "why"), *soft* (meaning "wait"), *enow* (meaning "enough"), and *rubs* (meaning "imperfections"). Visit the ThinkQuest site for additional information about topics treated at various grade levels and subject areas: http://www.thinkquest. org/library/. Courses for English-language learners focus on academic English because students must meet such grade-level expectations as those summarized above to be promoted from grade to grade and to graduate from high school.

HOME-LANGUAGE ARTS

When bilingual teachers and materials in students' home languages are available, courses in home-language arts (also referred to as heritage-language courses) may be offered in districts having enough English-language learners from the same language background to justify allocating a teacher. The goals of instruction parallel those in the English-language arts curriculum. For English-language learners, the transfer of concepts learned in the home-language arts class supports and promotes instruction in the ESL class, as is the case with initial literacy instruction in the home language. For students who are already proficient in English, the two-language arts courses are mutually reinforcing; they help students reach the biliteracy goals that are being established by district policy in an increasing number of districts. Home-language arts courses may be listed as foreign language or heritage-language offerings at both school district and postsecondary levels. For additional information on how district policies affect bilingual education, see Chapter 3.

ADULT SECOND-LANGUAGE LEARNING

English as a Foreign Language (EFL) is the name often assigned to courses for students who are learning English in countries where it is not a national language. International students attending colleges and universities in the United States who are English-language learners are typically enrolled in intensive English programs. Graduates from high schools in the United States who are English-language learners (as may be the case with students who established residence in this country late in their school careers) are sometimes placed in college basic skills programs rather than in ESL programs. For additional information on college-level ESL, see the position statement of the California Association for Teachers of English to Speakers of Other Languages (CATESOL) on the differences between ESL and basic skills instruction, available at http://www.catesol.org/eslbs.html.

Before World War II, ESL classes were rare; most were part of Americanization programs for adult immigrants, or were used to teach English to foreign diplomats and university students. Today, foreign or native-born English-language learners who are out-of-school adults aged sixteen or older may enroll in adult ESL courses when they are available. Adult ESL students, often the parents of school-aged children, have succeeded in overcoming multiple obstacles (such as access, conflicts with work schedules, cost, transportation, and need for child care) to attend ESL programs. Volunteer organizations, public school systems, and community colleges provide these programs. However, according to a national evaluation of federally supported adult education programs, the capacity of the adult education ESL service delivery system is exceeded by the demand (Fitzgerald 1995). This conclusion is supported by data collected by the National Center for ESL Literacy Education (NCLE 1997). Their compilation includes reports about how many people are waiting for space in ESL programs, including: 4,000 in San Jose, California; 500 in Fairfax, Virginia; and 15,000 in Massachusetts.

The waiting time in 1997 for placement in an adult ESL class in Massachusetts was up to three years. In Pennsylvania, the wait was from three to twelve months; in the state of Washington, from six months to a year. The National Center for Education Statistics (NCES) reports that, for various reasons, nearly 3 million adults were unable to participate in ESL classes across the nation in 1995 (NCLE 2000).

Estimates of the time it takes for an adult to learn English vary with contextual, curricular, and linguistic factors, and with the personal characteristics of the learners. The estimate available from NCLE is illustrative:

> Research done for the Mainstream English Language Training (MELT) project (1985) indicates that it would take from 500–1,000 hours of instruction for an adult who is literate in her native language, but has had no prior English instruction, to reach a level where she can satisfy her basic needs, survive on the job, and have limited social interaction in English. (NCLE 2000, online)

According to this estimate, if the adult ESL learner had access to instruction for five hours a week for a fifty-week school year, it could take four years of study to reach the specified level of survival and limited social language proficiency in English.

It takes a long time to reach survival levels of proficiency in other languages also, even under the most favorable conditions. The Defense Language Institute Foreign Language Center (DLIFLC) located at the Presidio in Monterey, California, provides a specialized type of adult language training to the military. The linguistics research undertaken at this site during World War II is credited with prompting the expansion of graduate-level applied linguistics programs and opportunities for training for foreign- and second-language teachers (Kreidler 1987). The DLIFLC featured an enriched staffing ratio of two instructors for each ten-student section. During the peak of U.S. involvement in Vietnam, eight-week military adviser "survival" courses were offered in the Vietnamese language. At the institution's typical schedule of seven hours a day, five days a week in classrooms and language laboratories (with additional time required to complete homework assignments), that survival-level training of 280 hours is equivalent to a one-and-a-half-year public school program delivered for one hour a day, five days a week. Additional information about the DLIFLC is available at the center's Web site at http://pom-www.army.mil/ and in Chapter 2.

ACQUIRING ACADEMIC LANGUAGE: PROGRAM DURATION

Over the past two decades, researchers with professional standing in the field of language education who have studied how long it takes to develop the more complex level of language proficiency needed for academic use have reached the conclusion that for students at the K–12 level, social and survival skills are not sufficient to enable English-language learners to meet required standards in the content areas. The United States General Accounting Office (GAO) estimated that LEP children need from four to eight years to become proficient enough in English to achieve the ability to read or communicate abstract ideas at grade level (GAO 2001). Based on the analysis of two school district data sets from the San Francisco Bay area and two from Canada, Hakuta, Butler, and Witt (2000) reported that it takes from four to seven years to develop the ability to use language that is needed for long-term success in school. The Center for Research on Education, Diversity & Excellence (CREDE), a research center funded by the U.S. Office of Educational Research and Improvement (OERI), also found that the amount of instructional time needed to become sufficiently proficient for academic purposes is from four to seven years (CREDE 1998). Collier's analysis of the test scores of English-language learners led to the conclusion that four to eight years of study are needed (Collier 1987; Thomas and Collier 1997). Cummins's (1981) research with immigrant second-language learners in Canada resulted in the conclusion that it takes from five to seven years or more for these students to reach grade-level norms (Cummins 1981). These findings for English-language learners in North America coincide with the conclusions of a World Bank–sponsored review of research on the use of first and second languages in education. In varied settings throughout the world, researchers determined that the development of academic language requires from four to seven years of instruction (Tucker 1999).

FUNDING FOR PROGRAMS IN BILINGUAL EDUCATION

Funding formulas of government bodies are sometimes congruent with the conclusions from research projects conducted by linguists, psychologists, and educators. Although funding for school programs is a local responsibility, legislative provisions in thirty-six states (NCBE 1999) provide supplements to local funds for bilingual programs for a given period. The duration and amount to be provided are periodically adjusted based on the amount of funding used by the districts or when legislative acts are reauthorized. These judgments are constrained, as are all public-funding decisions, by the prevailing political ideology at the time allocations are determined. See Chapter 6 for additional information about the politics of language.

Massachusetts, for example, the first state to pass a law for bilingual education in the 1970s, specifies in G.L. c. 71A, § 2 that English-language learners in elementary school are entitled to participate in state-funded transitional programs in bilingual education; the law specifies that each program should continue for three years or until students are proficient enough to perform successfully in classes instructed only in English, whichever occurs first. In Texas, elementary school English-language learners leave special programs when they meet state performance standards, according to the provisions of Chapter 89, BB, of the state code. Since the 1990–1991 school year, English-language learners in the state of New York have been entitled to participate in state-funded ESL or bilingual education programs until they score at or above the 40th percentile on an English-language assessment instrument, or up to a maximum of three years, unless this period is extended for an individual pupil by the commissioner. In Florida, three years of funding are provided, with an additional three years of funding available as needed, according to funding formulas adopted in 1990.

The U.S. Department of Education, through its Office for Bilingual Education and Minority Languages Affairs (OBEMLA), administers two five-year grant programs for educational reform related to linguistically diverse students, one three-year grant program for districts adopting new programs, and one two-year grant program for districts expanding or refining existing programs in bilingual education. Additional information about federal grants administered by OBEMLA is available from the agency's Web site at http://www.ed.gov/offices/OBEMLA/comgrant. html. See Chapter 4 for information about state initiatives and Chapter 5 for additional information about federal programs and regulations.

LINGUISTIC ISOLATION AND LOCAL CONDITIONS

How long English-language learners take to learn academic English, and how long programs for LEP students are funded are important considerations; the duration of ESL or bilingual education programs offered by school districts commonly coincides with the availability of state or federal funding for that purpose. The imposition of arbitrary or rigidly uniform time limits on funding can cause the widespread academic failure of LEP students by prematurely transferring them to settings in which all instruction is presented in English.

Although research findings support the conclusion that from four to eight years of instruction are needed for English-language learners to acquire the skills needed for academic English, the conclusion must be interpreted in light of local conditions such as those outlined earlier in this chapter. Important aspects of those conditions include the presence of native or near-native speakers of English in the home and in the community, as well as other out-of-school support for target language acquisition. Although a large co-ethnic community eases the adaptation process and provides invaluable assistance leading to incorporation of immigrants (Hernández and Charney 1998; Stepick 1998), it does not aid the social process of learning English. Without that support, language minority students may take much longer to develop proficiency in English than peers who live in less linguistically isolated settings.

A household with no one fourteen or older who speaks English "exclusively" or "very well" is defined by the Census Bureau as linguistically isolated. In 1990, from 70 to 78 percent of immigrant children lived with one or both parents who did not speak English; and from 30 to 60 percent of immigrant children from the twelve national-origin groups most likely to live in poverty lived in linguistically isolated households (Hernández and Charney 1998). Community-wide linguistic isolation, often associated with areas of concentrated poverty, is not uncommon. According to U.S. Census 2000 data presented in Table 1.1 (Census 2000, April 2, 2001), the listed counties in the United States are among those with a percentage of language minority persons greater than 75 percent and a child poverty percentage greater than 33 percent (see State and County Quick Facts at http://quickfacts.census.gov/qfd/ and Hispanic Percent of Total Population at http://www.census.gov/population/cen2000/phc-t6/tab05.txt for similar information about other locations).

The phenomenon of linguistic isolation is not limited to the border states listed above, or to counties having a high percentage of language minority residents. In Pennsylvania, Philadelphia County has a Hispanic population of only 8.5 percent (Census 2000, April 2, 2001). According to the Philadelphia Public Schools (http://saa.phila.k12.pa.us/tafs/elem_schools.taf), however, Isaac Sheppard Elementary has a Hispanic population of 92.9 percent, William H. Hunter Elementary has a Hispanic population of 80.9 percent, and Potter-Thomas Elementary has a Hispanic population of 80.7 percent. See http://saa.phila.k12.pa.us/tafs/elem_schools.taf.

Although San Diego County, California, is 26.7 percent Hispanic, 82.2 percent of the students at San Diego City School District's Martin Luther King Elementary are Hispanic, and 100 percent qualify for free or reduced-price lunches. See http://www.sandi.net/research/sarcs/sarc267.pdf. The school building is eighty-one years old. Central Elementary School, located in East San Diego, is a fifty-nine-year-old school originally designed to house 350 students. The school's enrollment in September 1999 was 1,200; 72 percent of the students were Hispanic and 10.4 percent were Indochinese. The school has a high student mobility rate; 45 percent of the students were new enrollees. Many students entered with no previous formal education. About 85 percent of Central's students are English-language learners.

Orange County, California, has a Hispanic population of 30.8 percent. The Santa Ana Unified School District (SAUSD), located in Orange County, is thirty-two miles southeast of Los Angeles. According to the district's Fact Sheet, the SAUSD is the fifth largest in the state; 92 percent of its enrollment of over 60,000 students are Latino and 4 percent Asian American. Approximately 70 percent of SAUSD students are English learners, Spanish, Vietnamese, and Khmer being the most common languages spoken at home. In 1999–2000, 73 percent of SAUSD students

Table 1.1

State and County		Percent American Indian	Percent Children below Poverty Level
ARIZONA			
Apache County		76.9	45.4

State and County	City	Hispanic	Percent Children below Poverty Level
ARIZONA			
Santa Cruz		80.8	36.4
NEW MEXICO			
Guadalupe		81.2	37.0
TEXAS			
El Paso	El Paso	78.2	38.6
Cameron	Brownsville Harlingen San Benito	84.3	45.2
Hidalgo	McAllen Edinburg Mission	88.3	47.9
Webb	Laredo	94.3	42.3

Source: U.S. Census 2000, April 2, 2001.

participated in free or reduced-price meal programs. See http://www.sausd.k12.ca.us/schooldistrict/office894479792/department888622769/links981421702/files/fact-sheet.htm.

Los Angeles County, California, is 44.6 percent Hispanic. The Los Angeles Unified School District (LAUSD) demographic profile for the 1999 school year shows that Hispanics constituted 69.9 percent of the district's student population. At LAUSD's Eastman Elementary, enrollment is 99.5 percent Hispanic. At Eastman, of a total of 1,472 students in the 2000–2001 enrollment, 1,076 are English-language learners. Hispanic students make up 85.5 percent of the students at Banning Senior High School, 89.8 percent of the students at Sepulveda Middle School, and 99.3 percent of the students at Garfield Senior High. See http://www.lausd.k12.ca.us/lausd/demographics/5_yr_review.html.

The Hispanic population of Miami-Dade County, Florida, is 57.3 percent. Nevertheless, according to the 1999–2000 District & School Profiles of Miami-Dade County Public Schools, Hispanic students constitute 83 percent of the students enrolled at Amelia Earhart Elementary, 85 percent of the students enrolled at Riverside Elementary, and 95 percent of the students enrolled at Palm Springs Elementary. Several Miami-Dade high schools are also linguistically isolated, including Miami Senior High School (83 percent Hispanic), Miami Coral Park Senior High (89 percent Hispanic), and Hialeah Senior High School (90 percent Hispanic). See http://www.dade.k12.fl.us/edp/profiles/Profiles.asp.

Recap: This examination of areas characterized as linguistically isolated illustrates the following points:

- ➡ Estimates of how long it takes to learn English must be interpreted within the context established by local conditions.
- ➡ In many homes, schools, and communities, conditions of linguistic isolation exist and are likely to increase the time needed by English-language learners for programs in bilingual education.
- ➡ Uniform funding guidelines for programs in bilingual education are not useful because local conditions are not uniform.
- ➡ The imposition of uniform funding guidelines may result in premature program exit for LEP students and lead to their academic failure.

CONTENT-AREA INSTRUCTION

School districts must teach LEP students English and give them access to other content areas in the curriculum. If they approach these dual responsibilities sequentially, teaching first English, then after four to eight years, beginning instruction in other content areas, English-language learners may well be so hopelessly below grade-level expectations that they never catch up. If both English and other content areas are taught simultaneously, in the sense that both sets of learning are presented during the school day to English-language learners from the beginning of their school experience, LEP students may not understand the content-area material presented through the language they have not yet mastered. The two principal solutions to this problem are sheltered English instruction and home language instruction.

SHELTERED INSTRUCTION

Sheltered English (called Specially Designed Academic Instruction in English, or SDAIE, in California) consists of instruction in various subjects; these are taught in English, with the aid of ESL techniques, to student groups composed exclusively of intermediate-level English-language learners. This component shelters English-language-origin students from competition with English-proficient students. Many K–12 ESL programs include sheltered instruction in one or more content areas, such as science, math, and social studies. By providing understandable subject matter instruction, development of academic English and achievement in other subject matter areas is fostered.

Sheltered instruction communicates meaning by presenting concepts in contextually rich environments; for example, with pictures, graphs, charts, maps, and models. Hands-on activities and cooperative learning (in-class projects in which students discuss the content while they work with it) augment the impact of the visual aids on the development of higher-order thinking skills and study strategies. For this component, teachers possessing credentials in the content area to be taught and in the applied linguistics fields of bilingual education and ESL or foreign-language education are needed. Teachers trained both in language and content areas are needed so that both content and language goals may be addressed and students may earn credit toward high school graduation requirements in both English and other content areas. Expertise in both language pedagogy and another content area is also needed so that the language used for instruction and instructional materials can be adapted without diluting the content. This component provides content-area instruction, at grade level, that students who have not yet mastered English can understand and use to promote their English language development.

In some school districts, ESL techniques for content instruction are used in classroom settings that include English-language learners and native speakers of English. In other districts, English-language learners spend a small part of their day in ESL classes; for the majority of their school day they are in the same classes attended by their English-language origin peers: content classes taught in English without adaptation to the language-learning needs of the language minority students.

HOME-LANGUAGE ARTS AND HOME-LANGUAGE CONTENT-AREA INSTRUCTION

Even with the help of sheltered English instruction, English-language learners face formidable obstacles to learning content material, at grade level, while also learning English. In consideration of the students' educational predicament and the districts' responsibility to provide access to the curriculum, many districts provide content-area instruction in the students' home languages as well as opportunities for continued development of home-language and literacy skills. Bilingual and biliterate teachers possessing credentials in the appropriate content areas are needed for this component.

Some districts offer home-language instruction in the content areas to students only during the time they are also enrolled in ESL classes. In other districts, they may be available as electives throughout the students' school careers, before and after the time of transition from ESL classes, for reasons similar to those that support requirements for English-language arts instruction at all grade levels for all students. An increasing number of bilingual charter schools have been established in response to parental demand for expanded opportunities for students to become biliterate. Preschool bilingual programs, bilingual-gifted or other exceptional-student education programs, migrant tutoring programs, newcomer schools and centers, magnet schools, and bilingual vocational education courses are examples of other ways schools are organized to provide home language arts and content instruction through the home language. See Chapter 3 for additional information about district policies that affect programs in bilingual education. There are many reasons why educators, elected officials, and parents prefer home-language components to traditional curricula. Even in districts whose policy goals focus only on English-language acquisition and content-area achievement, home-language courses may be offered because high literacy achievement in the home language is associated with high achievement in second-language learning.

INDIGENOUS STUDENTS

Districts with indigenous students (Native Americans or Hawaiian Natives, for example) offer heritage-language courses to help prevent or reverse language shift in observance of tribal preference and federal policy to "preserve, protect and promote the rights and freedom of Native Americans to use, practice, and develop Native American languages" established in the 1992 Native American Languages Act. The language maintenance and revitalization efforts of tribal communities were bolstered by the recent recognition of the critically important role of their heritage languages and of the contributions Native American Code Talkers made during World Wars I and II. See Chapter 2, the National Security Agency's Web site at http://www.nsa.gov/museum/talkers.html, or the National Archives Web site at http://www.nara.gov/exhall/people/newroles.html for additional information on the Code Talkers.

Biliteracy

Districts implementing policies supportive of multilingualism and biliteracy offer heritage-language courses to help prevent the loss of students' native language proficiency and the erosion of the language resources available in their communities. These policies are often adopted in districts located in areas where international trade and commerce are important to the local economy, and in schools that place a strong emphasis on advanced academic study.

PARENT AND COMMUNITY INVOLVEMENT

Although community and parental involvement goals are typically given high priority in all districts, only in districts offering home-language instruction is it possible for parents who don't speak English to oversee homework and serve as resource persons in the schools. According to a longitudinal study funded by the Department of Education comparing types of programs for language minority students, parents of students in bilingual programs were likely to report that they help their children complete school assignments. A majority of parents involved in all types of programs said they want their children to learn English and Spanish equally well (Ramírez et al. 1991).

DROPOUT PREVENTION

Employing the home language for instructional purposes increases academic success among English-language learners and helps keep more students in school. Districts with strong dropout prevention policies often include in home-language courses instruction on the history and culture associated with both the home language and the United States to ensure the development of students' self-esteem and pride in both cultures. All language courses of necessity teach associated cultures because language is inextricably linked with the lives of its speakers and cannot be taught effectively without reference to the communities that use them (Fishman 1994). Using the home culture as a reference point for teaching the culture of the United States, however, also applies the pedagogical principle of using what the students know as a means to aid new learning.

Access to Cultural Capital

Teaching the cultural component ensures that English-language learners will be better able to access the social and cultural capital available within their families, neighborhoods, and communities. Stepick (1998) explains the significance of social capital as the principal means for recent immigrants to obtain housing, food, and jobs. Nearly 70 percent of surveyed Haitians who arrived in south Florida in the 1980s, for example, reported that they found their first job in the United States as a result of help provided by family and friends. The home language gives the right of entry to the language minority community's informal exchange of information and assistance. By the same token, although visible or audible markers of minority status can impede participation in the majority's networks, loss of the home language can impede support from the minority community.

EARLY CHILDHOOD EDUCATION

Heightened concerns about school discipline prompted by tragic outbreaks of school violence highlight the importance of children's ability to communicate in the language of the home. Non-English-speaking parents cannot pass on traditional family values and provide direction to school behavior if the family's language is unavailable to the children. As Lily Wong Fillmore (1991) has described, language minority children have a fragile hold on their home languages; English-only programs for young children can therefore result in the loss of their home languages. In its 1995 position statement on language and cultural diversity, the National Association for the Education of Young Children (NAEYC) stated that language loss may result in the disruption of family communication patterns, lead to the loss of intergenerational wisdom, damage individual and community esteem, and retard children's potential mastery of their home languages or of English. The NAEYC statement supports programs that help children continue to enjoy full access to everything family members can teach them.

SHELTERED ENGLISH IMMERSION

The many ways in which the components of bilingual programs can be organized into complete programs reflect the traditions of decentralized local control of public education, adaptations in response to regional differences, the professional judgment of school district officials, and their knowledge of parental preferences in their communities. In two states, however, prominent activists have popularized alternatives to these traditions by organizing political campaigns that resulted in a uniform statewide approach to the education of language minority students. The voter initiatives are Proposition 227 in California and Proposition 203 in Arizona.

In both cases, the new approach, termed *sheltered English immersion,* is to be available during a temporary transition period expected to last no longer than one year. Both Proposition 227 and Proposition 203 define sheltered English immersion (SEI) as an English language acquisition process for young children in which nearly all classroom instruction is in English, but with the curriculum and presentation designed for children who are learning the language. In Arizona's Proposition 203, the definition is expanded to specify that all instructional materials are in English, and all reading, writing, and subject matter are taught in English, although teachers may use a minimal amount of the child's native language when necessary. Parents may request that their children be placed in programs for bilingual education under certain circumstances. The Arizona measure authorizes the denial of such requests by school authorities with no explanation or legal consequence, but requires that they prepare documents to justify the reasons for an affirmative response. It also stipulates that administrators and policymakers face personal liability risks and the danger of expulsion from school positions for five years if they violate these provisions.

Baker (1998), a former federal government employee with the Department of Education who is now an educational consultant in Utah, writes in support of structured English immersion. Baker points to the success of Canada's multiyear programs in bilingual immersion. He cites as successful several Canadian programs that exit students in two to three years; he believes these programs fit the definition of SEI, and observes that minimal use of the home language is helpful. Nevertheless, he predicts that English-language learners will need continued assistance in regular classrooms after they have completed a year in SEI. Baker's article is available in full-text form at the Web site of Phi Delta Kappa at http://www.pdkintl.org/kappan/kbak9811.htm.

Munro (2001), in a handbook (whose introduction was written by Linda Chávez, president of the Center for Equal Opportunity) that provides guidance on presenting programs in sheltered English immersion, inspires concern about these programs' compliance with equal educational opportunity requirements as he applies Baker's prediction to the high school level:

Clearly, older LEP students who arrive in U.S. schools at grade 10 or above with no knowledge of English will not be able to complete their academic curriculum in a normal four-year program. These students will have to go on to adult education in a local community college or in adult secondary-school programs (such as those awarding the General Education Diploma or GED). (Munro 2001, 20)

Recent studies indicate that GED holders' standing in the job market is more like that of dropouts than it is of high school graduates (Tyler, Murnane, and Willett 2000). For minority students, there seems to be no positive economic effect associated with the GED at all. Earning potential for dropouts and GED holders alike is at the $11,000 level, almost reaching the 1999 poverty guidelines established by the Department of Health and Human Services (DHHS) for a family of two and used for determining financial eligibility for certain federal programs. This income potential contrasts markedly with the 1999 median household income of $40,816 identified by the Census Bureau. Policymakers, parents, and the courts may determine that plans for English-language learners that require them to settle for a GED fail to provide prospects for economic mobility over their lifetimes. See Chapter 6 for a summary of school finance reform cases that include potential for economic mobility as part of the definition of an adequate education. For updates on poverty guidelines see the DHHS site at http://aspe.os.dhhs.gov/poverty/poverty.htm.

Because the statewide experiments in California and Arizona have been widely noted in the press, readers' curiosity about them may exceed the scope of this volume. See the State of California's Voter Information Guide's presentation of arguments for and against Proposition 227 at http://primary98.ss.ca.gov/VoterGuide/. For a side-by-side comparison of the Arizona and California measures, see James Crawford's Language Policy Web site at http://ourworld.compuserve.com/homepages/JWCRAWFORD/203–227.htm. For a detailed comparison of Canadian-style bilingual immersion and sheltered English immersion, see the Web page of Jill Kemper Mora at San Diego State University, at http://coe.sdsu.edu/people/jmora/Pages/SEIvCanadian.htm. See Chapter 6 for additional information on political processes affecting bilingual education.

SUBMERSION

In school districts where no programs designed for the educational needs of English-language learners are available, the districts may be described as using legally impermissible sink-or-swim, or submersion, approaches. In 1990, the Resource Center on Educational Equity of the Council of Chief State School Officers published the results of a multi-year study of what the states were doing to meet the needs of LEP students (CCSSO 1990). It found that many LEP students requiring special help to succeed academically were not receiving it. In 1994, the GAO reported that LEP students spent much of their time in subject-area classes with teachers who did not understand their native languages and who had little or no training in how to communicate with them. As recently as the latest year for which summary data from the states are available, approximately 16 percent of public school LEP students (and 52 percent of private school students) from states responding to survey questions were not enrolled in programs providing those special services (Macías 1998).

Language Majority Students

Programs for English-language-origin students (and for language minority students proficient in English) may include all the components described in the preceding sections, and may be found at pre-K-12 and postsecondary education levels. Language majority students may receive instruction in and through a foreign language, instruction in various subjects using the target language as the language of instruction, and opportunities for continued development of home language (in this case, English) skills.

Canadian-style programs in bilingual immersion for language majority students, where all or most content-area instruction is presented in the target language for several years, are increasingly popular. They may be combined with complementary developmental programs for English-language learners (i.e., programs to help students continue to develop the home language that also use that language as a medium of instruction for other content areas) to form two-way bilingual or dual-language education programs. Two-way models typically include equal numbers of language minority and majority students and use the target language for 40 to 90 percent of the school day. In this model, students from each of two language groups use their home language and the target language to learn material in the content areas. Both groups acquire a second language, develop cross-cultural communication skills, and continue to develop home-language skills. Although many variations to this basic model exist, the term *two-way* most often refers to the languages of the students, and the term *dual language* refers to the languages used in the curriculum. Two-way programs include native speakers of both languages, in contrast to some dual-language programs that are designed for students from only one of those language backgrounds. An online directory of a specific type of enriched language education, two-way bilingual immersion (TWI), is maintained by the Center for Applied Linguistics (CAL 2001), and includes a statement of the criteria for inclusion in the directory; see the CAL Web site at http://www.cal.org/twi/directory/.

Bilingual education or extended foreign-language courses may be part of Montessori's foreign-language immersion programs, International Baccalaureate programs, international education magnets, or gifted-children programs. For example, in the Montessori InterCultura School in Oak Park, Illinois, foreign-language immersion programs are available in Japanese and Spanish. Language majority parents enroll children as young as thirty-three months. Students may continue in the program until the end of third grade. Although the adults speak only the target language, the children are always free to speak in whichever language they please. Language-shift is not a danger in early childhood programs for language majority students because they receive ample support for their home language (English). For additional information about this program, see the American Montessori Society Web site at http://www.amshq.org/schls/index.html. For more information about early foreign-language learning see the National Network for Early Language Learning (NNELL) Web site at http://www.educ.iastate.edu/nnell/.

COMPARISON OF COMPONENTS

To further develop understanding of the wide range of possibilities inherent in the term *bilingual education,* its major components will be compared and contrasted in the following section.

Second-Language, Foreign-Language, and Language Arts Programs

Foreign-language and ESL programs are similar to each other in many ways, and very different from language arts programs. Because this deceptively simple statement masks important implications for the proper placement of English-language learners, it warrants extended consideration.

LANGUAGE ARTS AND ESL

The quintessential characteristic of English-language learners is that they are by definition learning English language skills, already developed by their English-speaking peers, that are prerequisite to learning in other areas of the curriculum. Second-language learners are learning a language, but native speakers are refining skills in a language they already know. The ESL Standards for Pre-K-12 Students developed by Teachers of English to Speakers of Other Languages (TESOL) (available for viewing at http://www.tesol.org/assoc/k12standards/it/11.html) shows that helping students to acquire language and to use it in culturally appropriate ways and at academically useful levels are the major tasks of ESL teachers, who address teaching goals related both to language acquisition and to overall academic achievement in other content areas. These functions are different from those involved in providing instruction in home-language arts in a language already known by the students. Penfield (1987) notes that this difference is particularly notable at the secondary level where teachers think of themselves primarily as content-area teachers and not as language specialists.

Valdés (2000) addresses the difference between ESL and English language arts by analyzing the composition of professional organizations. She points out that those who teach English to native speakers generally belong to organizations such as the National Council of Teachers of English (NCTE); those who teach English to nonnative speakers of English are generally members of TESOL or of the National Association for Bilingual Education (NABE). Valdés's conclusion is supported by the characteristics of NCTE's ESL Assembly. The ESL Assembly (with approximately eighty members from the total NCTE membership of 77,000) is intended primarily for teachers of English-language arts whose classes occasionally include only a few English-language learners.

Her description of current participation patterns is also consistent with the history of TESOL. The NCTE and four other organizations, the Modern Language Association (MLA), the Center for Applied Linguistics (CAL), the American Speech Association (later the American Speech and Hearing Association, or ASHE), and the National Association for Foreign Student Affairs (NAFSA), organized three ad hoc TESOL conferences. They took place in Tucson, Arizona, in 1964; San Diego, California, in 1965; and New York City in 1966. In 1966, a slate of officers and a constitution were approved and TESOL became an organization with Harold Allen (a former NCTE president and the author of the influential 1966 *Survey of the Teaching of English to Non-English Speakers in the United States*, known generally as the TENES Report) as the first president and Robert Lado as the first vice president. As president of TESOL, Allen presided over the first TESOL convention, held in Miami Beach, in 1967. TESOL Vice President Robert Lado, also dean of Georgetown University's School of Language and Linguistics, authorized his associate dean, James E. Alatis, to serve part-time as TESOL's first executive secretary (personal communication with James E. Alatis, September 22, 2000). The membership of the organization, which began with 337 members, now stands at 10,000.

The distinction between language learners and native speakers applies to all languages. Recognition of the pedagogical consequences of the difference has led to an increase in heritage language programs at both pre-K-12 and college levels. These programs are for students who want to maintain and develop their native language skills in a language other than English. They are the counterparts of English-language arts programs for native speakers of English. Traditional foreign-language classes are inappropriate for native speakers of heritage languages because they already possess the listening, speaking, syntax, and culture skills that other students in the class are acquiring. Arizona, California, Florida, New Mexico, and Texas are among the states where separate public school programs for native speakers of Spanish are available. At the college level, approximately 25 percent of postsecondary institutions offer both traditional foreign-language courses and those designed for the needs of heritage-language students (Rodriguez Pino 1997).

FOREIGN LANGUAGES AND ESL

The task of the ESL teacher is similar to that of the foreign-language teacher: They both teach a language and culture that are not native to their students. They differ in that the language taught by the ESL teacher is English; the goals of such instruction will merge with the goals of English-language arts instruction. The students experience a similar level of intellectual challenge and cognitive benefits from second-language learning, whether that language is English, another world language, an indigenous language, or sign language. Although all students of a second language face a similar intellectual task, credit toward meeting high school or college graduation requirements is not always accorded to ESL students.

Another major difference between the two fields lies in the extent to which fostering academic achievement in other courses is a program goal. English is a required part of the curriculum, and literacy in English is the means for achievement in other required subjects. Instruction in languages other than English is required for all students in North Carolina. In other states, it is required only for some students (the college-bound, for example), or at some grade levels (high school, for example). See Chapter 4 for additional information on this subject.

The 1996 statement of philosophy from the foreign-language standards document conveys the gist of the position of the American Council on the Teaching of Foreign Languages (ACTFL 1996). It demonstrates affinity with bilingual education through its vision of a future in which all students develop and maintain proficiency in English and at least one other language, including children who come to school from non-English backgrounds.

The ESL Standards for Pre-K–12 Students shares the emphasis on language use for communication purposes found in the foreign-language standards, but also emphasizes the foundational function of language as a tool by which other subjects are acquired. The ESL standards are organized around three goals: using English to communicate in social settings; using English to achieve academically in all content areas; and using English in culturally appropriate ways (TESOL 2001).

The foundational role is also present in foreign-language education, as evidenced by Standard 3.1 of the National Standards for Foreign Language Learning: "Students reinforce and further their knowledge of other disciplines through the foreign language." See the full statement of Standards for Foreign Language Education at http://www.actfl.org/index.cfm?weburl=/public/articles/details.cfm?id=33.

Further, since no pre-K–12 student studies bilingual education, but instead benefits from it, all second-language study can be considered foundational. Nevertheless, school districts are charged with the responsibility for providing English-language learners adequate opportunities to achieve to the level of the standards governing grade-to-grade promotion and graduation. Although parents have the right to opt out of programs in bilingual education, school districts are not thereby released from the responsibility to provide English-language learners with effective instruction in English and in other subjects in the curriculum. The ability to use English for academic purposes is prerequisite to meeting the standards in subject matter. Consequently, ESL teachers place high priority on helping their students meet those standards. Major federal legislation, policies, and court decisions that spell out the responsibilities of states and districts to language minority students are described in Chapter 5.

Bilingual Education and ESL

Although programs in bilingual education in the United States always include ESL goals, not all ESL courses are part of a program in bilingual education. In ESL classes, the English language is the object and the means of instruction. In bilingual education classes, where the home language is used as the medium of instruction for other content areas, home-language development may be a goal of the instruction; in this setting, learning is designed to transfer smoothly to English-language situations. Achievement of course goals in bilingual education supports the students' success with English learning tasks and contributes to the development of schooled levels of bilingualism for students whose home-language study is sustained over time. The TESOL Statement on the Role of Bilingual Education in the Education of Children in the United States, adopted by the TESOL executive board in 1992, recognizes the importance of English in the world community, that the home language of many students is a language other than English, that native-language literacy skills foster success in second-language development, and that it is beneficial to all children to learn a second language. Bilingual education and ESL are complementary, but not identical.

Bilingual Education and Foreign-Language Programs

Organizational factors have been and to a large extent still are different for the two areas. Foreign-language courses, unlike bilingual programs with home-language components, are offered in all states; they are required for high school graduation or for admission to state universities in many states. Teacher certification provisions for foreign-language teachers, but not for bilingual education teachers, exist in all fifty states. Historically, foreign-language courses were offered primarily at the high school level, but the majority of bilingual education programs are at the elementary school level. Language majority students are more frequently associated with foreign-language courses than with bilingual education courses; language minority students are more frequently enrolled in bilingual education courses.

The two fields are similar in that critical shortages exist in the availability of both foreign-language and bilingual education teachers. The GAO estimated a shortage of 175,000 bilingual teachers nationally (1994). Bilingual teachers are in such high demand that districts in Texas and California have offered them sign-up bonuses ranging from $2,000 to $5,000.

Both groups of educators teach a language other than English. Both groups of educators teach home-language arts to heritage-language students. Although this aspect of language education is much more prevalent in bilingual programs, since the 1970s, the foreign-language education profession has taken an increasing interest in this area. In 1972, the American Association of Teachers of Spanish and Portuguese (AATSP) recommended that special sections be established for developing literacy in Spanish and using it to reinforce or complement other areas of the curriculum, with correspondingly specialized materials, methods, and teachers, at all levels of education where native speakers of Spanish are enrolled (Roca 1997). A 1979 report by the President's Commission on Foreign Languages and International Studies added support to this recommendation and extended it to all language minority groups. The report noted that heritage-language speakers were a largely untapped resource who have great potential to make valuable contributions to the country's ability to deal persuasively and effectively with the world outside its borders. The first national heritage languages conference was sponsored in 1999 by the Center for Applied Linguistics (CAL), the National Foreign Language Center, and the California State University at Long Beach. See Chapter 4 for additional information about developments in heritage-language education.

Both groups of educators belong to organizations affiliated with the organization that is the national policy voice for the language professions, the Joint National Council on Languages (JNCL). The members of the JNCL constituent organizations support the proposition that all Americans must have the opportunity to learn and use English and at least one other language. Sixty state and national professional associations of language teachers and related groups, including NABE, ACTFL, TESOL, are members of JNCL.

The curriculum in both areas is evolving in ways that reduce the differences noted in this section. See Chapter 4 for descriptions of program innovations that bring together the two areas.

For Additional Information

Point-by-point descriptions of program models that combine the components described above, beyond the scope of this volume, are provided by Linquanti (1999), Rennie (1993), and Straight (1998). See Baker (1998) for a rationale for structured English immersion and Hakuta's First and Supplemental Declarations prepared for a motion for preliminary injunction for Proposition 227 at http://www.stanford.edu/~hakuta/EducationPolicy.html for an examination of whether structured English immersion programs in California can be developed on a sound theoretical basis. For an in-depth description of the assumptions that guide program development for language minority students, see Clair (1994).

REFERENCES

American Council on the Teaching of Foreign Languages (ACTFL). 1996. *Executive summary: Standards for foreign language learning: Preparing for the 21st century.* Yonkers, NY: Author [Online]. Available: *http://www.actfl.org/.*

Baker, K. 1998. Structured English immersion: Breakthrough in teaching limited-English-proficient students. *Phi Delta Kappan* (November). [Online]. Available: *http://www.pdkintl.org/kappan/kbak9811.htm.*

Census 2000 PHC-T-6. April 2, 2001. Table 5. Percent of population by race and Hispanic or Latino origin, for states, Puerto Rico, and places of 100,000 or more population. Washington, DC: U.S. Census Bureau. [Online]. Available: *http://www.census.gov/population/cen2000/phc-t6/tab05.txt.*

Center for Applied Linguistics (CAL). 2001. *Directory of two-way bilingual immersion programs in the U.S.* [Online]. Available: *http://www.cal.org/twi/directory/.*

Center for Research on Excellence and Diversity in Education (CREDE). 1998. Findings on the effectiveness of bilingual education. *Talking Leaves* 2, no. 3 (summer).

Clair, N. 1994. Informed choices: Articulating assumptions for language minority students. *ERIC/CAL News Bulletin* 18, no. 1 (September). ERIC Clearinghouse on Languages and Linguistics.

Collier, V. 1987. Age and rate of acquisition of second language for academic purposes. *TESOL Quarterly* 21, no. 4 (December).

Council of Chief School Officers (CCSSO) Resource Center on Educational Equity. 1990. *School success for limited English proficient students: The challenge and state response.* Washington, DC: Author.

Cummins, J. 1981. Age on arrival and immigrant second language learning in Canada: A reassessment. *Applied Linguistics* 11, no. 2.

Fishman, J. 1994. Interview with Joshua Fishman conducted by Dan Holt and David Dolson, July 18. Sacramento, CA: California Department of Education. [Online]. Available: *http://www.cde.ca.gov/iasa/fishman.html.*

Fitzgerald, N. July 1995. ESL instruction in adult education: Findings from a national evaluation. *ERIC Digest* EDO-LE-95-03. Washington, DC: National Center for ESL Literacy Education. [Online]. Available: *http://www.cal.org/ncle/DIGESTS/FITZGERA.HTM.*

Government Accounting Office (GAO). 1994. *Limited English proficiency: A growing and costly educational challenge facing many school districts.*

GAO/HEHS-94–38. Washington, DC: Author. [Online]. Available: *http:// frwebgate.access.gpo.gov/cgibin/useftp.cgi?IPaddress=162.140.64.88 &filename=he94038.txt&directory=/diskb/wais/data/gao.*

Hakuta, K., Y. Butler, and D. Witt. January 2000. *How long does it take English learners to attain proficiency?* Policy Report 2001. University of California Linguistic Minority Research Institute. [Online]. Available: *http://www. stanford.edu/~hakuta/Docs/HowLong.pdf*.

Hernández, D. J., and E. Charney, eds. 1998. *From generation to generation: The health and well-being of children in immigrant families.* National Research Council and Institute of Medicine. Washington, DC: National Academy Press. [Online]. Available: *http://www.nap.edu/books/0309065615/html/ index.html.*.

Krashen, S. 1996. *Under attack: The case against bilingual education.* Culver City, CA: Language Education Associates.

Kreidler, C. November 1987. *ESL teacher education. ERIC Digest ED289361.* Washington, DC: ERIC Clearinghouse on Languages and Linguistics. [Online]. Available: *http://www.ed.gov/databases/ERIC_Digests/ed289361. html.*

Linquanti, R. 1999. *Fostering academic success for English language learners: What do we know?* San Francisco, CA: WestEd. [Online]. Available: *http://www.wested.org/lcd/RandP1.htm.*

Macías, R. 1998. *Summary report of the survey of the states' limited English proficient students and available educational programs and services, 1996–97.* The SEA Report. Washington, DC: National Clearinghouse for Bilingual Education.

Munro, R. January 2001. *Teaching English to high school students: The ABC's of English immersion: A teachers' guide.* Washington, DC: Center for Equal Opportunity (CEO).

National Center for ESL Literacy Education (NCLE). 1997. The waiting game. *NCLEnotes* 6, no. 1 (summer).

———. November 22, 2000. Frequently asked questions in adult ESL literacy. [Online]. Available: *http://www.cal.org/NCLE/FAQS.HTM#Three.*

National Clearinghouse for Bilingual Education (NCBE). September 1999. Which states have legislative provisions for additional funding of instructional programs for limited English proficient students? [Online]. Available: *http://www.ncbe.gwu.edu/askncbe/faqs/19fund.htm.*

Penfield, J. 1987. ESL: The regular classroom teacher perspective. *TESOL Quarterly* 21, no. 1.

Ramírez, D., S. Yuen, D. Ramey, and D. Pasta. 1991. *Final report: Longitudinal study of structured immersion strategy, early-exit, and late-exit transitional bilingual education programs for language-minority children.* Vols. 1 and 2. San Mateo, CA: Aguire International.

Rennie, J. 1993. ESL and bilingual program models. *ERIC Digest* (September). Washington, DC: ERIC Clearinghouse on Languages and Linguistics.

Roca, A. 1997. Retrospectives, advances, and current needs in the teaching of Spanish to United States Hispanic bilingual students: *ADFL Bulletin* 29, no. 1 (fall). [Online]. Available: *http://www.adfl.org/adfl/bulletin/v29n1/291037.htm.*

Rodriguez Pino, C. 1997. Teaching Spanish to native speakers: A new perspective in the 1990s. *ERIC CLL News Bulletin* 21, no. 1.

Stepick, A. 1998. *Pride against prejudice: Haitians in the United States.* Boston: Allyn and Bacon.

Straight, H. S. 1998. Languages across the curriculum. *ERIC Digest* (October). Washington, DC: ERIC Clearinghouse on Languages and Linguistics. [Online]. Available: *http://www.cal.org/ericcll/digest/lacdigest.html.*

Teachers of English to Speakers of Other Languages, Inc. (TESOL). 2001. *The ESL standards for pre-K-12 students: Table of contents.* Alexandria, VA: Author. [Online]. Available: *http://www.tesol.org/assoc/k12standards/it/01.html.*

Thomas, W., and V. Collier. 1997. School effectiveness for language minority students. NCBE Resource Collection Series, no. 9. Washington, DC: National Clearinghouse for Bilingual Education. [Online]. Available: *http://www.ncbe.gwu.edu/ncbepubs/resource/effectiveness/index.htm.*

Tucker, G. R. 1999. A global perspective on bilingualism and bilingual education. *ERIC Digest* (August). EDO-FL-99-04. Washington, DC: ERIC Clearinghouse on Languages and Linguistics. [Online]. Available: *http://www.cal.org/ericcll/digest/digestglobal.html.*

Tyler, J. H., R. H. Murnane, and J. B. Willett. June 2000. Estimating the labor market signaling value of the GED (NCSALL Research Briefs). Cambridge, MA: Harvard Graduate School of Education, National Center for the Study of Adult Learning and Literacy. [Online]. Available: *http://gseweb.harvard.edu/~ncsall/research/report_extra.html.*

Valdés, G. 2000. Nonnative English speakers: Language bigotry in English mainstream classrooms. *ADE Bulletin* 124 (winter). [Online]. Available: *http://www.ade.org/ade/bulletin/N124/toc/124toc.htm.*

Wong Fillmore, L. 1991. When learning a second language means losing the first. *Early Childhood Research Quarterly* 6, no. 3.

Chapter Two

●◆ Chronology: The Evolution of Teacher Education

A summary of key events in the evolution of bilingual education follows. Selected social, legal, and political developments that illustrate the context for those events or for current language, immigration, and race relations controversies are also included in the timeline. Headings indicate the significant characteristics for each period; they are not definitive, as themes emerge at several points in the timeline.

Precolonial Times to 1879: Open Door for Immigrants and Their Languages

1565   Don Pedro Menéndez de Avilés becomes Spain's governor of Florida and founder of St. Augustine, the first permanent European settlement in the continental United States. Two miles north of St. Augustine, Fort Mose is established in 1738; it is the first officially sanctioned community of free Africans in the present-day United States. Its residents are runaway slaves, including Mandingos, Congos, Carabalis, Minas, Gambas, Lecumis, Sambas, Gangas, Araras, and Guineans, who accept the Spaniards' offer of freedom for those who swore allegiance to Spain and embrace the Catholic religion. A free integrated school, funded by Spanish government funds, is established i n St. Augustine in 1787. See Hispanic USA, Inc. for additional information about the school at http://www.neta.com/~ 1stbooks/integ.htm, and the Archaeological Institute of America at http://www.archaeology. org/9609/abstracts/ftmose.html for information on Fort Mose.

1598   The first permanent European settlement in what is now the western United States is established north of present-day Santa Fe, New Mexico, by Don Juan de Oñate. The expedition group of

1598,   six hundred soldiers, priests, and family includes Spaniards, in-
cont.   digenous people, and Africans.

1607   Jamestown is founded in Virginia, the first permanent English
colony on the continent.

1608   Quebec in present-day Canada becomes the first permanent
French colony on the continent.

1620   English pilgrims land at Plymouth, Massachusetts.

1654   Descendants of Jews expelled from Spain and Portugal in the
fifteenth century come to New Amsterdam (now New York) in
1654. They had lived in Dutch settlements in Brazil until the
Portuguese regained control of the area.

1682   Robert Cavelier, Sieur de La Salle, and Henri de Tonti claim the
Mississippi Valley for France, naming it Louisiana. New Orleans is
founded in 1718.

1683   German Quakers found Germantown in what is now Philadelphia, Pennsylvania.

1734   A German school opens in Lancaster, Pennsylvania.

1763   Sephardic Jews (Jews whose ancestors came from the Iberian
Peninsula) build the Touro Synagogue in Newport, Rhode Island,
the only colony to permit a permanent Jewish settlement. The
synagogue is the oldest in the United States and the only Jewish
house of worship still standing from colonial times. See the National Humanities Center's Web site at http://ipmwww.ncsu.
edu:8080/tserve/nineteen/nkeyinfo/judaism.htm for additional
information about Jewish settlement in the United States.

1776   The American Revolutionary War officially begins with the signing of the Declaration of Independence.

1784   Russia's first North American colony is established on Kodiak
Island.

1787   The opening ceremony of Franklin College, founded as the first
bilingual college in the United States, is held in German and En-

glish. In 1853, it became Franklin and Marshall College, in Lancaster, Pennsylvania, after merging with Marshall College.

1790 Under the provisions of the Uniform Rule of Naturalization enacted by the Seventh Congress, any free White alien is eligible for admission and may become a citizen after two years of residency in the United States.

1804 President Jean-Jacques Dessalines proclaims the independence of Haiti, the first Black republic, from France. Napoleon Bonaparte, abandoning his plans for an empire in the New World, sells the Louisiana Territory to the United States for $15 million. This acquisition doubles the size of the United States.

1810– Mexico's War of Independence against Spain begins in 1810
1821 with the "Grito de Dolores" of Miguel Hidalgo y Costilla. It ends with the signing of the Treaty of Córdoba, which establishes Mexico's independence on September 16, 1821.

1828 The *Cherokee Phoenix,* the first newspaper in an American Indian language, is published.

1829 Slavery in Mexico is officially abolished.

1837– Two schools employing German-speaking teachers for German
1920 American immigrant students open in New York City. German-language schools are established in the Carolinas, Colorado, Illinois, Iowa, Indiana, Kentucky, Maryland, Minnesota, Missouri, Nebraska, Oregon, Pennsylvania, Virginia, and Wisconsin. German and Czech schools are established in Texas. Chinese, Japanese, German, Italian, and French schools are established in California. Spanish is used as a language of instruction in Arizona, New Mexico, and Texas. Ohio authorized instruction in English, German, or both languages. Louisiana authorized instruction in English and French.

1837– Irish Catholics, the first large group of poor refugees to the
1960 United States, face religious discrimination. Hostility against Irish Catholic immigrants grows violent in 1837, when mobs burn down a convent in Boston. In 1844, anti-immigrant riots take place for a week in Philadelphia. Catholic churches and neighborhoods are destroyed and a dozen immigrants are

1837–   killed. Baltimore, St. Louis, New Orleans, and Louisville, Ken-
1960,   tucky, are also sites of anti-Irish violence. Their greatly increased
cont.   numbers (along with those of Italians, Poles, Hungarians, Slo-
         vaks, and other Catholic immigrants who arrived in the nine-
         teenth century) are equated with increased power for the Pa-
         pacy and considered a threat to the political independence of
         the United States. The Ku Klux Klan aims its attacks at Catholics
         as well as African Americans and Jews. Although Catholics even-
         tually gain an advantage through their voting power, their labor
         union affiliations, and their status as English-speaking U.S. citi-
         zens of European origin, not until 1960 is their full acceptance
         marked by the election of an Irish Catholic, John Fitzgerald
         Kennedy, as the 35th president of the United States. Kennedy is
         the great-grandson of a famine immigrant (Patrick Kennedy
         from County Wexford) who left Ireland in 1849. For additional
         details about the history of the incorporation of Irish immigra-
         tion, see http://www.historyplace.com/worldhistory/famine/
         america.htm.

1838–   The Cherokee Indians are relocated by the army, in accordance
1839   with the Indian Removal Act sponsored by President Andrew
         Jackson, from Georgia to Oklahoma along what became known
         as the Trail of Tears. Approximately 25 percent of the Cherokee
         died on the enforced march.

         The survivors establish an educational system that achieves a 90
         percent literacy rate in their native language.

1845   The newly proclaimed Republic of Texas is annexed by the
         United States, exacerbating conflicts with Mexico. The following
         year, the invasion of Mexico marks the beginning of the Mexican
         War.

1846   Copies of the proposed Wisconsin constitution are printed in
         Norwegian (as well as in English) as authorized by resolution of
         the constitutional convention.

1848   The Treaty of Guadalupe Hidalgo is signed at the conclusion of
         the war between the United States and Mexico. According to its
         terms, Mexico's northern states are annexed and Mexicans re-
         siding in the annexed area are incorporated into the newly ac-
         quired U.S. territories of the Southwest. Treaty provisions to

protect the property and human rights of Mexicans who chose to stay in the United States are agreed to by the United States.

Gold is discovered in California.

1850 The Territory of New Mexico authorizes instruction in English and Spanish.

1861 The Civil War begins when Confederate forces fire on Fort Sumter, in Charleston, South Carolina.

1862– The Homestead Act entitles citizens or those eligible for citizen-
1880 ship to buy 160 acres of land after they pay a modest filing fee and reside continuously on the land for five years. Many of the settlers face financial difficulties and are forced to sell their land to speculators because 160 acres are not enough to ensure access to water in arid zones. This procedure for the individual acquisition of public lands runs counter to the concept of the common ownership of land held in Indian communities and by Mexican land-grant holders. Members of both groups have prior claims to land made available through the Homestead Act. Nonetheless, when the provisions of treaties made with Indian tribes are unilaterally revised, tribal groups are relocated.

Mexicans whose families and communities have acquired property from Spain and have lived on it for centuries lose their common grazing lands if they cannot present documentation acceptable to the courts of the United States. Grants established though Spanish civil and customary law are evaluated through the system of law in North America, which is derived from English common law. Misunderstandings ensue. At the same time, the discovery of gold and silver in the West, the convenience of the railroad, and the need to employ veterans of the Civil War add impetus to the encroachments on lands owned by Mexicans and Indian tribes. By the 1880s, the majority of the former Mexican landowners in the Southwest have lost their land and become impoverished workers and agricultural laborers. For details about land-grant claims and lawsuits, see the Center for Land Grant Studies at http://www.southwestbooks.org/lgintro.htm.

1863 A German high school opens in Pittsburgh, Pennsylvania.

1867   The United States purchases Alaska from Russia.

1869   Work is completed for the Central and the Union Pacific transcontinental railroads connecting Omaha, Nebraska, and Sacramento, California. The majority of those who built the railroads are Chinese laborers.

1871   The San Carlos Institute is founded by Cuban exiles who came to Key West during the war for Cuba's independence from Spain. One of America's first bilingual and integrated schools is housed at the institute for more than a century.

1878–   A German-English teacher training institution is established in
1919   Milwaukee.

1879–   Indian children are separated from their families and forced to
1934   attend off-reservation English-language boarding schools where students are punished if caught using their home languages.

1880–1939: Territorial Expansion; Immigration and Language Regulation

1882–   The first of a series of Chinese Exclusion Acts (later expanded to
1943   include other Asian groups) and the first law to bar a group's immigration on the basis of a named nationality suspend Chinese immigration for ten years and prohibit the naturalization of Chinese persons. This prohibition (and previous legislative provisions restricting eligibility for naturalization to free White persons) prevents Chinese immigrants from acquiring the right to vote, and in some states, from owning land. Section 6 exemptions to the act do permit the admission of Chinese teachers, students, merchants, and travelers. Still, a tax is levied on immigrants. The Chinese Exclusion Act is extended twice, and finally repealed in 1943.

1885   In Rock Springs, Wyoming Territory, Chinese workers for the Union Pacific Railroad Company's coal mines are attacked by White miners, who shoot the unarmed Chinese and set fire to their homes. Eleven of the Chinese miners are burned to death and others are killed by gunfire; there are twenty-eight victims of the all-day riot. The massacre has resulted from an argument over the Chinese workers' right to employment in the mines. Although all workers are paid on the same scale, there is widespread concern that the employment of Chinese workers will depress wages.

1887–
1934
The stated purpose of the Dawes Severalty Act is to protect indigenous land rights during the Oklahoma Land Rush by granting Indians prior claim to apply for up to 160 acres, and eligibility to apply for citizenship. Indian lands not allocated according to the formula set forth in the act are to be declared surplus and sold. The process results in huge loss of land communally held by Indian tribes; individual members of the tribes often end up with arid land, unsuitable for farming. Very few Indians apply for citizenship.

The Indian Reorganization Act of 1928 protects the Indian land base and extends recognition of the federal trust responsibility to Indian tribes. Nevertheless, by 1934, Indian landholdings of 138 million acres have been reduced to only 48 million acres.

1890
In the Edgerton Bible case (*State ex rel. Weiss v. District Board of School Dist. No. 8 of the City of Edgerton*), the Wisconsin Supreme Court determines that Bible reading in public schools is in violation of Article X, Section 3 and Article I, Section 18 of the Wisconsin Constitution. German members of the Roman Catholic Church object to the reading of the King James Version of the Bible to pupils during school hours. As members of the Roman Catholic Church, they adhere instead to the Douay Version. Because the Edgerton school is a public school, the parents prevail in their argument that the Bible readings violate the separation of church and state.

German and other immigrant voters in Wisconsin sweep Republicans out of office for the first time in twenty years in retaliation for the Bennett law supported by Governor William D. Hoard's administration. The measure, introduced by Assemblyman Michael Bennett, imposes English-only requirements on German-language private schools. The schools conducted classes in German, not English, because the Germans considered the schools essential to preserving their native language, culture, and religion. The law is repealed at the next session of the legislature by the newly elected representatives.

1891   The Immigration Act establishes an Office of Immigration, the initial designation for the current Immigration and Naturalization Service (INS) in the Department of Justice.

1892–   Over 12 million immigrants are received at Ellis Island, which
1953   opens in 1892.

1893   Queen Lili'uokalani tries to adopt a new constitution to restore her government's autonomy and the voting rights of Hawaiians. American businessmen and planters in Hawaii respond by creating a Committee of Safety. With the help of four boatloads of armed United States Marines, who are acting without congressional authorization, the committee declares an end to the government of the Kingdom of Hawaii and the reign of Queen Lili'uokalani. To avoid bloodshed, she surrenders to and requests help from the United States, which is party to four treaties with the kingdom. Sanford Dole is proclaimed president of a provisional government, and he petitions the United States for annexation. The business community in Hawaii, fearing loss of favorable tax treatment for their agricultural products, wants annexation to guarantee tariff protection. The petition for annexation is granted by 1898. Territorial status is granted by 1900. Hawaii became a state in 1959. English is required as the language of instruction in the schools; using the Hawaiian language is forbidden.

Although 100 percent of Hawaiian land was owned by Native Hawaiians during the 1800s, only 6.23 percent of the islands' property is held by Native Hawaiians in 1919. According to Professor Jon M. Van Dyke of the University of Hawaii, Native Hawaiians are members of the only native group in the United States that has never been allowed to seek restitution for its losses, including 1,800,000 acres of lands acquired by the federal government. Although Native Hawaiians live in the most literate nation in the world in 1874, in 2001 only 45 percent complete high school, and only 7 percent earn college degrees. For additional information on Hawaii's history and current issues, see the state's Office of Hawaiian Affairs Web site at http://www. oha.org/and the Native Hawaiians' site at http://www. nativehawaiians.com/hawn_future. html.

1896   In *Plessy v. Ferguson,* upholding a Louisiana statute requiring that railway companies provide separate accommodations for Blacks and Whites, the United States Supreme Court gives federal legal sanction to racial segregation under the principle of "separate but equal."

Suomi College and Theological Seminary is established at Hancock, Michigan, by the Finnish community to prepare Lutheran pastors who could minister to the Finns in their own language. In 1932, as the only institution of higher learning in the United States that offers courses in Finnish, it is recognized as a department at the University of Michigan. Finnish is the medium of instruction in the Finnish courses and some of the branches of theology; all other courses are taught in English. Suomi College is renamed Finlandia University on July 1, 2000.

1898   In *Tape v. Hurley,* the right of Chinese children in California to attend the same public schools attended by others in their neighborhoods is confirmed by the California Supreme Court. However, the segregation of Chinese children in northern California continues in accordance with state law that requires "Chinese or Mongolian" children to attend separate schools when such schools are provided.

According to the terms of the Treaty of Paris, which formally closes the Spanish-American War, Spain cedes Puerto Rico and Guam to the United States. It relinquishes control over and title to Cuba and places it under U.S. military occupation, which ends in 1902. Because Spain granted a Charter of Autonomy to Puerto Rico in 1897, giving it home rule, Puerto Rico seeks continued autonomy.

Spain acquiesces to the offer of the United States of payment of $20 million for the transfer of sovereignty over the Philippines to the United States. The Philippines disputes the authority of Spain and the United States to enter into this transaction and continues its war for independence, first from Spain, later from the United States. The Philippine-American War ends in 1901 with the capture of the president of the Philippine Republic, Don Emilio Aguinaldo, and his Proclamation of Formal Surrender to the United States. Although Spanish has been the language of instruction in the schools when the Philippines were under Spanish rule, English instruction is required during the military occu-

1898, cont.	pation by the United States (as it is in Guam and Puerto Rico). Both Pilipino and English are used as languages of instruction in the 1990s, and some eleven languages and eighty-seven dialects are spoken in the Philippines.

1899   Through the Treaty of Berlin, the United States acquires exclusive rights from the United Kingdom and Germany to the eastern islands of Samoa, now administered by the United States Department of the Interior. The people of American Samoa are United States nationals. English and, of late, Samoan are the languages of instruction.

1901   Congress confers citizenship on all American Indians in the Oklahoma Territory.

1902   Under the provisions of the Platt Amendment, the United States reserves the right to approve treaties and financial transactions between Cuba and other countries, and the right to build a naval base in Cuba. After these restrictions are written into the constitution of Cuba, the United States returns control of other aspects of the sovereignty of Cuba to the Cuban people.

Both English and Spanish are adopted as the official languages of Puerto Rico.

1903   Congress authorizes funds for building a canal on the Isthmus of Panama, but Colombia does not agree to the terms offered. Business interests associated with the New Panama Canal Company engineer an uprising in Panama, supported by the military presence of the United States. The United States recognizes the Republic of Panama and completes treaty negotiations with the new government. The terms of the treaty granting the United States control of the Canal Zone in perpetuity are resented by Panamanians. The United States negotiates revised terms in 1977; these terms give Panama control of the Canal Zone and increased payments while protecting the interests of the United States.

1904   The post of resident commissioner is created to apply to Puerto Rico and the Philippines. Resident commissioners, like delegates, have voice and vote in committees of the House of Representatives, and voice but no vote in House debate. Resident commissioners serve four-year terms; delegates serve for two years. Currently, there is one delegate for the District of Columbia, the Virgin Islands, Guam, and America Samoa, as well as a resident commissioner from Puerto Rico.

1905   The Nelson Act provides for the establishment of Alaskan schools outside of incorporated towns for "white children and children of mixed blood who lead a civilized life." The boarding school education of Native Alaskans in the district of Alaska remains under the control of the secretary of the interior.

1906   San Francisco school authorities order the ninety-three Japanese children in the city (as well as Chinese and Korean students) to be placed in a separate Oriental Public School. Although public outrage and talk of war in Japan over the insult move the president to act to reverse the order, anti-Japanese riots in the city cause additional embarrassment to the United States government. Japanese workers were originally recruited to California as a source of cheap labor in the 1880s. Their growing prosperity and the defeat of Russia by Japan in a conflict over claims to Korea and Manchuria inspire antagonism toward the Japanese in the United States. Hostility is fueled by newspaper accounts of the "yellow peril" represented by Japan's emergence as a great power, and by the specter, being repeated in those articles, of White people deprived of their jobs by Japanese immigrants.

The Naturalization Act of 1906 combines the immigration and naturalization functions of the federal government. The Bureau of Immigration becomes the Bureau of Immigration and Naturalization. Knowledge of English becomes a requirement for naturalization. See Mertz (1982) at http://ccat.sas.upenn.edu/~haroldfs/540/theory/mertz1.html for a summary of court decisions illustrating the belief that the political principles of the United States must be understood to inspire allegiance, that they can be understood only in English, and that knowledge of English must, therefore, be required of those who seek citizenship.

The Race Betterment Foundation in Battle Creek, Michigan, is established by J. H. Kellogg. Beginning in 1914, the foundation sponsors a series of conferences on eugenics, the now discredited theory that genetic differences exist between racial or nationality groups. The trait of feeblemindedness, according to

1906,   this view, is carried in the genes of inferior groups and creates
cont.   social problems such as poverty, crime, and militant labor
        unions. Concern with feeblemindedness fosters the develop-
        ment of intelligence testing, which produces scores presumed
        to support eugenics theory. Among the solutions favored by
        eugenicists are racial segregation, restrictions on immigration,
        selective breeding, and sterilization. The eugenics movement
        becomes influential, leaving its imprint on immigration law
        enacted in 1924, and on public school and university curric-
        ula. See the American Eugenics Movement Archives for addi-
        tional information about the theory and its followers at
        http://vector. cshl.org/eugenics/ and the Archives for the Study
        of Academic Racism at http://about.ferris.edu/isar/archives/
        mental.htm for a discussion of the history of mental testing and
        immigration law. Also, see the Anti-Defamation League's article
        on the Federation for American Immigration Reform (FAIR) for
        a description of the links between immigration and language
        restrictionist organizations and eugenics at http://www.adl.
        org/Civil_Rights/ Is_Fair_Unfair.pdf. Visit Cornell University's
        Mak-ing of America Archives at http://cdl.library.cornell.
        educgi-bin/moa/ pageviewer?coll=moa&root=/moa/cent/cent
        0046/&tif=00643. TIF&view=50&frames=1 to read an article in
        an 1893 issue of *The Century* asserting that militancy among
        unions stems from their control by foreigners.

1907   The Dillingham Commission is appointed by the United States
        Senate to study immigration patterns in response to pressure
        from groups such as the Immigration Restriction League who
        blamed immigration for social problems and labor unrest. Ac-
        cording to Dillingham Commission reports, immigrants who
        have arrived since 1880 are inferior to the immigrants from
        northern and western Europe, who arrived before 1880.

1910–   The Angel Island Immigration Station is established on Angel
1940   Island in the San Francisco Bay. The station operates as the
        main entry point into the United States for people arriving from
        the Pacific until sections of the facility are destroyed by fire in
        1940. The station processes more than 1 million people. The fa-
        cility is a means of enforcing the Chinese Exclusion Acts; over 75
        percent of the arrivals are admitted to the United States after
        being held in detention, which in some cases lasts as long as two
        years. During the detention, Immigration Service officials ques-

tion the Asian arrivals to determine their eligibility for entrance. Poetry composed by the detained Chinese, which describes the conditions at the facility, is etched in the walls of their barracks and is today preserved by the National Archives.

1911   The constitution ratified by New Mexico includes several provisions to protect the rights of Spanish speakers. Article XII, Education, Section 8, directs the legislature to provide for the training of teachers in both the English and Spanish languages and so qualify them to teach Spanish-speaking pupils and students in the public schools and educational institutions of the state, and to provide proper means and methods to aid the teaching of the English language. Section 10 of Article XII guarantees the educational rights of children of Spanish descent in the state of New Mexico. Article XX, Miscellaneous, Section 12, provides for publication in English and Spanish of all laws passed by the legislature, and thereafter as the legislature may provide. New Mexico is admitted to statehood on January 6, 1912, as the forty-seventh state.

1917   Under the terms of the Jones-Shafroth Act, Puerto Ricans are granted status as United States citizens. Consequently, they are eligible to be drafted for military service six weeks later when World War I is declared. The act confirms continued exemption for Puerto Ricans from the internal revenue laws as established in the Foraker Act that ends military rule on the island.

The United States enters World War I with a declaration of war on Germany.

1918–
1923   Laws requiring that all instruction be provided in English are adopted in more than thirty states as patriotic measures prompted by the hostilities of World War I.

1923–
1924   The National Origins Act creates the United States Border Patrol and reduces immigrant admissions to 2 percent of each nationality group's representation in the 1890 census. This quota system gives preferential treatment to immigration from northern and western Europe and excludes all aliens ineligible for citizenship from entering the United States as immigrants. Non-whites, with the exception of Africans, are ineligible to become citizens.

The Citizenship Act of 1924 confers citizenship upon all American Indians born within the United States.

1926   In *Yu Cong Eng, et al., v. Trinidad, Collector of Internal Revenue,* the United States Supreme Court reviews Act No. 2972 of the Philippine legislature, known as the Chinese Bookkeeping Act, which declares it unlawful for any profitmaking entity in the Philippines to keep its account books in a language other than English, Spanish, or any local dialect. The Court finds the act to be a fiscal measure chiefly directed against a large group of Chinese merchants (who are proficient only in Chinese languages) and that enforcement of the law would prevent them from staying advised of the status of their businesses and directing its conduct. The Court's ruling strikes down language-based discrimination in the case of Chinese bookkeepers as denial of equal protection of the laws.

1931   School authorities in Lemon Grove, California, require Mexican children to leave the school they have attended jointly with White children, and reassigns them to a newly built but inferior, separate, barnlike structure; the children's books and equipment are secondhand. The parents of the Mexican children form El Comité de Vecinos de Lemon Grove, refuse to enroll their children in the designated school, and sue the school district. In *Alvarez v. Lemon Grove School District,* an early court victory in favor of school desegregation, Judge Claude Chambers orders the immediate reinstatement of Mexican children to their previous school.

1940–1959: Military Challenges and Renewed Interest in Language Education

1940   The first teachers of English as a Foreign Language enroll at the University of Michigan.

1942   A Marine Corps project using the Navajo language for radio and telephone communications in the Pacific during World War II begins at Camp Eliot in San Diego. The code, an encrypted version of the Navajo language invented and committed to memory by Navajo volunteers, is never broken. The Navajo Code Talk project is classified information until 1968. April 14, 1982, will be proclaimed National Navajo Code Talker Day by President Ronald Reagan. The proclamation will express appreciation for the similar work carried out by Choctaws, Chippewa, Creek, Sioux, and other tribes during World Wars I and II.

1942–
1945

After the Japanese Empire bombs Pearl Harbor, Executive Order 9066 is signed by President Franklin D. Roosevelt authorizing a series of military orders that result in the internment of 120,000 Japanese Americans in ten relocation centers and the confiscation of their homes and property. In 1988, President Reagan signs legislation offering an apology and a $20,000 check to every former internee.

1942–
1964

The Bracero Program (the Mexican Farm Labor Supply Program and the Mexican Labor Agreement) authorizes the temporary admission to the United States of agricultural and railroad workers from Mexico and other Latin American countries to fill acute labor shortages caused by the manpower demands of defense work and of the military draft for World War II. The federal government issues contracts to those willing to undertake temporary work without the right to unionize. Applicants are required to sign contracts written in English, a language they do not understand.

1946

The Military Intelligence Service Language School is established at the Presidio of Monterey. It is renamed as the Army Language School in 1947; the Defense Language Institute, West Coast Branch, in 1963; and the Defense Language Institute Foreign Language Center in 1976.

The Philippines becomes independent from the United States on July 4.

In *Mendez v. Westminster,* United States District Judge Paul J. McCormick rules in a case supported by the League of United Latin American Citizens (LULAC) that the Westminster, Santa Ana, Garden Grove, and El Modena districts in California cannot force Mexicans to attend segregated "Mexican" schools. His ruling is upheld in the Court of Appeals in 1947. At the appeal level, amicus curiae briefs are filed by the following organizations: the American Jewish Congress, the American Civil Liberties Union, the National Lawyers Guild, the Japanese American Citizens League, and the National Association for the Advancement of Colored People (NAACP). This is the first time that a federal court has concluded that the segregation of Mexican Americans in public schools is contrary to California law, thereby violating Fourteenth Amendment due process and

1946,   equal protection clauses. The ruling presages the *Brown* deci-
cont.   sion in its reliance on social science and education research.

1947   Puerto Rico is accorded Commonwealth status. Puerto Ricans
          can vote in presidential and congressional elections only if they
          are registered in one of the fifty states or in Washington, D.C. Al-
          though federal taxes are not imposed, Puerto Rican taxes are.
          Puerto Rico is not currently automatically eligible for equal treat-
          ment with the states under major social programs.

1948   Luis Muñoz Marín becomes the first governor of Puerto Rico
          elected by Puerto Ricans. The following year, his appointed
          commissioner of education establishes Spanish as the language
          of instruction in the schools and English as a required subject.

          The Displaced Persons Act permits 400,000 persons displaced
          by World War II who meet security criteria and have proof of
          employment and housing to enter the United States.

1950   The United States government enacts the Guam Organic Act,
          conferring United States citizenship on the people of Guam.
          Guam is an unincorporated, organized territory of the United
          States. Chamorro and English are the official languages of
          Guam.

1952   The McCarran-Walter Act adds immigration quotas for aliens
          having skills needed in the United States, removes race as a
          basis for exclusion, and permits exclusion on the basis of an
          alien's political ideology.

1953–   The Refugee Relief Act (RRA) of 1953 and its 1954 amendments
1957   authorize the admission of 214,000 refugees from Europe and
          escapees from Communist-dominated countries. Admissions
          to the United States under the provisions of this act include Ital-
          ians, Germans, Yugoslavs, and Greeks. The category of escapees
          from Communist domination is expanded to authorize entry for
          refugees from the unsuccessful 1956 Hungarian revolution. The
          Refugee-Escapee Act of 1957 expands the definitions of the RRA
          to authorize entry for escapees such as the Hungarians, Kore-
          ans, Yugoslavs, and Chinese.

1954   In *Brown v. Board of Education of Topeka,* the United States

Supreme Court unanimously concludes that the doctrine of "separate but equal" has no place in the field of public education because separate educational facilities are inherently unequal.

In *Hernandez v. Texas,* the United States Supreme Court finds that the systematic exclusion of persons of Mexican descent from service as jurors in the Texas county in which a petitioner is indicted and tried for murder deprives him, a person of Mexican descent, of the equal protection of the laws guaranteed by the Fourteenth Amendment. The conviction of Hernandez is reversed. In extending the protection of the equal protection clause to Hispanics, the Court observes that although Texas recognizes only two classes (White and Negro) within the contemplation of the Fourteenth Amendment, the Court does not support that view.

1957   The Soviet Union launches Sputnik I, the first manmade satellite to orbit the Earth. This event is seen as an intellectual challenge and as a military threat. Confidence in the superiority of the United States in matters of science and national security is shaken. Congressional hearings are held to explore ways to restore national security and primacy in science, goals widely accepted by the public. The need for major investment in curriculum development for K–12 classrooms as a means of reaching those goals, and to help the United States reach the moon before the Russians do, becomes apparent. These considerations lead to passage of the National Defense Education Act (NDEA).

1958   The National Defense Education Act provides assistance to state and local school agencies for strengthening instruction in science, mathematics, modern foreign languages, and other critical subjects, as well as for foreign-language study and training provided by colleges and universities.

1959   Rebel leader Fidel Castro assumes control of the government in Cuba. Refugees from that country begin arriving in the United States.

Alaska becomes the forty-ninth state to join the Union.

Hawaii becomes the fiftieth state in the American Union.

1959,   Hawaii's constitution contains provisions protecting the rights
cont.   of Native Hawaiian–speaking residents.

1960–1979: Expansion of Civil Rights and Reemergence of Bilingual Education

1960   From late 1960 until the October 1962 missile crisis, Operation
        Pedro Pan (the Unaccompanied Cuban Children Program)
        brings 14,048 children to the United States. Father Bryan O.
        Walsh from the Catholic Church in Miami arranges for their fos-
        ter care while they are separated from their parents, who are un-
        able to obtain visas to leave Cuba. Ramón Grau Alsina and Polita
        Grau, leaders of the Cuban underground movement, will spend
        years as political prisoners for their clandestine activities in
        shepherding the children out of Cuba. Octavio Visiedo, a former
        superintendent of the Dade County Schools in Florida, is an ex-
        ample of the success achieved in adult life by the children helped
        by this program.

1962   The Migration and Refugee Assistance Act authorizes funding to
        educate and train refugees.

1963   With the assistance of a Ford Foundation grant, Coral Way Ele-
        mentary in Miami, Florida, begins operation as a two-way bilin-
        gual education school, where English-language-origin and
        Spanish-language-origin children each spend half the school
        day studying in and through their home language, and half the
        school day studying in and through their target second lan-
        guage. In 2000, Coral Way is one of only thirty-six schools in the
        district to earn an A grade on the state's accountability system.
        The model will be replicated in many parts of the country. On-
        line profiles of 248 current two-way immersion programs in
        twenty-three states and the District of Columbia are maintained
        by the Center for Applied Linguistics at http://www.cal.org/twi/
        directory/.

1964   The Civil Rights Act of 1964 prohibits discrimination on the
        ground of race, color, or national origin in all federally funded
        school activities and authorizes support for training and techni-
        cal assistance programs for assisting instructional staff in deal-
        ing with problems caused by desegregation, including national
        origin desegregation.

Title VII of the Civil Rights Act protects individuals against employment discrimination on the basis of national origin as well as race, color, religion, and sex. English-only workplace rules may violate Title VII unless an employer shows the rule is necessary for conducting business.

The National Defense Education Act authorizes summer institutes to provide training for teachers of English as a second language.

1965   The National Education Association (NEA) sponsors the 1965–1966 Tucson Survey on the Teaching of English to the Spanish-Speaking and a symposium on The Spanish-Speaking Child in the Schools of the Southwest. Reports from symposium sessions are shared with Congress and figure in deliberations prior to passage of the Bilingual Education Act in 1968.

The Elementary and Secondary Education Act (ESEA) authorizes grants for educational components of the war on poverty through compensatory programs for elementary and secondary school children of low-income families. This act accelerates the trend away from general federal aid to education and toward categorical aid, and to closer relationships between education legislation and national policy concerns such as poverty, defense, and economic growth.

The Hart-Caller Immigration and Nationality Act Amendments abolish nationality quotas, initiate quotas for immigration from the Western Hemisphere, and institute a visa system for family unification and for the admission of aliens with needed skills. With this law, the United States officially ends the quota system established in reaction to massive immigration from southern Europe and exclusions based on race. Applications from people from anywhere in the world previously precluded from entry henceforth are to be placed on an international waiting list. Annual admission levels are increased.

Freedom flights begin, bringing 150,000 exiles from Communist Cuba to the United States by 1973.

1966   The organization for Teachers of English to Speakers of Other Languages (TESOL) is founded. The organization's focus is

1966,   teaching English to speakers of other languages to help students
cont. foster effective communication in diverse settings while re-
specting individuals' language rights.

The Cuban Adjustment Act authorizes the adjustment of the
immigration status of an alien who is a native or citizen of Cuba,
who has been inspected and admitted or paroled into the
United States subsequent to January 1, 1959, and has been
physically present in the United States for at least one year to
that of an alien lawfully admitted for permanent residence.

1967   The American Council on the Teaching of Foreign Languages
(ACTFL) is founded by the Modern Language Association of
America (MLA). ACTFL is the only national organization repre-
senting teachers of all languages at all education levels.

The Supreme Court decision in *Loving v. Virginia* strikes down
Virginia's antimiscegenation law as unconstitutional. Briefs of
amici curiae are filed by the Japanese American Citizens
League, the National Catholic Conference for Interracial Justice,
the National Association for the Advancement of Colored People (NAACP), and the NAACP Legal Defense & Educational
Fund, Inc. Prohibitions on interracial marriage have been enacted as early as 1661 to protect the property interests of slave-
holders in the offspring of their slaves. Since then, more than
forty states have adopted such laws. In 1967, sixteen states still
enforce such laws. In California, the intermarriage of White persons with "Chinese, Negroes, Mulattos, or persons of mixed
blood" is prohibited; Arizona prohibits persons of mixed race of
any kind from marrying anyone. In 2001, there are 3 million
mixed interracial and interethnic marriages, a tenfold increase
over the corresponding total for 1960, according to an analysis
conducted by demographer Bill Frey of the Milken Institute of
data from the Census Bureau's 2000 Current Population Survey.

1968   The Bilingual Education Act is enacted as Title VII of the Elementary and Secondary Education Act of 1968 for economically
disadvantaged language minority students. It recognizes the
unique educational disadvantages faced by non-English-speaking students.

1970   A memorandum stating the applicability of Title VI of the 1964

Civil Rights Act to language minority students is widely distributed to school authorities on May 25, 1970, by the director of the Office for Civil Rights in the Department of Health, Education, and Welfare (HEW).

1971   Massachusetts passes the first state bilingual education act of the decade.

In *Serrano v. Priest,* the California Supreme Court finds the state system of school funding based primarily on local property taxes to be in violation of the equal protection clauses of the Fourteenth Amendment to the United States Constitution and of the state constitution.

1972   Austin, Texas, is the site for the First Annual International Bilingual/Bicultural Education Conference.

1973   *Keyes v. School District No. 1* is the first school desegregation case to reach the United States Supreme Court that involves a major city outside the South. The court holds that Hispanos (the term used by the Colorado Department of Education to refer to a person of Spanish, Mexican, or Cuban heritage) and Blacks in Denver have suffered identical discrimination in treatment in comparison to the treatment afforded Anglo students. Schools with a combined predominance of the two minority groups cannot be considered desegregated.

Florida's Dade County Commission declares the county bilingual and bicultural.

1974   The *Aspira, Inc. v. the Board of Education of New York City* consent decree provides a timetable (by September 1975) for implementing a bilingual education program.

The United States Supreme Court decision in *Lau v. Nichols* requires that school officials take action to provide limited-English-proficient students appropriate services to permit their meaningful participation in the district's educational programs.

The Office of Bilingual Education (now the Office of Bilingual Education and Minority Languages Affairs in the Department of Education) is established within the federal Department of Health, Education, and Welfare.

1974, Passage of the Equal Educational Opportunity Act prohibits dis-
cont. crimination by the states whether or not federal funds are involved. Its provisions require states and school districts to take
appropriate action to overcome language barriers that impede
equal participation in the instructional program.

Amendments to Title VII, the Bilingual Education Act, eliminate
the requirement that children receiving assistance must come
from low-income families; establish regional support centers, a
research program, and an information clearinghouse; and require capacity-building efforts by grantees. Bilingual education
is defined as instruction in English and in the native language of
the student to allow the student to progress effectively through
the educational system.

1975 The National Association for Bilingual Education (NABE) is established as the only national organization exclusively concerned with the education of language minority students in U.S.
schools. It is incorporated in Texas in 1976.

The Indochina Migration and Refugee Assistance Act of 1975
authorizes funds to be used to educate and train Cambodians
and Vietnamese.

The Education of the Handicapped Act (Public Law 94-142) requires all districts to provide handicapped children access to a
free appropriate education designed to meet their unique
needs. It is later reenacted as the Individuals with Disabilities
Education Act (PL 105-17) (IDEA), amended in 1997. Use of languages other than English is authorized as needed for testing
procedures, instructional purposes, and communication with
students and parents.

The Indian Self-Determination and Education Assistance Act
provides for increased participation of Native Americans in the
establishment and conduct of their education programs and
services.

The Office for Civil Rights (OCR) distributes to its regional of-
fices Task Force Findings Specifying Remedies Available for
Eliminating Past Educational Practices Ruled Unlawful under
Lau v. Nichols. This document contains an outline for remedies

to be undertaken by districts found out of compliance with the *Lau* decision. The document is prepared by OCR after consultation with educators who are experts in bilingual education.

1976　Alaska state education authorities are required to establish a high school program and expand opportunities for parental decisionmaking (including decisions related to language of instruction) in every one of the 126 villages covered by the terms of a detailed consent decree in the case of *Tobeluk v. Lind.* This case is more commonly known as the Molly Hootch case, after the Native Alaskan student who is the first named plaintiff in a 1972 suit against the state for failing to provide village high schools.

1977　Amendments to Title VII, the Bilingual Education Act, changes the means of designation of eligible children from criteria based on limited English-speaking ability (LESA) to limited English proficiency (LEP), in recognition of the role of literacy in success in school and later life. It emphasizes the strictly transitional nature of native language instruction, and permits the enrollment of English-speaking students in bilingual programs. Teacher training programs for undergraduate students preparing to become bilingual teachers, fellowships for graduate students, and the establishment of the National Advisory Council on Bilingual Education are authorized.

In *Regents of the University of California v. Bakke,* the judicial system is asked to resolve affirmative action issues. Allan Bakke, a Vietnam veteran turned down by eleven medical schools, learns that the University of California (UC) at Davis Medical School has accepted minority students who are less qualified academically than he is. The Supreme Court, in a 5–4 ruling, upholds the constitutionality of affirmative action, but also rules that Bakke must be accepted to the UC Davis Medical School because race has been used as the sole reason for reserving sixteen places for minority students. The university may consider race in admitting students, but a system of strict quotas based on race is in violation of the Civil Rights Act of 1964 and is thus unconstitutional. Although critics have asserted that affirmative action programs are giving unfair opportunities and advantages to minorities, the majority of the Court holds that the government has a compelling interest in allowing public colleges to

1977,   give consideration to race in admissions because students need
cont.   to be prepared to live in a diverse society.

1978   Journalist Noel Epstein, writing for the Institute for Educational
Leadership, completes a synthesis of information regarding federal policy in bilingual education titled *Language, Ethnicity, and
the Schools* to serve as a basis for discussion among policymakers in Washington, D.C., and elsewhere. The analysis raises
questions regarding the legal and pedagogical basis for bilingual education, its effectiveness, and its long-term impact on
interethnic relations. He quotes critics who attribute self-serv-
ing motives to Hispanic Americans who actively support bilingual education. He identifies as the central issue in the discussion the delineation of the appropriate federal role in financing
and promoting student attachments to their ethnic languages
and cultures. In a response included as part of the report, Dr.
José Cárdenas decries Epstein's assertion that bilingual education leads to separatism, affirmative ethnicity, un-Americanism,
and minority power, and rejects suggestions that the immersion
of LEP students represents an innovative alternative. He explains that bicultural programs lead children from the known to
the unknown by using information about their own groups as
background for concept acquisition. The concerns summarized
by Epstein are incorporated in repeated criticisms of bilingual
education in the 1980s.

In *Debra P. v. Turlington,* plaintiffs, represented by Multicultural
Education Training and Advocacy, Inc. (META), challenge the
Florida Functional Literacy Examination (SSAT II). META claims
that its use, and the denial of high school diplomas for those
who fail the test, are instituted with inadequate notice of graduation requirements and with inadequate time to prepare for the
exam in violation of due process guarantees. The plaintiff class
consists of three groups of students: African American students
in Florida, African American students in Hillsborough County,
and all students in Florida. The Federal District Court holds that
use of the SSAT II as a diploma sanction for students who have
attended the de jure segregated schools violates the Fourteenth
Amendment, Title VI, and the Equal Educational Opportunities
Act (EEOA). Use of the SSAT II will not be valid until the school
system no longer serves students who have attended school
under a dual system of segregated schools. The court further

rules that all students have a due process right to timely notice of the exam when used to deny them diplomas. For notice of the exam to comport with due process requirements, four to six years should pass between announcement of the SSAT II's objectives and the implementation of the diploma sanction.

1980–2001: Education Reform; Demographic Changes; Immigration and Language Restrictions

1980 The contemporary English Only campaign begins in Miami, marked by the passage of Dade County's Anti-Bilingualism Ordinance prohibiting the use of county funds for the use of any language other than English.

The Refugee Act of 1980 is enacted. Prior to passage of this act, the United States has not had a permanent, formal refugee program. Instead, refugees have entered the country under a variety of immigration provisions, including those of conditional entrant and parolee.

Shirley Hufstedler, the first secretary of education for the newly created Department of Education in the Carter administration, publishes in the Federal Register a Notice of Proposed Rulemaking (NPRM), titled Nondiscrimination Under Programs Receiving Federal Financial Assistance Through the Department of Education, Effectuation of Title VI of the Civil Rights Act of 1964, in compliance with agreements entered into with the state of Alaska in *Northwest Arctic v. Califano.* Although the proposed regulations are supported by a few national organizations, including the National Education Association (NEA), they are vigorously opposed by many school districts and by the organizations of their administrators and board members. After the 1980 elections, Terrell Bell is appointed secretary of education in the Reagan administration. Secretary Bell withdraws the NPRM, describing the proposed regulations as inflexible, burdensome, and costly.

The Cuban government grants permission for those who want to leave Cuba to do so. Cuban Americans in Florida organize the Mariel boatlift to pick up the Cuban exiles at Mariel Harbor. More than 125,000 Cubans are admitted under the INS category of Entrants.

1980,   More than 25,000 Haitians also arrive by boat. Considered "eco-
cont.   nomic" refugees by the INS, they are subject to deportation.

The Refugee Act of 1980 removes the ideological definition of
refugee as one who flees from a Communist régime.

United States District Judge James Lawrence King rules that INS
deportation orders that ignore claims of political asylum from
one of the most oppressive régimes in the Americas systematically discriminate against Haitians.

General aid to 32,000 Cuban and Haitian entrants ends. Refugees were receiving $119 a month.

1981   President Ronald Reagan declares bilingual education ab-
solutely wrong and against American concepts because it is
dedicated to preserving native languages but never teaches the
English language needed in the workplace.

An amendment to the Constitution of the United States establishing English as the official language of the United States is introduced as the first appearance of English Only legislation in
the United States Congress. See James Crawford's language policy Web site at http://ourworld.compuserve.com/homepages/
jwcrawford/langleg.htm and the U.S. English Web site at http://
www.us-english.org/inc/official/states.asp for ongoing information on language legislation.

English Only legislation is enacted in Virginia to designate English as the language of the Commonwealth. This is the first
state in the decade to enact English Only language legislation.

1982   A three-point test to determine the effectiveness of an alternative program for LEP students and the extent to which the plan
complies with the Equal Educational Opportunity Act of 1974 is
set forth in *Castaneda v. Pickard.*

The United States Supreme Court rules in *Plyler v. Doe* that
states may not deny public education to students on the basis of
their immigration status.

1983   The National Commission on Excellence in Education publishes a report titled *A Nation at Risk*. This report raises fears, reminiscent of those of the Sputnik era, that the inadequacy of the nation's schools will cause the United States to lose its competitive status in global economic competition. Federal and state legislative action seeking rigorous academic requirements soon follows.

1984   Amendments to Title VII provide program funding for LEP students with special needs, support family English literacy programs, and emphasize the importance of teacher training. Set-asides are established for special alternative instructional programs, which do not require that native languages be used. School districts are also permitted to apply for funding for transitional bilingual education program, or for developmental bilingual education programs whose goal is to develop students' competence in English and a second language. Additional requirements for parent notification and for parents' rights to decline participation in Title VII–funded programs are instituted.

The Carl D. Perkins Vocational Education Act replaces the Vocational Education Act of 1963, and provides aid to the states to make vocational education programs accessible to all persons, including individuals who have limited proficiency in English.

1986   The Immigration Reform and Control Act offers amnesty to undocumented aliens able to prove continuous residence in the United States since January 1, 1982; introduces sanctions for employers of undocumented aliens; and increases border enforcement.

1987   The English-Plus Information Clearinghouse is established.

1988   The Augustus F. Hawkins–Robert T. Stafford Elementary and Secondary School Improvement Amendments of 1988 (Public Law 100-297) reauthorize through 1993 major elementary and secondary education programs, including Chapter 1, Bilingual Education, Magnet Schools, Impact Aid, and Indian Education. Amendments to Title VII, the Bilingual Education Act, include increased funding to state education agencies, expanded funding for "special alternative" programs that provide instruction using only the English language, and increased funding for

1988,	training programs. Emphasis is placed on grade-to-grade pro-
cont.	motion and high school graduation standards. The research
	agenda is expanded.

1989   The New Mexico legislature adopts House Joint Memorial 16, "Supporting Language Rights in the United States." The resolution notes that the fostering of proficiency in other languages on the part of its citizens is needed for survival in the twenty-first century. According to Crawford, New Mexico becomes the first state to adopt an English-Plus resolution, soon followed by Oregon and Washington State. See *Language Loyalties: A Source Book on the Official English Controversy* (1992), edited by James Crawford, or his Language Policy Web site at http://ourworld. compuserve.com/homepages/JWCRAWFORD/nm.htm for detailed accounts of state and national language legislation.

1990   With the Native American Languages Act, Congress declares that the status of the cultures and languages of Native Americans is unique and the United States has the responsibility to act together with Native Americans to ensure the survival of these unique cultures and languages.

In Florida, a Federal District Court hands down a consent decree with statewide requirements for identification and assessment of LEP students, access to the curriculum, parental involvement, monitoring and reporting, teacher training, and other requirements for services to LEP students in *LULAC et al. v. Fl. Board of Education, et al.* The decree requires that any teacher who teaches any subject to LEP students must be appropriately trained for that task, with requirements ranging from the equivalent of fifteen semester hours of training for ESL teachers to three semester hours of training for teachers of other subjects. As the plaintiffs are represented by attorneys from Multicultural Education Training and Advocacy, Inc. (META), the decree is often referred to as the META Consent Decree. For additional information about META, see the organization's Web site at http://www.mindspring.com/ ~allumete/metapages/index.htm.

The Hate Crimes Statistics Act provides for data collection by the attorney general from state and local law enforcement agencies about crimes that manifest evidence of prejudice based upon race, religion, sexual orientation, or ethnicity.

The Immigration Act of 1990 increases authorization for employment-based immigration, establishes a diversity admissions category for underrepresented countries, offers naturalization to Filipino veterans of World War II, and offers permanent residency to immigrants agreeing to invest at least $1 million in urban areas or $500,000 in rural areas. The McCarran-Walter Act of 1952 is amended to eliminate provisions that deny admittance to the United States on the basis of an alien's beliefs, statements, or associations.

1991   The National Security Education Act establishes the National Security Education Program (NSEP), whose aim is to lead in developing the national capacity to educate United States citizens to understand foreign languages and cultures, strengthen United States economic competitiveness, and enhance international cooperation and security.

The National Literacy Act of 1991 establishes the National Institute for Literacy, the National Institute Board, and the Interagency Task Force on Literacy. It amends federal laws to establish and extend various literacy programs, including those serving persons of limited English proficiency.

Spanish becomes the official language of Puerto Rico.

1992   The Native American Languages Act is enacted by the U.S. Congress as a grant program whose purpose is to ensure the survival and continuing vitality of Native American languages.

1993   One of the initial acts of the first Dade County Commission, whose members are elected from minority-empowering single-member districts, is to rescind the county's 1980 Anti-Bilingualism Ordinance.

A bill to declare English the official language of the United States, H.R. 739, is introduced in the U.S. House of Representatives.

English and Spanish are restored as the official languages of Puerto Rico.

A Resolution is passed by Congress and signed by President William J. Clinton to offer an apology to Native Hawaiians on

1993,   behalf of the United States for the January 17, 1893, overthrow of
cont.   the Kingdom of Hawaii, and to urge that steps be taken to bring
         about reconciliation.

1994   The Goals 2000: Educate America Act states the nation's educa-
         tion goals and establishes the National Education Goals Panel.
         Students having limited English proficiency are specifically
         identified as part of the group of "all students" to be included in
         school reform.

         The School-To-Work Opportunities Act establishes a national
         framework within which states and communities can develop
         School-To-Work Opportunities systems to prepare all young
         people for first jobs and continuing education.

         The Bilingual Education Act, part of the Improving America's
         Schools Act (IASA) of 1994, is amended to reinforce professional
         development programs, increase attention to language mainte-
         nance and foreign language instruction, improve research and
         evaluation at state and local levels, and supply additional funds
         for immigrant education. The emphasis of IASA is on school-
         wide reform. Title I eligibility for LEP students is stipulated.

         California voters approve Proposition 187, whose provisions re-
         move undocumented children from public schools, deny emer-
         gency health care and social services to people who are living in
         the state illegally, and require teachers, police, and health care
         providers to notify federal immigration officials and others of
         the identities of persons (including students or their parents)
         "reasonably suspected" of being in the country illegally. Imple-
         mentation is enjoined by the courts. The measure's education
         provisions are struck down as unconstitutional by United States
         District Court Judge Mariana Pfaelzer in 1995. Judge Pfaelzer
         rules that denying undocumented students a K–12 education
         violates the 1982 Supreme Court decision in *Plyler v. Doe*. Not-
         ing that only the federal government has the right to set immi-
         gration policy, other key provisions are ruled unconstitutional
         in 1998. Governor Gray Davis withdraws the state's appeal of
         these decisions in 1999.

         Thousands of Cubans (called Balseros, from the Spanish word
         "balsa," meaning "raft") en route to Miami are rescued at sea

and interned in camps at the United States Navy base at Guantanamo Bay. In a reversal of the policy of the previous thirty years of automatic admission for Cubans, the federal government announces that after the 25,000 Balseros at Guantanamo are brought to the United States, other rafters will be returned to Cuba. The policy change is presented as a humanitarian effort to remove incentives for a journey that costs many refugees their lives. In addition, the repetition of a massive migration such as that of the Mariel period is considered beyond the ability of agencies in the south Florida area to accommodate. Speculations of anti-immigrant, anti-Hispanic, or anti-Cuban motives for the policy change, however, are widespread.

1996 California voters approve Proposition 209, now Section 31 of Article I in the California state constitution. The measure eliminates affirmative action preferential programs throughout the state.

The Illegal Immigration Act doubles the size of the Border Patrol, establishes a telephone system for verification of the immigration status of potential employees, and mandates the construction of fences at selected sections of the border between the United States and Mexico.

The Personal Responsibility and Work Opportunity Reconciliation Act restricts access to public assistance programs (such as food stamps and Supplemental Security Income, a program originally geared for older, blind, and disabled people) for legal immigrants who are not citizens, and sets a lifetime limit of five years for eligibility for public assistance for any individual regardless of nationality or immigration status. Undocumented aliens become eligible only for emergency medical care, immunization programs, and disaster relief. Criteria for eligibility for specific programs are amended by the Illegal Immigration Reform and Immigrant Responsibility Act ("Immigration Law" PL 104-208); the Balanced Budget Act of 1997 (PL 105-33); the Agricultural Research, Extension, and Education Reform Act of 1998 (PL 105-185); and the Noncitizen Benefit Clarification and Other Technical Amendments Act of 1998 (PL 105-306).

1997 The GI Forum and Image de Tejas, represented by the Mexican American Legal Defense and Education Fund (MALDEF), files

1997, cont.	suit in federal district court in *GI Forum v. Texas Education Agency,* alleging that the Texas Assessment of Academic Skills (TAAS) test for high school graduation is discriminatory. On January 7, 2000, Judge Edward C. Prado dismisses the lawsuit, ruling that although there is an achievement gap between majority and minority students, the TAAS examination does not have an impermissible adverse impact on minority students in Texas and does not violate their right to the due process of law.

Congresspersons Jose Serrano and Ileana Ros-Lehtinen introduce an English-Plus Resolution in the United States House of Representatives.

1998   The United States Commission on Civil Rights presents a report to Congress and to the president titled Equal Educational Opportunity and Nondiscrimination for Students with Limited English Proficiency: Federal Enforcement of Title VI and *Lau v. Nichols.* The commission notes that as immigration rates are unlikely to lessen in the near future, the urgency of ensuring that this growing minority of American children has equal access to the nation's educational system is likely to continue into the next century as one of the most pressing civil rights needs confronting the nation, which must find a way to provide educational equity and educational excellence to all students.

Proposition 227 is approved by California voters. Its provisions require schools to teach LEP students solely in English, and to limit instruction in ESL to one year, with some limited waivers and exceptions. Exit polls show extensive opposition among Latino, Asian, and African American voters. Voter surveys conducted by Zoltan Hajnal and Mark Baldassare in March 2001 by the California Public Policy Institute yield findings that coincide with exit poll results. The full report on the surveys, *Finding Common Ground: Racial and Ethnic Attitudes in California,* is available at http://www.ppic.org/publications/PPIC145/ppic145.rb.pdf.

1999   The Census Bureau issues diversity projections. By 2050, White North Americans are expected to constitute less than 50 percent of the population of the United States. California, New Mexico, and Hawaii have no majority group, and the District of Columbia has a Black majority. The country as a whole, however, is still predominantly White.

The United States District Court decision in *Carbajal, et al. v. Albuquerque Public School District v. Burciaga, et al.* supports state bilingual education provisions that provide for Spanish and Navajo lessons for LEP and other students and improvements in the program being offered by the Albuquerque Public Schools. Both the state and local policies are challenged in the suit with the financial backing of the Center for Equal Opportunity (CEO), an organization that also supported Proposition 227 in California. The Carbajal court rejects CEO's challenge to New Mexico's Bilingual Multicultural Act, and accepts improvements negotiated by META and MALDEF in Albuquerque's program, including extra financial incentives for bilingual teachers.

2000   According to an opinion published by the attorney general of California, a school district may not deny a parent's request for a waiver from the statutory mandate that all students be instructed in English because the district has no alternative bilingual program. See http://www.usc.edu/dept/education/CMMR/227/AGopinion227.pdf for the text of the opinion.

A memorandum is issued by President William J. Clinton underscoring the importance of international education to the future of the United States and emphasizing the need to ensure that our citizens develop a broad understanding of the world, proficiency in other languages, and knowledge of other cultures.

Executive Order 13166, Improving Access to Services for Persons with Limited English Proficiency, is issued by President William J. Clinton on August 11, 2000. The Order requires federal agencies to develop and implement a plan to provide services to those with limited English proficiency (LEP) to ensure meaningful access to programs and activities conducted by those agencies. Implementation of the Order is halted by the administration of President George W. Bush pending congressional review of its implications.

Proposition 203 is approved by Arizona voters. Its provisions require schools to teach LEP students in English, and to limit instruction in ESL to one year, with some limited waivers and exceptions.

2000,   The Education Law Center in Philadelphia complains to the Of-
cont.   fice for Civil Rights that Pennsylvania's teacher-certification
policies discriminate against LEP students because the state requires certification in many other areas, but not in ESL. No disposition in the matter has been taken as of this writing.

Recommendations that the Office for Civil Rights of the United
States Department of Education conduct an analysis to determine whether current testing practices for Hispanic students in
the fifty states violate professional testing standards and federal
laws barring discrimination are presented in the President's Advisory Commission on Educational Excellence for Hispanic
Americans report, titled *Testing Hispanic Students in the United
States: Technical and Policy Issues.*

The United States Department of Education Office for Civil
Rights publishes *The Use of Tests as Part of High-Stakes Deci-
sion-Making for Students: A Resource Guide for Educators and
Policy-Makers* to provide guidance on the educationally sound
and legally appropriate uses of tests for students (including LEP
students).

2001   The United States Supreme Court rules five to four in *Alexander
v. Sandoval* that although individuals can sue over alleged inten-
tional state-sponsored discrimination, they do not have the right
to challenge state actions under Title VI of the Civil Rights Act of
1964 on the theory that the disputed actions have a "disparate
impact" on minorities. The lower courts in Alabama had invali-
dated the state's policy of offering written driver's license tests
only in English as a violation of federal antidiscrimination law.
The state does not require the verification of English proficiency
of applicants who hold a valid driver's license from a foreign
country, and provides special accommodations for illiterate and
handicapped driver's license applicants, including those who are
deaf. Pro-English (formerly known as English Language Advocates), the Center for American Unity, U.S. English, and the English First Foundation are among those who filed amicus briefs
on behalf of the state of Alabama. The Center on Race, Poverty
and the Environment; the NAACP Legal Defense & Educational
Fund, Inc., et al.; and the National Women's Law Center, et al.
filed amicus briefs on behalf of the petitioner Sandoval, represented by the Southern Poverty Law Center and the ACLU.

New York State Supreme Court Justice Leland DeGrasse issues a landmark ruling in favor of the petitioners in *The Campaign for Fiscal Equity v. The State of New York,* finding that the state's system of allocating money to school districts fails to provide the opportunity for a sound basic education to New York City public school students in violation of the state constitution. As this failure affects New York City's high percentage of minority students, it is a violation of the federal Title VI regulations. In its ruling, the court orders that the New York state legislature remedy the inequities in its school funding system.

The New York City Board approves changes to its bilingual education programs to include four options from which parents may choose: traditional bilingual classes, classes in English as a second language, a more intensive version of such classes, and dual language instruction. The board does not elect to challenge the *Aspira* Consent Decree that forms the basis for its bilingual education policy; it votes instead to negotiate changes in the decree with the *Aspira* plaintiffs. A key point in those negotiations is whether students will continue to be placed in bilingual programs when appropriate, with parents entitled to withdraw them as provided in the decree, or whether parents will have to affirmatively request bilingual programs.

Arizona Attorney General Janet Napolitano issues an opinion that federal law guarantees the right to teach native languages and cultures in Arizona schools. Napolitano says that Native American language and culture instruction cannot be prohibited in tribal, state, and federal schools because of provisions of the Native American Languages Act of 1990 and the sovereign rights of American Indian nations to self-rule and self-determination. These rights are not affected by the passage of Proposition 203.

President George W. Bush's proposed education plan would eliminate requirements that the federal government give preference to requests for funding from the Bilingual Education Act for bilingual education rather than English-only programs. The plan proposes Title III, Moving Limited English Proficient Students to English Fluency, for programs that ensure LEP children achieve English fluency within three years. Penalties of 10 percent of states' administrative funds could be withheld for failure

2001,
cont. to meet this goal. See the proposal titled Leave No Child Behind at http://www.ed.gov.

A related bill is introduced by Senator Joe Lieberman and ten other original Senate cosponsors and a corresponding group of New Democrats in the House. Their "Three R's" bill aims at overhauling the Elementary and Secondary Education Act (ESEA) by combining more than sixty programs into five performance-based grants (including those funded by the Bilingual Education Act) to the states.

The House/Senate Democratic Caucus, led by Representative George Miller, Representative Dale Kildee, Senator Tom Daschle, and Senator Edward Kennedy, introduces its education bill in the Senate (S.7). Both Democratic bills feature quality control by keeping the Bilingual Education Act as a competitive grant program, increase accountability procedures, and streamline requirements.

According to Census 2000 reports, 12.6 percent (35.3 million of the country's 281 million people) are Hispanic, in addition to the 3.8 million residents of Puerto Rico. Colombians become the fastest growing Hispanic group. The Census Bureau estimates that over 1 million Hispanics are not included in the count. Identifying themselves as Black are 34.7 million people. In addition, 1.76 million persons say they are Black and at least one other race. Non-Hispanic Whites remain the majority at 69 percent of the population. Asians constitute 3.6 percent, Native Americans 0.7 percent, and Native Hawaiians 0.1 percent of the population. A new census category of Multiracial includes 6.8 million people, or 2.4 percent of the population.

The results of the first national poll on Latino and Jewish public opinion in the United States reveal that Jews and Latinos are united on issues such as universal health care: More than 90 percent of both groups favor it. The opinions of a majority within each of the two groups are less congruent with each other on issues such as bilingual education: 63 percent of Hispanics and 19 percent of Jews surveyed strongly support bilingual education. More Latinos (65.9 percent) than Jews (55 percent) think that children are not taught enough about the Holocaust in school.

Utah's English Only law, a voter initiative passed by the voters in November 2000, is upheld as constitutional by the Third District Court in Utah. Judge Ronald E. Nehring concludes that the law is a symbolic gesture of no constitutional consequence and would not discriminate against those who want to communicate with government officials or employees. An appeal is pending in the Utah Supreme Court.

Congressman Bob Stump of Arizona and thirty-one cosponsors (as of August 8, 2001, including one Democrat, twenty-nine Republicans, and one Independent) introduce Bill H.R. 969 to provide that Executive Order 13166 shall have no force or effect, and to prohibit the use of funds for certain purposes related to that Order. The August 11, 2000, Executive Order requires all government agencies to provide services to those with limited English proficiency to ensure meaningful access to programs and activities conducted by those agencies.

In *Kasayulie v. State of Alaska,* Superior Court Judge John Reese reaffirms an earlier decision that the state's rural schools receive inequitable and inadequate funding for facilities in violation of the Alaska constitution and federal regulations prohibiting discrimination under Title VI of the Civil Rights Act. Discrimination against rural schools when money is allocated for school construction has a disparate impact on Alaska Natives, who make up the majority of the students enrolled in rural schools. The judge warns that he will order specific funding levels for rural school construction if the legislature does not act to correct the disparities. Some members of the legislature urge the state to appeal the judge's ruling.

The University of the Incarnate Word, a private Catholic university in San Antonio, agrees to pay $2.4 million in the largest legal settlement to date over English Only rules in the workplace. The federal lawsuit involves Hispanic housekeepers, represented by the Equal Employment Opportunity Commission (EEOC), who claim they are ordered to speak only English, are subjected to ethnic slurs, and are physically abused by their supervisor.

On May 5 (Cinco de Mayo), President George W. Bush becomes the first to deliver a version of the weekly presidential radio ad-

2001,   dress in Spanish. The date commemorates the Battle of Puebla
cont.   in 1862 and the defeat of a French army of 8,000 well-armed
men by approximately 4,000 Mexicans.

REFERENCES

Mertz, E. July 1982. Language and mind: A Whorfian folk theory in United States language law. Sociolinguistics Working Paper Number 93, Southwest Educational Development Laboratory, Duke University, Raleigh, NC.

Chapter Three

✒ Local Bilingual Education Policies and Curriculum

This chapter presents descriptions of the students, teacher preparation programs, and districts whose characteristics affect the implementation of bilingual education programs. Summaries of school district policies from a cross section of the United States illustrate curriculum patterns employed in various school systems. As two-way bilingual programs are increasingly popular, summaries of interviews with principals from schools with those programs are presented to provide an in-depth view of this model.

OVERVIEW

Patterns of bilingual education curriculum are formed by the interaction among basic elements of public education (students and community, teachers, and districts) with language education components (such as ESL, sheltered content, and heritage language instruction). Frequently selected combinations of those components are called *models*. Programs use those models, each program reflecting the array of economic and political forces at play in its district while conforming to the boundaries established by fiscal constraints and state and federal law. The result is a wide variation on the theme established by each model.

Two types of variations must be considered: organizational and idiosyncratic. Organizational differences are the variations that exist from district to district in the choice of model, as incorporated into program descriptions and board policies. Idiosyncratic differences are those within a district that stem from individual actions taken during program implementation. As theoretically defined curricular patterns are translated into political and programmatic reality, inevitably slippage occurs from model to practice.

In instructional programs designated as English-only, for example, the students' home languages may nevertheless be used for diagnosis, placement, supplementary instructional materials, extracurricular activities, tutoring, guidance, community outreach, or parental involvement. Home language use in these activities may be mandated, prohibited, or ignored in district policy. However, individual actions create differences in implementation from school to school, and even within each school. Board policy may authorize the use of the home language in parent outreach activities, but a principal might unilaterally enforce an English Only policy within a school. Board policy may require subject matter instruction through the home language for English-language learners, but a school might place students from several language groups in the same classroom where instruction is presented in only one of the students' languages. Board policy may require that all instruction be presented in English, but a teacher might nevertheless use the home language behind the closed doors of the classroom. Bilingual students might whisper translations. Parents might provide literacy activities in the home language. Teachers, students, and parents might find Web sites in their home languages to supplement official textbooks. Consequently, program titles only suggest, but do not define, which components and languages are included or excluded.

CHARACTERISTICS OF LANGUAGE MINORITY STUDENTS

There were approximately 3.5 million limited English proficient (LEP) students (English-language learners who have a non-English-language background and difficulties with speaking, reading, writing, and understanding English) enrolled in public schools for the 1997–1998 school year, or 8 percent of the total public school population for that year (Macías 1998). Almost half of all English language learners attended schools in which 30 percent or more of the students are also LEP students.

Location, Ethnicity, and Home Languages

English-language learners were concentrated in the western states, in large school systems in urban areas, and in schools with 750 or more students. Schools with concentrations of 20 percent or more minority students, and 20 percent or more students from families whose incomes meet eligibility standards for free or reduced-price lunches, were also more likely to enroll LEP students. Students classified as LEP included 31 percent of all American Indian, Alaska Native, Asian or Pacific Islander, and Hispanic students enrolled in public schools in 1993–1994 (National Center for Education Statistics 1996). Ruiz-de-Velasco and Fix (2000) reported that approximately 20 percent of LEP students at the high school level and 12 percent in middle school had missed two or more years of schooling.

In California, the state with the most LEP students enrolled in public schools, one of every five students was identified as LEP, and two of every five adults providing bilingual instruction were not teachers, but bilingual aides. Texas, Florida, and New York have the second through fourth largest enrollments of LEP students (Macías 1998).

The eleven districts with the highest LEP enrollments (NCBE 1995) are located in Los Angeles, California; New York, New York; Chicago, Illinois; Miami-Dade County, Florida; Houston, Texas; Santa Ana, California; San Diego, California; Dallas, Texas; Long Beach, California; Fresno, California; and Garden Grove, California.

Spanish speakers comprised 73 percent of the LEP student population. The next most common language groups among LEP students were Vietnamese, Hmong, Cantonese, Cambodian, Korean, Laotian, Navajo, Tagalog, Russian, and Creole (French). For additional and regularly updated information on the ethnolinguistic composition and distribution of English language learners, see the National Clearinghouse for Bilingual Education (NCBE) Web site at http://www.ncbe.gwu.edu/askncbe/faqs/index.htm.

English-language learners may be children of native-born citizens of the United States, a group that includes Puerto Ricans and many Mexican Americans, Filipinos, and Haitians. They may be from indigenous communities, a category that includes American Indians, or from communities composed of descendants of Spaniards and Mexicans in the Southwest who were living in those territories before they became annexed to the United States. They may be members of communities of Bosnians, Cubans, Haitians, Iraqis, Russian Jews, Somalis, or Vietnamese refugees. They may be recently arrived immigrants from any country in the world.

Educational Status of Language Minority Students

President George W. Bush's 2001 education agenda was titled "No Child Left Behind." Moving LEP students to English fluency was listed as one of the seven high-priority education goals for his administration. Bush summarized the educational status of LEP students by reference to their standing on accountability measures used to determine whether all students were meeting content-area standards. Noted were indications that

LEP students were not receiving the services they need to make the transition to English. English-language learners, when compared with their English-fluent peers, tended to receive lower grades and often scored below the average on standardized math and reading assessments.

The president's concern is supported by reports summarizing data provided by seventeen to thirty-three state education agencies (Macías 1998), revealing that:

- 37,837 LEP students were retained one or more grades during 1995–1996.
- 14,032 LEP students dropped out of school the previous year.
- 211,433 LEP students scored below state norms in mathematics.
- 52,880 LEP students scored below state norms in science.
- 51,388 LEP students scored below state norms in social studies.

The limited data available on LEP student achievement take on more meaning when more recent information on school achievement by ethnic groups—compiled by the National Center for Educational Statistics (NCES) and presented in *The Condition of Education* (2000)—is considered. Available information on Hispanic American, Asian and Pacific American, and American Indian students was contrasted with data on the performance of non-Hispanic White students. The data summaries were based on combined reports of achievement levels of both English-proficient and English-language learners.

According to Census Bureau reports on the school population based on a 1999 sample survey of households (*San Francisco Chronicle,* March 23, 2001), White non-Latino students were 63 percent of the K–12 student population. This contrasts with the comparable figures of 15 percent for Latinos, 16 percent for Blacks, and 5 percent for Asians. Results of the 1998 National Assessment of Educational Progress (NAEP) on writing skills indicated that Whites were more likely to score at the Proficient level and less likely to score below the Basic level when compared with Hispanic and American Indian students. White students have consistently outperformed their Hispanic classmates on this indicator. On the NAEP assessment in mathematics, results for White and language minority twelfth graders ranked in the following order: Asian, White, American Indian, and Hispanic. Asian and Pacific Islander and White high school graduates were usually more likely than others to complete advanced levels of mathematics and science coursework, courses considered part of the college preparatory track.

White non-Hispanic students comprised 74 percent of the college population, in contrast to the comparable figures for Hispanics of 9 percent, for Asian and Pacific Islanders of 6 percent, and for American Indians of 1 percent. Young adults with college degrees earned more than their peers with less education. In 1998, male and female college graduates earned 56 percent and 100 percent more, respectively, than their peers who completed high school only. Those who received a high school diploma earned approximately 30 percent more than their peers who dropped out of high school. According to educational attainment data presented by the National Education Association (NEA) for 1998, the percentage of sixteen to twenty-four-year-olds without a high school credential was 7.7 percent for White non-Hispanics, 4.1 percent for Asian and Pacific Islanders, and 29.5 percent for Hispanics.

American Indian Students

According to the National Indian Education Association, the Indian population stands at 2 million. The federal government recognizes 550 American Indian tribes and Alaska Native groups.

By rights confirmed in treaties between the United States and tribal governments, the Indian nations are sovereign political entities authorized to control persons, property, and resources within the geographical boundaries of the tribes' lands. Through those treaties, the government of the United States assumed trust responsibility and the obligations flowing from that responsibility. As members of tribes, American Indians and Alaska Natives enjoy dual citizenship as citizens of their Indian nation and of the United States.

Reyhner (2000) recapitulates the history of Indian education under the administration of the Bureau of Indian Affairs (BIA). For most of its history, the BIA acted on the assumption that divesting Indian children of their languages, religions, and other aspects of their culture was in the best interests of the students and the country. Reyhner reports that assimilation, the policy of replacing the home culture and language, has contributed to the poor performance of American Indian students (and dropout rates as high as 25 percent). The schools' requirement that students reject the home language and culture has resulted instead in rejection of schooling by many Indian children and their parents. Reyhner also reports a rise in gang activity among Indian youth who have lost their indigenous languages and are thereby cut off from the counsel of their family members. He cites current research findings that Indian students who are more traditional, who acculturate by adding a second language and culture to their repertoire rather than assimilate by replacing the first language with the second, do as well or better academically than students who are more assimilated. Self-determination for American Indians and Alaska Natives has been the policy of the United States only since the 1970s. Reyhner's article is available in full text at http://jan.ucc.nau.edu/~jar/LIB/LIBconts.html.

An example of the effects of additive and subtractive bilingualism (adding a second language, or subtracting the first acquired by substituting a second language) is provided by *Education Week* in "Bilingual Education Traces," a description of literacy among Cherokee Indians in Oklahoma after 1838. They achieved a 90 percent literacy rate in their own language, and a higher English literacy level than the White populations of either Texas or Arkansas. In 1879, the government began forcing Indian children into off-reservation English Only schools. Gradually, the Cherokee became one of the least literate tribes.

ASIAN STUDENTS

Siu (1996) reviewed an extensive body of research on Asian American and Pacific Islander (APA) students and communities. She concludes that the extent of diversity within APA communities is so great that there are few if any valid generalizations that can be made about them. The category includes over twenty-five ethnic groups with no common language, country of origin, religion, socioeconomic level, length of residence, or generational history in this country. Further, information about Pacific Islanders is lacking. Because government reports group information about Asian and Pacific communities together, the omission is not always evident.

Although the average percentage of Asian Americans not speaking English well is 15 percent, the range on which that average is based includes the percentage for Laotians of 69 percent, and that for Asian Indians of only 5 percent. Members of the APA group also experience wide variation in income. The median income for Asian Indian Americans, Filipino Americans, and Japanese Americans is over $40,000, while that of Hmong Americans is less than $15,000.

Many Asian students do exceptionally well in school. However, the presumption that all APA students will do well (the model minority myth) harms students from that group who are at risk of failure in school. Among the predictors of school failure are low family income and education levels, immigrant status, emotional trauma, non-English-language background, lack of ethnic-group identification, interrupted prior schooling, underdeveloped home-language literacy skills, and age at entry into this country. School factors contributing to at-risk status include inequity in access to the curriculum and to resource allocations, untrained teachers, unrealistically high or low expectations by school staff, the absence of parent-friendly and culturally sensitive policies, biased testing practices, inappropriate placements and tracking based on those test results, and a hostile racial and social climate. Siu's article is available in full text at http://scov.csos.jhu.edu/crespar/Reports/report08entire.html.

HISPANIC STUDENTS

The President's Advisory Commission on Educational Excellence for Hispanic Americans (September 2000) defines Hispanic Americans as persons having historical origins in Spanish-speaking cultures and uses the term *Latinos* interchangeably with *Hispanics* in its reports (1996, 2000). Like Asians and Pacific Islanders, Hispanics are characterized by diversity in race, national origin, socioeconomic status, and cultural traits, and are affected by similar risk factors. Like American Indians, some Hispanics have been living on land now within the borders of the United States since before it was a nation, and 64 percent of Hispanics are native-born citizens of this country. Like other minority groups in the United States, Hispanics have been subjected to discrimination. For the most part, the educational achievement of significant percentages of all three language minority groups continues to lag behind that of the rest of the nation. Unlike either Asians or American Indians, the majority of Hispanics speak a common world language, Spanish.

The combination of rapid population growth, serious shortcomings in the educational systems serving Hispanics, and resulting educational achievement gaps for Hispanics in this country prompted the President's Advisory Commission on Educational Excellence for Hispanic Americans to recommend educational reform in quantum leaps rather than in a series of small improvements. The commission predicts that Hispanics will be the largest minority in the United States by the year 2005; they already make up 25 percent of the school-aged population in California, Texas, Florida, New York, and in many urban centers. According to Census Bureau reports for the year 2000, Hispanics constitute 12.6 percent (35.3 million people) of the country's 281 million people, in addition to the 3.8 million residents of Puerto Rico. By the year 2025, Hispanic children will make up 25 percent of the country's school population. Population projections are that by 2050, Hispanics will represent approximately 25 percent of the *total* U.S. population. Hispanic students are dropping out of school at more than three times the rate of White students and almost twice the rate of Black students, according to "Study: Hispanic Students," 2000.

According to all the traditional indicators, the benefits of educational reform have yet to lift schools serving English-language learners and other language minority students from the depths of the educational doldrums.

TEACHER PREPARATION

The similarities among the components of bilingual education programs (described in Chapter 1) have been recognized in recommendations for teacher education programs. Peyton (1997) recommends that rather than separating language teacher preparation into different departments, English as a Second Language (ESL), foreign language, bilingual, and immersion teachers should be prepared to teach in more than one second-language context and grade level. There is and has long been great similarity in teacher training programs for educators in bilingual programs and foreign and second languages (Fanselow and Light 1977), and in the preparation of university-level faculty who provide the teacher training programs in these fields.

Language Educators

The content of training programs for teachers of English-language learners of limited English proficiency must be different from programs for teachers of students who already know the sounds and grammatical forms of English when they begin their school years, as do native speakers of English and English-proficient students (Kreidler 1987). For ESL teachers, that content typically includes studies in English linguistics; educational anthropology, psychology, and sociology; and educational foundations, curriculum, and methodology.

The preparation program for university-level TESOL faculty (faculty who prepare ESL teachers) typically includes twenty-four graduate semester-hours credit distributed over the following courses:

- Language Acquisition Research
- Language Teaching Methodology
- Syntax
- Sociolinguistics
- Language Testing

- Language Research
- Statistics
- Curriculum/Materials Development
- Phonology
- Practicum (Castro Feinberg, Reiss, and Killian 1997)

In addition to the coursework outlined above, proficiency in a language other than English is required in twenty-three out of thirty-four doctoral programs listed in the *Directory of Professional Preparation Programs in TESOL in the United States and Canada, 1995–1997* (Garshick 1995).

Among the fields of linguistics pertinent to the work of TESOL faculty are applied linguistics, language planning and policy, studies of endangered languages, sociolinguistics, discourse analysis, pragmatics, anthropological linguistics, and dialect and language contact studies. The research agenda for the Center for Research on Education, Diversity & Excellence (CREDE) has an explicitly sociocultural basis. Its emphasis is on critical research and development in the education of linguistic and cultural minority students and those placed at risk by factors associated with race, poverty, and geographic location. Those issues lead to the consideration of the history of culture contact and the nature of relationships among speakers of different language varieties in the home countries and in the United States, description of community attitudes about linguistic groups, and delineation of the distribution of influence along ethnic and linguistic lines. These matters are central concerns in the fields of language education because they frame language learning environments. Preparation programs for language teachers, incorporating research findings from centers such as CREDE, are accordingly grounded in research from the disciplines of psychology, linguistics, sociology, and anthropology of education (and are ultimately related to the philosophical basis for the aims of education in a democratic society).

Recap: The distinguishing areas in the preparation of second-language and bilingual educators are studies in:

- Language and linguistics
- The processes of first- and second-language acquisition
- Culture and its influence on the learning process
- Curricular and instructional approaches best suited to put knowledge about language and culture to use in the classroom

ENGLISH-LANGUAGE ARTS

The content of training programs for second-language teachers contrasts with the guidelines for the preparation of teachers of English that were in place when experienced professors and teachers in English-language arts were trained. The following statement summarizes the content of those guidelines:

> The organization of the guidelines in this document recognizes the division of English into language, literature, and composition, but emphasizes the skills, knowledge, and personal qualifications which contribute to effective teaching. By language is meant the study of the structure and historical development of present-day English. By literature is meant chiefly British and American writing of distinction, but also any writing of distinction in good English translation. By children's literature or literature for adolescents is meant literature which has particular interest and value for children or adolescents. By composition is meant oral and written composition and their relations to rhetorical theory. (Association of Departments of English, November 1966)

These two sets of teacher preparation programs (for bilingual and second- or foreign-language teachers on the one hand, or for language arts teachers on the other) are different, because they prepare teachers to undertake different teaching responsibilities.

ELEMENTARY AND SECONDARY EDUCATION

An even starker contrast exists when the preparation of second-language and bilingual teachers is compared to that of elementary and secondary teachers specializing in areas other than language. Few requirements exist for courses that prepare teachers specifically for instructional duties with English-language learners in the illustrative programs outlined in the following section.

For example, the basic program of studies for the Department of Education at a college in Michigan includes the courses required for elementary education certification in that state:

200: Tutorial Experience, or 300: Clinical Experience
200/4: Tutorial Experience/Special Education
204: Educational Psychology and Observation-Participation

205: Education of Exceptional Students and Observation-
   Participation
330/1: Teaching-Learning Processes and Clinical Experience
350: Instructional Technology
363: Teaching Handwriting
365: Teaching of Reading I and Clinical Experience
366: Teaching of Reading II and Clinical Experience
367: Teaching of Mathematics and Clinical Experience
400: Associate Teaching
403: School Law
444: Associate Teaching Seminar
471: Social Foundations of Education
489: Senior Research in Education

In addition, one course from the following:

368: Teaching of Language Arts and Clinical Experience
369: Teaching of Science and Clinical Experience
370: Teaching of Social Studies and Clinical Experience

A university in Indiana identifies the following courses required
of all secondary education majors preparing for teacher certification in
that state:

EDUC P250: Educational Psychology
EDUC K205: Introduction to Exceptional Children
EDUC K200: Introductory Practicum in Special Education (0 cr.)
EDUC W200: Microcomputing for Education: An Introduction
EDUC: F201 Exploring the Personal Demands of Teaching:
   Laboratory Experience (2 cr.)
EDUC F202: Exploring the Personal Demands of Teaching: Field
   Experience (1 cr.)
EDUC M310: General Methods
EDUC R301: Audiovisual Production of Materials (1 cr.)
EDUC H340: Education in American Culture

A minimum of twelve credit hours completed in a major with at least a
2.5 major area GPA.

The widespread nature of patterns of teacher training such as
those outlined above is confirmed by data compiled by the National
Center for Educational Statistics (NCES). Based on a nationally repre-

sentative survey of full-time public school teachers, NCES (1999) concluded that although 54 percent of the teachers taught English-language learners, only 20 percent of those teachers felt well prepared to do so. The Urban Institute reports that in California, for example, "the 1996–97 ratio of fully credentialed bilingual teachers to LEP students was 1:85 for Spanish-speaking students, and 1:889 for Vietnamese-speaking students" (Ruiz-de-Velasco and Fix 2000, 47). The U.S. needs 100,000 to 200,000 bilingual teachers, according to Díaz-Rico and Smith (1994), depending on the teacher/pupil ratios in the various districts.

The extent to which teachers in the regular classrooms are trained for their roles with English-language learners is important because these students spend only a portion of their school years and generally only part of their school day with ESL and bilingual education specialists. Some students (almost a fifth of all identified as English-language learners) are not enrolled in any program designed for their needs (Macías 1998). Almost half of all pre-K-12 English-language learners reside in the states of California (with 41 percent of the English-language learners in the United States) and Arizona (with 6 percent), where access to specialized services is now expected to last no longer than a year. Ron Unz, the author of Proposition 227, reports that by September 1998, only 20 percent of California's students enrolled in bilingual education programs before the Proposition 227 election in June 1998 were still in bilingual education programs (Unz 1999). Before the election, no more than 30 percent of the state's English-language learners were in bilingual education programs.

Training All Teachers

The shortage of teachers trained to work with LEP students and the rapid increase in the number of these students have led to increased interest in revising preparation programs for elementary and secondary school teachers. Typically, the goal of such revisions is to prepare preservice teachers to cooperate effectively with ESL and bilingual education specialists. These efforts have resulted in various suggestions for ways to prepare all teachers to instruct English-language learners. They include:

- Inclusion of language minority student issues in teacher education diversity courses and in teachers' guides to textbooks used at the K–12 level
- Modification of the teacher preparation curriculum to include new courses or revamp existing courses through infusion of LEP issues

•• Revision of requirements from state or national accreditation agencies that teacher preparation programs address these concerns

•• Adoption of teacher certification requirements that all teachers who teach any subject to English-language learners must document successful completion of training for that task

•• Expansion of staff development programs managed by school districts to include LEP issues

•• Initiation of professional development programs for university faculty whose expertise is in areas other than language to enable them to prepare pre- and in-service teachers for their duties with English-language learners

Teacher Credentials

Every state establishes the requirements that must be met to qualify for and renew a license to teach in the public schools. The license, often called a teaching certificate, lists the subjects and levels for which authorization to teach is granted. Areas of coverage added to the certificate after initial certification has been granted may be called endorsements.

By 1999, thirty-seven states and the District of Columbia offered ESL teacher certification or endorsement. In twenty-three states and the District of Columbia, ESL teachers are required to have ESL certification or endorsement. Similarly, bilingual education or dual language certification or endorsement is available in twenty-three states and the District of Columbia, and required in seventeen states (NCBE 2000).

In Pennsylvania, which offers teaching credentials in many teaching areas but neither offers nor requires a license to teach ESL, the Education Law Center in Philadelphia has filed a complaint with the Department of Education Office for Civil Rights (OCR) about the state's teacher certification policies, alleging discrimination (Zehr 2000). As of this writing, a disposition on the matter is pending.

University Faculty Credentials

Students depend to a great extent on the skill of their instructors, a function of a teacher's professional preparation. Because teacher training is an important consideration, many states require districts to report and make public annually how many teachers are assigned instructional duties in subjects for which they do not hold teaching credentials. Equivalent reports for postsecondary instructors teaching courses other than those in their fields of expertise in teacher training institutions are not required. Colleges and universities are instead reviewed periodically by national and regional accrediting agencies. The review is voluntary, based on the principle of academic self-governance. Typically, criteria are established for minimum standards of quality and integrity regarding academics, administration, and related services.

The Southern Association for Colleges and Schools (SACS) Commission on Colleges, for example, conducts reviews every ten years. Criteria for the academic and professional preparation of faculty in undergraduate programs state that faculty members teaching credit courses leading toward the baccalaureate degree must have completed at least eighteen graduate semester hours in the teaching discipline and hold at least a master's degree. At the graduate level, the expectation is that faculty members teaching credit courses enjoy professional standing (including clinical experience and published research) and hold the terminal degree (usually the earned doctorate) in the teaching discipline or in a closely related discipline.

Graduate and undergraduate students are becoming more sophisticated consumers. Many regularly review student evaluations of college instructors and request the opportunity to review instructors' resumes (often posted on faculty Web pages) before selecting courses. This may well be a prudent course of action for prospective teachers as courses to "prepare all teachers" proliferate in the scramble to increase the supply of teachers for English-language learners.

School Districts

Districts with the largest percentages of English-language learners are located in California, Florida, Illinois, Massachusetts, New York, and Texas. Of the twenty districts with the highest LEP enrollments, fifteen are members of the Council of Great City Schools (CGCS), an organization of the nation's largest urban public school systems. Increasingly, urban schools in the states attended by English-language learners are racially and economically segregated, and located in neighborhoods marked by concentrated poverty (Orfield 1993; Rumbaut 1998).

Racially isolated schools, and associated divisions in social class and anti-immigrant sentiments, are among the features of contemporary society that affect the attitudes of students and school personnel. English Only legislation, attacks on affirmative action, and limitations on how many years students are eligible for instruction in ESL or in bilingual programs are perceived as expressions of anti-immigrant and antiminority bias (Attinasi 1998). These sentiments are sometimes expressed violently, as indicated by an increasing incidence of hate crimes directed against language and other minority persons. In a press release issued March 27, 2001, by the National Council of La Raza (NCLR) urging passage of hate crimes legislation (the Local Law Enforcement Enhancement Act of 2001), Raul Yzaguirre, president of NCLR, pointed out that the Latino community is increasingly a target of hate-motivated crimes. According to the Federal Bureau of Investigation's (FBI) annual *Hate Crimes Statistics Report,* 7,876 bias-motivated criminal incidents were reported in 1999.

The frangible state of schools in the large urban centers has often been noted. The challenges district officials face include difficulties in coping with growing fiscal deficits, overcrowding, shortages of fully trained and credentialed teachers, and isolation from other community institutions (McDonnell and Hill 1993). Although minority students are the numerical majority in many school districts, the teaching force has become increasingly dominated by White females (Baca, Escamilla, and Walton 2000). Accordingly, school districts need to allocate funds for diversity training and for recruiting a diverse teaching force.

Two aspects of this description are of particular importance in any discussion of school district policy development. First, what is the extent to which adequate classroom space is available? Schools are not only overcrowded but they are in need of maintenance. Nationwide, the average public school is forty-two years old; one-third of these buildings should be repaired or replaced (Riley 1999). Second, are enough appropriately trained teachers available? The United States needs 100,000 to 200,000 teachers trained to work effectively with language minority students (Díaz-Rico and Smith 1994).

Rural schools cope with problems similar to those noted above; they affect 25 percent of all U.S. schoolchildren attending schools in rural areas. According to Beeson and Strange (2000), minority group members constituted 17 percent of all rural residents in 1997. Where there is a concentration of English-language learners, the number of rural minority children as a percentage of all rural students ranges from 63 percent in New Mexico to 27 percent in Florida. In the same states, the percentage of all children living in rural areas whose family income is below the federal poverty level ranges from 37 percent in New Mexico to 16 percent in California.

Problems common to all schools are often greater in rural areas. It is difficult, for example, to recruit rural educators to isolated posts that offer salaries lower than those in other areas (nationally, the difference between the average rural teacher's salary and teachers' salaries in the rest of the state amounted to $6,124 in 1993–1994). District budgets must finance greater transportation costs associated with the distance and sparsity. As noted in the 2001 Alaska Supreme Court decision in *Kasayulie v. State of Alaska,* the distribution of political power in a state can generate biased systems for the distribution of capital outlay funds. In this case, the bias resulted in discrimination against rural areas and their minority students. For additional information on the condition of rural education, see the Rural School and Community Trust Web site at http://www.ruraledu.org/index.html.

The problems noted above divert limited district funds from instructional improvements and mark boundaries within which policymakers must work in authorizing curriculum development or program implementation. Even when qualified teachers are available, for example, if there is no vacant classroom space in overcrowded school buildings, new teachers will not be hired as there would be nowhere for them to conduct classes. If funds allocated for building and repair are consumed by emergency maintenance projects, no funds will be left for new construction. If new teachers for bilingual programs must nevertheless be hired to comply with nondiscrimination requirements, they often become "floating" or "roaming" teachers, pushing a cart with their teaching materials as they travel from room to room to meet their charges in the students' "home rooms"; sometimes, they even travel from school to school. Constant turnover is the result as new itinerant teachers are hired to replace those who have acquired the seniority they need for assignment to other programs.

POLICYMAKERS AND ADMINISTRATORS

School district policy and budget decisions in over 15,000 school districts, affecting students in over 100,000 schools, are made by elected school board members (or, for 15 percent of the districts, by members appointed by other elected officials, such as mayors or governors). Their major concerns include student achievement, finance and budget issues, increasing enrollment, facilities, and curriculum (Educational Vital Signs 1998).

The majority of board members are White (81 percent) and middle- to upper-middle-class (28 percent with incomes above $100,000, 17 percent with incomes from $80,000 to $99,000, and 21 percent with incomes from $60,000 to $79,000). They are advised by administrators who are also predominantly White (84 percent of principals) and economically secure (Education Vital Signs 1998). In contrast, the majority of K–12 students in a growing number of school districts are ethnically, culturally, and linguistically diverse, and financially vulnerable. The

Children's Defense Fund (2001) reports that 17 percent of all children in the United States live in poverty. In the fifty-seven member districts of the Council of Great City Schools, however, the extent of concentrated poverty can be gauged by the districts' average 58 percent rate for the number of students eligible for participation in the free or reduced-price lunch program (Council of Great City Schools 1999). The growing social distance between school officials and their students and patrons constitutes an additional constraint (compounded under conditions of linguistic or cultural mismatch between staff and parents) in the policy-development process.

Public accountability measures instituted as part of state educational reform plans include standardized tests based on increasingly rigorous goals for instruction; the test results will be published along with other indicators of a school's effectiveness (Editorial Projects in Education, Inc. 1999). The reputation of the districts, the career prospects of their personnel, and the reelection prospects of their board members become linked to increased student achievement as measured by test scores. A school with low student test scores can be marked by state officials as a low-performing school. In some states, legislative provisions give state education officials authority to assume control of schools whose students chronically fail to achieve the required standard on state examinations. Such a takeover can result in replacement of the board members and superintendent with new officers selected by the state. These pressures inevitably affect the district staff's attitudes toward English-language learners, who must demonstrate their knowledge through a language in which they are not proficient on examinations whose stakes are high for students and staff members alike.

FUNDING

One of the major duties of school board members is to approve their districts' budgets. In times of burgeoning enrollment or downturns in the economic base for state revenue, the recurring need to balance resources with anticipated income typically results in pruning programs as competing requests for allocations are evaluated. In the priority-setting process, the constituents best served are typically groups whose economic standing and educational preferences are similar to those of the people with the power to make decisions, groups that infrequently included language minority communities.

An alternative to reducing allocations and cutting services is to seek additional funding. In districts with taxing authority, the board may increase the tax levy on local property or seek additional local tax-ing authority. Rather than tap local resources, school boards may re-quest additional appropriations from other levels of government. None of these strategies is entirely without political cost, or likely to be effec-tive when the pursuit of lower taxes conflicts with goals for educational reform and improvement. See Chapter 6 for additional information on the relationships between the political process and education funding.

Challenges to Consider When Selecting Programs

Bilingual education programs are initiated for various reasons. District officials may select language education models according to recommen-dations by staff members with technical expertise in language education. On occasion, staff proposals may be prompted by requests from individ-ual board members or by official directives from the board. In many dis-tricts, bilingual programs are initiated as a result of parent requests or community demands, the enforcement of state curriculum requirements or state or federal civil rights mandates, or court orders. Staff members tend to resist mandates that come from outside their school systems. Al-though resistance has negative effects on the success of the required pro-gram, there might be no program at all without the requirement.

The views of district advisory committee members, professional associations, or parent and civic groups are often solicited and incorpo-rated within policy proposals. No matter the nature of the input provided by those groups, staff members must draft their plans in accord with what they believe the majority of the board will approve; failure to gain board approval of a plan recommended by staff may be perceived as a public setback for the superintendent who employs them. As elected officials, board members need positive media coverage and contributions suffi-cient to cover the expenses of a campaign to attract the voters. Continued tenure for board members often reflects the degree to which their deci-sions are compatible with the interests of those who control resources.

With rare exceptions, board meetings are open to the public; some jurisdictions provide gavel-to-gavel television coverage. Board members act on the basis of their finely tuned attention to community preferences and their own knowledge. Members within the same board may represent different (and sometimes competing) groups within the community, and may even aim their comments at different segments of the local media.

Discussions prompted by those sometimes competing allegiances illustrate the advantages (and, at times, challenges) of the democratic de-cisionmaking process. The following summary of board deliberations from a large urban system illustrates the point. The board's only language minority member suggested that translated report cards be provided for the two major language minority groups in the district so that parents of English-language learners might be more adequately informed about their children's progress. Staff members responded that translated materials could be easily developed for most, but not all, of the students' home languages, and that type fonts for some languages were very expensive. The teachers' union president offered his opinion that parents would have no incentive to learn English if materials in the home language were made available. Other board members agreed that although it's important to keep parents informed, report cards should not be translated until funds were available for the type fonts needed to translate each of the twenty-three languages spoken by students in the district (in other words, never). The reader may decide whether this decision is an example of an advantage of the majority rule aspect of legislative deliberations (because by providing English-language report cards to all parents, it represents support for the principle of treating all students and parents in the same way) or a limitation of the process (because in failing to direct the resources that are available to 95 percent of the language minority parents in the district, it denied their claim for the different treatment required to achieve benefits equal to those available to English-language-origin parents).

A comparison of the program of studies usually available for English-language-origin students with that of English-language learners will help shed light on additional curriculum development and program selection challenges. Dick and Jane (English-language-origin students) will study the English language each of the twelve years of their public school experience. In the first three grades, the majority of the school day will be devoted to the development of the literacy skills needed as a learning tool in the later grades. During the elementary school years, their teacher will have credentials in elementary education and may also qualify for certification as a reading specialist based on graduate study in reading instruction.

During the secondary school years, their teachers are likely to have teaching credentials that correspond to assigned areas of teaching. In addition to English, the required program of studies will include science, social studies, mathematics, and possibly art, computer applications, foreign languages, and physical education. At the secondary level, Dick and Jane may have room in their schedules for elective courses. They may choose electives that prepare them for college, for healthy leisure-time pursuits, or for vocational areas.

Dick and Jane (and their parents) can expect to understand the language of their teachers, their peers, their textbooks and other instructional materials, and the examinations they will be required to pass to demonstrate achievement and to qualify for promotion or high school graduation. By the time they graduate from high school, their elementary and secondary education will have prepared them to continue to learn in academic settings, to earn a living in the high-tech global economy of the twenty-first century, to take part in the civic and political life of their community, and to help solve social problems as knowledgeable voters and jury members.

Maria and Victor (English-language learners) need to reach the same academic, economic, political, and social goals as Dick and Jane, and in addition they need to learn the English language and its associated culture. While Dick and Jane are learning to read in their home language, Victor and Maria can be developing a foundation for literacy skills in their home language, which will later transfer to English, or they can attempt the far more difficult task of simultaneously learning the second language and literacy skills taught through the second language (English). During the elementary school years, they may have a teacher who holds an elementary school certificate, a teacher with both an elementary school certificate and training in how to teach English as a second language or bilingual education, or a group of teachers during the school day, each of whom is prepared in a different aspect of teaching English-language learners. In some districts, their instructors will be teachers' aides, long-term substitutes, or teachers who are not fully credentialed.

During the secondary school years, they may or may not have teachers trained in teaching English-language learners through ESL or home-language methods in addition to subjects such as science or social studies. Throughout their school careers, their teachers may or may not be bilingual. They may have access to English instructional materials, or to both English and home-language materials.

While Dick and Jane are studying content areas through their home language (English), Maria and Victor can do the same through their home language, or they can attempt the far more difficult task of simultaneously learning the English language and other content areas taught through that language. While Dick and Jane are studying a foreign language, Maria and Victor will be studying English as a Second Language (ESL). Dick and Jane (and their parents) will understand the teachers, their peers, their textbooks, and the questions on the examinations they will be required to pass to demonstrate achievement and to qualify for promotion or high school graduation. Maria and Victor may not.

English-language learners and English-language-origin students alike need to develop English-language literacy skills and learn science, social studies, mathematics, and other required content areas within the twelve-year time span allocated for elementary and secondary education. English-language learners, however, must also learn a new language within the same period.

Programs and Models

The components (described in Chapter 1) most frequently selected by school districts include ESL, sheltered content-area instruction, and home-language instruction in the content areas. Frequently selected configurations of those components are referred to as models. District officials select from or develop models to implement as programs.

Programs Using English Only

Some school districts provide formal instruction in English-language skills through an ESL component. They may offer content-based ESL structured around academic content rather than or in addition to a skills-based approach. Content ESL is an approach to teaching the English language based on the assumption that modification of language and curriculum will lead to comprehensible instruction in the subject areas; this in turn will result in students' learning English the way they learned their native tongues. The principal goal is English-language acquisition.

Districts making exclusive use of English often offer a component in sheltered content instruction. Sheltered content-area instruction is an approach to teaching content areas other than English through the English language to class groups composed solely of intermediate-level ESL students, based on the assumption that understandable instruction will assist second-language learners to achieve at grade level in the various subject areas. The principal goal is content mastery in subjects such as science and social studies, as well as the acquisition of academic English. Understandable instruction is provided through modifications in the language, curriculum materials, and methods used in instruction.

To implement these programs, students are grouped according to their levels of English-language proficiency and grade level. To the extent they are available, teachers with credentials in ESL and, in the case of sheltered content-area instruction, credentials in the areas of subject specialization, are selected for these programs. Major program variables include duration during the school day and in the number of years the instructional program is provided for each student, and the extent to which supplementary home-language services (such as diagnostic screening, orientation and counseling, and parent involvement) are available.

Arrangements to deploy staff and use school buildings constitute a third major variable among ESL programs. Elementary school "pull-out" ESL programs move groups of English-language learners from their regularly assigned classrooms, shared with language majority students, to another setting where they are gathered to receive ESL instruction. In "self-contained" ESL programs, English-language learners receive instruction in ESL and in all other subject areas in the same room, generally from the same teacher. A self-contained classroom may be composed exclusively of English-language learners or may include both English-language learners and English-proficient students.

In California and Arizona, sheltered English immersion has been required for almost all English-language learners (except for those whose parents succeed in gaining an exception for their children) since voters approved Proposition 227 (adopted in 1998) in California and Proposition 203 (approved in 2000 and adopted in the fall of 2001) in Arizona. This program aims to bring about English-language acquisition during a one-year period through modified curriculum and instruction designed for children who are learning English.

PROGRAMS USING ENGLISH AND
THE HOME LANGUAGE

Transitional Bilingual Education (TBE) programs combine ESL, sheltered English, and home-language instructional components. The goal of a TBE program is to teach English so that students can transfer to an all-English-language curriculum. To avoid academic retardation in required subject areas, the students' home languages are used for content area instruction while the students are learning English.

English-language learners are grouped according to their grade and level of English-language proficiency in ESL and sheltered content courses, and according to their home-language background and grade in classes taught in the home language. To the extent they are available, teachers with credentials in ESL and bilingual education and, in the case of content-area instruction, credentials in the areas of subject specialization are selected for these programs. Often, bilingual paraprofessionals are employed to assist with home-language instruction. When students meet the criteria for transfer to the all-English-language curriculum, no additional home-language instruction is provided.

Maintenance or Developmental Bilingual Education programs arrange language-education components in the configurations described above, but increase the duration of home-language instruction.

Heritage language arts instruction, in other words, is provided for students who are English-proficient as well as for English-language learners. Some subjects may be taught through the home language to provide opportunities for its academic use. Program goals include the development of academic proficiency in the students' home languages and reinforcement of skills in English-language arts.

Foreign Language Immersion (also known as Canadian Bilingual Immersion) is designed for language majority students. All or part of the district curriculum is presented in the target language by bilingual teachers. The students acquire the target language as they focus on learning the various subjects presented through that language. Like Content ESL, immersion programs share the emphasis on language learning; but in the long term, they share the emphasis of sheltered English instruction on grade-level achievement in the content areas. In some districts, students participate in immersion programs for the full school day, gradually adding instruction in English when they reach the upper grades. In less intensive programs, students participate in immersion programs for only part of the school day; English is the language of instruction for the remainder of the day.

Two-Way Bilingual Programs (also known as Two-Way Immersion Programs, or TWIP) combine developmental bilingual education for language minority students with Canadian-style bilingual immersion for language majority students. Language majority and minority students are grouped together for instruction according to their grade levels, each group studying in and through the home language for a portion of the day and through the second language for a portion of the day. Biliteracy goals are explicitly addressed for both groups of students. The amount of time during a school day devoted to home-language instruction varies from program to program. Many programs aim for a half-day of instruction through each language; others schedule 90 percent of the school day in the non-English language during the early grades, gradually increasing the amount of time devoted to instruction in the English language. The goal of the program is to develop proficiency in both languages for both groups of students, and to foster grade-level achievement in the content areas through each language. The integration of both sets of students in the same program also helps students achieve cross-cultural communication goals.

Two-way bilingual programs are sometimes called "dual-language" programs; But in some districts, dual language refers to a program of instruction with a biliteracy goal; during the school day, it distributes two languages of instruction in programs serving students of English-language origin exclusively. Two-way programs are bilingual and bi-ethnic, but dual-language programs may be bilingual and mono-ethnic. A directory of Two-Way Immersion Programs in the United States is available at http://www.cal.org/twi/directory/.

Program goals for developmental, immersion, and two-way bilingual education programs include grade-level achievement in the content areas, transfer and reinforcement of language arts skills between first and second languages, and the addition of a second language to the student's linguistic repertoire.

NEWCOMERS

Although English-language learners who are gifted, or whose schooling in the country of origin was accelerated, pose program development and student placement issues, the pressing needs of English-language learners whose former schooling was limited or interrupted have received more attention. English-language learners who begin their education in the United States during their secondary school years also face formidable challenges in meeting graduation requirements.

In recognition of these difficulties, some districts have established newcomer centers or schools. This organizational arrangement helps target resources to English-language learners because all teachers in the program or school are working full-time toward the same goal. Some newcomer schools adopt home-language components, others do not. The Center for Applied Linguistics maintains an online searchable database with profiles of 115 newcomer programs in twenty-nine states at http://www.cal.org/newcomerdb/.

Because language minority students in newcomer schools are in a segregated and ethnically identifiable setting, the Department of Education Office for Civil Rights (OCR) has established guidelines for reviewing these programs. Their basic criteria for approval of newcomer schools include voluntary participation on the part of minority students, temporary placement in the isolated program, access to enriched resources equal to or better than those available in other settings, and documentation of the educational justification for placement in a segregated setting (Schnaiberg 1996).

PUBLIC SCHOOL DISTRICT POLICIES AND PROGRAMS

The two states with the largest concentrations of students in bilingual programs are California and Texas. The district profiles presented in this section describe the largest urban and one of the smallest rural districts in Texas, and a suburban district from California. For each profiled district, a specific school and program are described. These profiles include descriptions of each district's students and community, teachers, and districts; the language-education components selected by the district; and the variety of ways these factors are combined to fit local conditions.

The Houston Independent School District

The Houston Independent School District (HISD) is the largest school district in the state and the seventh largest in the United States. Its former superintendent, Dr. Rod Paige, was nominated by President George W. Bush to be the secretary of education for the U.S. Department of Education. The district operates 295 campuses and educational programs. This urban school system serves the Harris County community of 4.5 million residents. The county's economy is based on a broad spectrum of industries, including petrochemical production, medical research and health care delivery, high technology, international import and export, commercial fishing, agriculture, banking and finance, manufacturing, and distribution.

Policies are established for this district by a board of trustees composed of nine members who are elected from single-member districts and who serve staggered four-year terms. Single-member districts typically foster ethnic representation reflective of the ethnic composition of the community in legislative bodies. According to the district's mission statement (available online at http://www.houstonisd.org/Pubs/Purpose/purposeintent.htm), the district's mission is to strengthen the social and economic foundation of Houston by assuring its youth the highest-quality elementary and secondary education available anywhere. Judging by the voters' approval of the 1998 bond issue election authorizing the district to issue $678 million in bonds for capital construction, the district enjoys a high degree of public confidence.

Salaries for HISD teachers with a bachelor's degree range from $33,750 to $50,846. In addition, stipends of up to $3,000 per year are provided for teachers with certification in ESL or bilingual education. As an additional recruiting tool, four-year scholarships are awarded to future bilingual teachers.

As reported by the district in student ethnicity reports for October 2000, the ethnic composition of the student population is 55 percent Hispanic, 32 percent African American, 10 percent White, 3 percent Asian and Pacific Islander, and less than 1 percent American Indian or Alaskan Native. Almost two-thirds of the students are economically disadvantaged, and one-quarter are not fluent in English.

To be eligible for promotion in elementary school, a student must maintain an overall average of seventy or better for the year and an average of at least seventy in reading, other language arts, math, and either science or social studies. An additional requirement is a passing score on specific parts of the Texas Assessment of Academic Skills (TAAS) test and a passing score on the Stanford 9 or the Aprenda 2 (a Spanish-language standardized test).

To be promoted in middle school, a student must maintain an average of at least seventy in any three of the four core courses (language arts, math, science, and social studies) and an overall average of seventy or above for all courses in which the student is enrolled in grades six through eight, as well as a passing score on specific parts of the TAAS and a passing score on the Stanford 9 or the Aprenda 2. The Language Proficiency Advisory Committee (LPAC) makes promotion decisions for students with limited English proficiency.

To graduate and receive a diploma, students must earn twenty-four credits; in addition, students must pass the exit-level (tenth-grade) TAAS or appropriate end-of-course exams. English is a required subject each of the four high school years, as four credits in English are required for graduation. One credit in a language other than English is required to graduate from the district's Core Program, two credits to graduate from the Advanced Program, and three credits to graduate from the Distinguished Achievement Program.

The district offers various options in language education, including Transitional Bilingual, Developmental Bilingual, Two-Way Bilingual Immersion, and ESL programs at the elementary school level. At the secondary level, both ESL and bilingual programs are offered.

In July 1999, the HISD school board approved the district's mission statement, statement of beliefs, and goals for its multilingual programs. The mission statement speaks to the need to strengthen the social and economic foundations of Houston by ensuring that its students achieve their full academic potential and by providing opportunities for all students to graduate proficient in multiple languages. Limited-English-proficient children are to learn to read, write, and speak English as rapidly as individually possible. The statement of core beliefs emphasizes the importance for English-language learners to learn English rapidly, but without sacrificing long-term academic success. English-language learners and all other students are strongly encouraged to develop fluency in two languages. Bilingualism is described as crucial to Houston's economic prosperity and to individual success in a competitive global marketplace. Policy goals include the improvement of identification procedures for English-language learners eligible for gifted and talented programs, and increasing communication with parents to be sure they are aware of program options. To assist in communicating with parents, schools are to be provided with bilingual brochures and videos. The program guidelines are available online at http://www.houstonisd.org/multilingual/Program%20Descriptions/Bilingual_ESL/Bil_ESL.htm.

Bilingual and ESL programs in Texas must comply with the state's rules under Chapter 89, set forth at the Texas Education Agency Web site at www.tea.state.tx.us/rules/tac/chapter089/ch089bb.htm. These state guidelines require districts to provide bilingual education programs to elementary school students and an ESL program to all students who are not entitled to bilingual education, and authorize dual-language programs at the option of the district. In grades three through eight, English-language learners may be eligible for exemption from the Texas Assessment of Academic Skills (TAAS), or for the administration of a Spanish-language version of the test. Additional state requirements for the identification, assessment, classification, and placement of LEP students are incorporated into district procedures. Written notice of the recommended placement and a request to parents for written approval must take place within ten days from the date a student is classified as LEP.

Beginning in the second grade, students are reclassified as English-proficient and exit the bilingual or ESL language support program when they demonstrate the ability to participate equally in an all-English, instructional program according to state performance standards; students may be reclassified if they later fail to meet those standards. Because bilingualism is encouraged by the district, home-language instruction may continue after students are classified as English-proficient.

Notable School

The Rice School (La Escuela Rice), a dual-language school that focuses on technology, serves students in kindergarten through the eighth grade. Based on performance on the TAAS, and on dropout and attendance rates, the Rice School was awarded the rating of "Recognized" by the Texas Education Agency Accountability Rating System for the year 2000. A recognized rating means the district or campus had a TAAS passing rate of 80 percent or more and a dropout rate of 3.5 percent or less for all students and each student group, as well as an attendance rate of at least 94 percent. In 2000, the performance of students in the third through sixth grades who took the Spanish TAAS was considered when determining ratings.

The Rice School is one of HISD's many magnet schools. Parents must apply to enroll their children in this school and prospective students may have to take entrance auditions or examinations. These theme-based schools are established to attract students from a cross-section of the community and thereby foster social integration. At the elementary and middle school levels, Houston's list of magnet schools includes those emphasizing the fine arts, math, science and technology, technology and Spanish, communications, foreign languages and cultures, dual language, literature, architectural and graphic design, and Vanguard Programs for gifted students. At the high school level, magnet programs are available in aviation sciences, business administration, careers, classical humanities, communications, computer technology, engineering professions, environmental sciences, foreign languages, health professions, hotel and restaurant management, international studies, law enforcement and criminal justice, leadership, math, science and technology, the meteorology and space sciences, music and fine arts, performing and visual arts, research and technology, teaching professions, and technology careers. In addition, a Vanguard high school for gifted students features advanced placement courses.

The design of the Rice School, which opened in 1994, resulted from a partnership between HISD and Rice University. The school is intended to serve as a model for innovative, effective instruction and professional development for teachers throughout the area. The planning team for this school included officials from both institutions as well as parents and teachers. The popularity of the school can be gauged from the number of students who apply for admittance. In its opening year, more than 7,000 students applied for 1,290 places; a lottery system was adopted to determine the final selection of students.

Acting on the belief that it is essential for children to develop proficiency in communication in English and another language, the planning team's design included small, bilingual, and socioeconomically mixed classes. Student advancement to higher grade levels is based on achievement, not age. Students in grades six through eight have their own computers, and younger students share equipment. These features flow from the school's statement of philosophy and lead to small, family-like communities of learners, considered to be the key to more effective schools. Teachers work in teams; they include teachers and parents, who develop plans for the active involvement of students in setting goals, self-evaluation, and planning and carrying out learning activities.

The school features a challenging academic program that provides students opportunities to develop skills in English and Spanish by participating in a dual-language program that integrates the study of mathematics, science, social studies, language, the arts, technology, and physical development. Its programs are characterized by active learning projects and "mini courses," many of which are conducted by members of the Rice University faculty.

The school program is supported by a professional development center staffed by HISD specialists and Rice University faculty members; the center focuses on innovative instructional practices for urban students. Rice University's Precollege Science Education Program staff members offer the school's teachers professional development courses in science and technology, assist with student projects, and provide expertise in the design and maintenance of the school's Web site. In September 1999, Rice University was able to extend a $10,000 grant to the school to fund a School Yard Habitat that will feature wetlands, prairie, and pond habitats.

Additional information about the Rice school is available at the school's Web site at http://www.rice.edu/armadillo/Rice/rice_school.htm.

Dumas Independent School District

Dumas Independent School District is located in the small city of Dumas, Texas, in the Texas Panhandle. It includes one senior high school, one junior high school, and five elementary schools. This rural school system serves the Moore County community of 15,000 persons, whose economic base includes oil and gas refineries, farms and ranches, and meatpacking plants.

Policies are established for this district by a seven-member board of trustees. According to the district's online policy manual, which can be viewed at http://www.tasb.org/cgi-pol/do-policy-frame-verity. perl?orgno=171901&policy=EHBE(H)-P.html, the district's mission is to provide academic excellence through collaboration with students, parents, and community.

To be eligible for grade-to-grade promotion, students must earn an overall average of 70 on a scale of 100 based upon course-level, grade-level standards for all core subject areas; and an average of 70 or above in mathematics and reading. English-language learners' knowledge and competencies are assessed independently of their English-language skills.

To graduate and receive a diploma, students must complete the minimum units of credit mandated by the state and additional units required by the district, and perform satisfactorily on secondary exit-level assessment instruments, according to requirements currently in effect. Special provisions for LEP students permit recent immigrants to postpone the initial administration of exit-level tests.

The district offers bilingual education and ESL programs; their goals are to enable LEP students to become competent in the comprehension, speaking, reading, and composition of the English language. Programs emphasize the mastery of English-language skills and achievement in the other content areas so that LEP students can participate equitably in school activities. State guidelines require districts to provide bilingual education programs at the elementary school level, and an ESL program to all students who are not entitled to bilingual education.

In grades three through eight, English-language learners may be eligible for exemption from the Texas Assessment of Academic Skills (TAAS) or may take a Spanish-language version of the test. Additional state requirements for the identification, assessment, classification, and placement of LEP students are incorporated into district procedures. Written notice of the recommended placement and a request for written approval by parents must take place within ten days from the date a student is classified. Beginning in grade 2, students exit from bilingual or ESL programs when they are reclassified as English-proficient after meeting state performance standards. Students can be reclassified if they later fail to meet the required standards.

Notable School

Dumas Junior High School is a 1999–2000 National Blue Ribbon School (also recognized as a Texas Blue Ribbon School and a Region XVI Middle School of the year). Since 1982, the Department of Education Blue Ribbon Schools Program has been a means of identifying and recognizing schools that are models of excellence and equity, demonstrating a strong commitment to educational excellence for all students. These schools have achieved high academic standards or have shown significant academic improvement over a five-year period. The following description is drawn from the nominations package submitted by Dumas Junior High School to the Blue Ribbon Schools committee judges. The nominations package is available online at http://www.ed.gov/offices/OERI/BlueRibbonSchools/NominationPack_2000/17txm03.doc.

The ethnic composition of the student population at Dumas Junior High is 42 percent White non-Hispanic, 55 percent Hispanic, and 3 percent Other. Almost half the students (49 percent) are economically disadvantaged, and 42 percent are highly mobile and served in the migrant program.

Programs at Dumas Junior High are enhanced by several nonacademic components. For example, an on-campus registered nurse provides first aid and emergency care, supervises sick and injured students, provides health advocacy; maintains health and immunization records; screens for dental care, immunizations, vision, hearing, and scoliosis; oversees height and weight measurement; administers prescribed medications; and refers students and parents to community organizations that provide free glasses. Substance-abuse education and group counseling on decisionmaking, goal-setting, divorce, grief, teen marriage, teen sexuality, and family and community relationships are offered in the seventh and eighth grades.

To create a safe, nurturing environment that promotes student attendance and academic achievement, class meetings are used for introducing new students, recognizing students' birthdays, and identifying personal successes. Prizes of cash, gift certificates, and lunch with the principal are awarded for meeting attendance goals and for participating in extracurricular activities. The school provides transportation, meals, and entry fees for extracurricular activities to stimulate optimum involvement.

An Academic Awards Assembly is held each spring. Students and staff are organized into academic teams of five teachers and a hundred students each. The teachers on each team are assigned joint planning time to share information about their students.

To provide additional educational opportunity to students whose family obligations present obstacles to their attendance at after-school or summer-study sessions, an evening study hall has been established in the nearby Hispanic community of Cactus, home to the largest meatpacking plant in the United States and a major employer in the area. Students provide free child care for evening parent meetings in Dumas and Cactus. School bulletins are printed in English and Spanish, and translators are available to help parents. Dumas Junior High programs try to provide stability to students whose lives are marked by mobility and change.

The student population includes 240 students for whom English is a second language and 72 students with limited English proficiency. English-language learners at intermediate levels participate in regular classes and receive extra academic assistance from a certified ESL teacher and an assistant in a newly remodeled Content Mastery Super Lab for students with special learning needs. English-language learners at beginning levels are mainstreamed into exploratory classes and receive sheltered English instruction in the content areas. All language arts teachers in the school are required to have ESL certification so that they can provide further support to second-language learners.

The foreign-language program is strengthened by the incorporation of Spanish speakers as teachers' aides and by the service of ESL students as after-school tutors for Spanish I students.

Capistrano Unified School District

The Capistrano Unified School District (CUSD) is located approximately midpoint between Los Angeles and San Diego, in suburban South Orange County in Southern California. Retail trade, professional services, and light industry fuel the local economy.

The district operates forty-six campuses and educational programs serving 44,000 children from the cities of Aliso Viejo, Capistrano Beach, Coto de Casa, Dana Point, Ladera Ranch, Laguna Niguel, Las Flores, Rancho Santa Margarita, San Clemente, San Juan Capistrano, Talega, Wagon Wheel, and portions of Dove Canyon and Mission Viejo. With more than 4,000 full- and part-time employees, it is the largest employer in the 195-square-mile area of the district. Public support for the district's education programs was demonstrated in 1999 with the passage of Measure A, a local $65 million bond measure, with 73 percent of the voters approving. To accommodate increasing enrollment, eighteen new schools have been built since 1993.

The district's student ethnicity reports for the 1999–2000 school year show that the ethnic composition of the student population is 73 percent White, 17 percent Hispanic, 5 percent Asian, 2 percent African American, 1 percent Filipino, less than 1 percent Pacific Islander, and less than 1 percent American Indian or Native Alaskan. English-language learners comprise 13 percent of the student population. The students' home languages include Spanish, Vietnamese, Korean, Farsi, and Russian. The socioeconomic levels represented in the student population ranges from children living in million-dollar seaside custom homes to a few children who live in local motels. Title I eligibility has been established for 25 percent of the children in the district, 19 percent of whom have a high mobility rate.

The salary scale for teachers starts at $36,040. Teachers with twenty-four years of service and the requisite number of credits for advanced study may earn up to a maximum of $73,783. Since 1998, the district has offered training for teachers of foreign languages; many have earned credentials in Cross-Cultural Language and Academic Development, Bilingual/Cross-Cultural Language and Academic Development, and Specially Designed Academic Instruction in English. These are the credentials required in California for ESL and bilingual education teachers. The district's noninstructional staff includes nurses, health technicians, and specialized health assistants. Health technicians provide services to schools once a week.

A board of trustees composed of seven members establishes policies for this district. Each trustee must reside in a separate trustee area, although all trustees are elected district-wide. District-wide election systems typically foster representation from all geographic areas of the district. According to the district's board-approved strategic plan available online at http://www.capousd.k12.ca.us/pdf/Capo%202000% 20.pdf, the district's mission is to educate students and to assist them in realizing their full potential as responsible, productive, contributing members of society by providing an educational environment in which students meet challenges, excel academically, and value differences.

In 1999, the board revised its promotion and retention policies in accordance with changes in state law. Grades and other indicators of achievement are selected by the district to measure student achievement levels for purposes of retention.

English-language learners are promoted according to differentiated criteria. At the conclusion of three years of intensive English-language and academic-intervention programs, the final determination of whether English learners will be retained or promoted is based on the students' all-around progress. English learners who are achieving academically commensurate to their rate of English-language acquisition are promoted. English learners who are not achieving academically commensurate to their rate of English-language acquisition attend Saturday School or receive after-school remediation. If they are still unsuccessful, they are referred for retention; however, district administrators are confident that students who receive remediation will be successful.

To graduate and receive a diploma, students must earn 220 credits (5 credits are awarded for each semester course), including 40 credits in English and 10 in foreign languages or fine arts. As required by the state, beginning with the graduating class of 2004, students will also be required to pass the state's High School Exit Exam.

English-language learners who have lived in the United States for less than one year may defer taking the High School Exit Exam for an additional year. Starting in 2004, however, they must earn a satisfactory score on the examination to receive a diploma.

The district established Capistrano Affirms Family English (CAFÉ) Projects in twelve schools to assist parents with their parenting skills. The program teaches parents how to speak English and how to help their children become successful in school. CAFÉ classes meet from two to four times each week. In addition, many schools host evening Parent Institute, family literacy, and math sessions.

As one of six district-wide priority goals, the board agreed that all CUSD students will demonstrate conversational ability in a second language. Several district programs address this goal. An International Baccalaureate (IB) Diploma Program (with an enrollment of 150 students as of 2001) was established at San Clemente High School. This program has a rigorous and comprehensive curriculum, spans two years, and consists of courses in language, science, mathematics, individuals and societies, and several electives. All diploma candidates are examined in a second language and must demonstrate the ability to use it in written and spoken form in a range of contexts. Colleges and universities throughout the world recognize the academic integrity and intellectual promise of the IB Program. Only 378 schools in the United States are listed as participants in this prestigious program on the Web site of the International Baccalaureate Association at http://www.ibo.org/ibo2/en/services/ib_worldschool_results.cfm.

Chinese, French, German, Japanese, Latin, Spanish, and American Sign Language are offered in the district's high schools. Each course is available to all students through open enrollment. For the past three years, Latin, French, and Spanish classes have been offered at the district's middle schools.

An elementary school dual immersion program was initiated to provide students with instruction in Spanish and English, with the goal of bilingualism and biliteracy by grade 6. The program was subsequently expanded to include the middle school. After approval of Proposition 227, the district's Division of Student Services conducted a successful campaign to enable the dual immersion program to continue with an alternative school waiver.

The district also offers elementary school programs in Japanese and in Mandarin Chinese. The Mandarin program also provides a Chinese Cultural Center where students study Chinese culture and history. Fourteen elementary schools have also adopted after-school foreign-language programs.

Notable School

Concordia Elementary School, located in San Clemente, has been honored as a National Blue Ribbon School and a California School of Distinction. In 1998, the school's Project Japan received the prestigious Golden Bell award from the California School Boards Association. The Golden Bell Awards Program, now in its twenty-first year, promotes excellence in education by recognizing outstanding programs in school districts and county offices of education throughout California.

Concordia is a Title I school (136 students qualify for free and reduced-cost lunches) that is a center for CUSD gifted students. It serves approximately 640 students in grades K–5. The school fosters high academic achievement for all students, and cultivates various forms of intelligence, including mathematical, linguistic, spatial, interpersonal, intrapersonal, musical, and kinesthetic. The school's creed states that each student excels in one or more of these areas.

The ethnic composition of the student population at Concordia is 76 percent White non-Hispanic, 19 percent Hispanic, 7 percent Black, 2 percent Asian, and less than 1 percent for each of the Filipino, Alaska National, Pacific Islander, and Multiple Ethnicity groups. Approximately 13 percent of the student population speak Spanish.

Over 85 percent of Concordia's teachers reside in San Clemente. Of the teachers who have children, over 73 percent have children currently or previously attending Concordia. Instructional aides, library clerks, English Language Development (ELD) aides, reading support staff, and Gifted and Talented Education (GATE) staff are also available at the school. Some staff members work full-time and some work on an as-needed basis.

Parent and community input is welcomed at this school. The Concordia Joint Council, consisting of representatives of the Parent Teacher Association (PTA) Executive Board, the School Site Council, the GATE Parent Council, the English-Learning Students Parent Committees, and teachers, meets each spring to evaluate the previous year's goals and discuss the upcoming school year's goals and direction. Businesses adopt and interact with classrooms throughout the year. City officials participate in school celebrations, retired teachers return to volunteer, and parents, students, and teachers all dance at the traditional sock hop. Ten percent of the parents of Concordia's students attended the school when they were students.

School-wide goals include student-centered uses of technology, the continuation of a school-wide literacy focus, and the identification of multiple intelligences. Concordia's teachers plan to use technology to provide students with real-life opportunities to interact with other students around the world, integrate Japanese-language studies, and encourage global understanding. As part of an overall program on human diversity, Concordia's faculty members aim to prepare students linguistically and culturally for successful interaction at home and abroad as citizens in the global community. Home-language support is provided so that English-language learners master the English language and the CUSD CORE Curriculum.

Concordia Elementary School, now over forty years old, was the first school in the school district (with the exception of schools newly constructed) to install Internet access in every classroom. The school-wide emphasis on technology and the faculty's awareness of business applications both of technology and of the Japanese language led to the creation of Project Japan, through which all Concordia students receive foreign-language instruction in Japanese.

The Japanese Language Program at Concordia focuses on conversational ability. A team of Japanese-language instructors provides instruction to all classes. During the first year of the project, Japanese instruction was provided on the following schedule:

- Kindergarten students: twice a week for a total of forty minutes
- First graders: twice a week for a total of eighty minutes
- Second and third graders: twice a week for a total of sixty minutes
- Fourth, fifth, and sixth graders: once a week for thirty minutes

Students' progress in Japanese has been measured through materials provided by Berlitz International and by locally developed language proficiency assessments designed by the Japanese Language Team. Some Spanish-speaking English-language learners were among the group called star Japanese students.

Kathy Oshima, former principal and project director at Concordia Elementary School in San Clemente, noted that Project Japan was expanded into Shorecliffs Middle School to allow students to continue their Japanese studies. Two levels of instruction in Japanese are offered at San Clemente High School, which also schedules courses in Spanish Levels One through Three, Spanish for Native Speakers, French Levels One through Three, and German Levels One and Two. In 2001, students from Concordia's first Japanese class were freshmen at San Clemente High School. They have strong conversational ability and can read and write the language; a few have completed writing assignments in Hiragana and Katakana, parallel modern Japanese syllabaries.

Additional information about Concordia Elementary School is available on the school's Web site at http://intergate.capousd.k12.ca.us/schools/concord.html.

Summary

In Houston, Texas, an urban area with significant international trade and commerce, Hispanics are the majority student group. The school board includes several Hispanic members, elected under the single-member district voting system. The district requires English-language learners to acquire English-language skills as quickly as is consonant with continued academic achievement. It also strongly encourages all students to become proficient in two languages, and offers a variety of means by which language minority and majority students can reach that goal. Biliteracy is viewed as an academic and economic asset for all students and as an important part of meeting the labor force needs of the business community. At least one year of foreign language credit is required for graduation for all students. These program features reflect assumptions that multilingual and multicultural skills are resources that can help students from any language group earn a good living.

Guided by the same set of state regulations for bilingual education, Dumas Middle School in rural Texas concentrates on English-language acquisition goals. At the secondary level, it offers language support programs only in the English language (ESL and sheltered content instruction), but uses students' home languages extensively for parent outreach, counseling, and tutoring. Using English-language learners as tutors for students of Spanish as a foreign language creates informal peer-tutoring arrangements akin to those in two-way bilingual education programs. The school staff uses Spanish as a means of providing assistance to students and parents. Although language majority students may choose to study Spanish as an elective, it is not required for graduation as it is in Houston. These program features reflect an assumption that adults in the local community will not require a language other than English.

In Capistrano, in ethnically diverse suburban California, the district has a strong focus on academic preparation and achievement. Foreign-language study is encouraged for language majority and minority students, to begin in the elementary school years. Opportunities to continue language studies at secondary schools are provided. Even after the passage of Proposition 227, the district found ways to continue dual-language programs. Although biliteracy is stressed in IB and dual-language programs, fluency is the goal for most students. The district's graduation standards require a year of credit in fine arts or foreign languages. These program features reflect an assumption that an introduction to either area (but not necessarily mastery of either) is necessary to the formation of a well-rounded person.

The three profiled districts, each of which has been recognized for exemplary instruction, implement programs congruent with their resources, community needs, and economic and political realities. They prepare students for the lives they are expected to lead. Although the three language-education programs are different, they nevertheless exhibit common characteristics. All three districts include bilingual programs that accord priority to teaching English and other content areas; all anticipate that an extended period is needed to acquire English and other second languages; and each offers a variety of options and sup-port services to promote success in learning a language. Teacher prepa-ration and development, technology, and parental involvement goals are included in plans developed by each of the three districts.

AN IN-DEPTH LOOK AT TWO-WAY PROGRAMS

In two-way schools, language majority and minority students are grouped together for instruction according to their grade level, each group studying in and through the home language for a portion of the day and through the second language for a portion of the day. All stu-dents are expected to participate in the dual-language program. More districts than ever are adopting two-way bilingual education, which prompts an in-depth look at its implementation features.

The issues identified during a review of the literature on two-way bilingual schools were incorporated into a protocol; this was used as the basis for semistructured interviews, each two hours long, with fourteen current and former principals of a set of well-established two-way Span-ish-English bilingual schools from three jurisdictions on the eastern seaboard. Each principal had from nine years to several decades of ex-perience with the program. For the historical context for this study, see Castro Feinberg (1999). The following summaries of interview tran-scripts are presented in relation to management and leadership func-tions of the principal in a two-way school. Whenever possible, the par-ticipants' exact words are used, sometimes combined with those of other participants and edited to form a composite statement presented as a quotation. The transcripts were also edited as needed to maintain the anonymity of the participants and of their school districts. The par-ticipants' comments explain why or how the administration of two-way schools is considered unique, and thereby shed light on the nature of dual-language instruction. The pronouns "she," "her," and "hers" are used throughout the summary section regardless of the gender of the person interviewed. The title of "Principal" is used for all who are or have been principals of two-way schools, regardless of current role; the title of "Participant" is used to refer to the total group of informants.

Management

Is the administration of two-way bilingual elementary schools different from the administration of other schools? Yes, according to the partici-pants in this study. Save for one full and two partial exceptions, all participants immediately answered this question in the affirmative. The full dissent was stated by one of the original architects of dual immersion plans. In this view, the unique characteristics of specialized schools are acknowledged, although persons deemed qualified to run a school are considered qualified to run any school. She went on to add that this point of view assumes that to be so qualified, for any school, adequate instruction in diversity has been provided as part of the generic administrative preparation program.

Scheduling

As one principal put it, "Scheduling is more complicated in a two-way school. You have to learn it on the job. It's not taught anywhere." Another asserted that "staffing, scheduling, and a belief in what you are doing are critical to the success of the school."

Paired Teachers

Without exception, every principal stressed the importance of the scheduling function in a two-way school, and the difficulties involved in drawing up a schedule faithful to the model. A key feature of this model is that each group of students spends a portion of the day with a teacher who presents content in one language, and the other part of the day with another teacher who presents content in the other program language (in the participants' schools, the time distribution ranged from 50 percent of the day in each language to 60 percent in the English language). In some models, two teachers are assigned to each class group, one for each target language, who are present in the same classroom at the same time. In most models, students receive instruction from only one teacher at a time, shifting from one teacher to another. In either case, each of the paired teachers is responsible for joint planning, instruction, evaluation, recordkeeping, and parental involvement for two groups of students. In the latter model, each teacher is accountable for sixty students, or twice the students she would be responsible for in other elementary schools.

In two-way schools, the presentation of content between the two languages is coordinated, not duplicated; teachers have to work together as members of a team to effect this coordinated approach. The principal therefore considers teachers' language skills in each language, their expertise in delivering instruction in various subject-matter areas, and the likelihood that the paired teachers will get along well with each other. "How do you do all this? You build from the strength of each teacher. The older teachers, who immigrated to the USA from another country and were educated in that other country, generally have balanced skills in both languages. The younger teachers are generally English-dominant. Place them in the lower grades where there is less need for Spanish language literacy skills. You move teachers around to find the right place; look for teachers' strengths; change the pairs as needed to maximize their strengths until you have built the perfect schedule."

Joint Planning

A key factor is scheduling time for common planning periods not only for the paired teachers but for all teachers in a grade level. This is important because the English-language teachers and the Spanish-language teachers must contribute to the same theme and therefore they have to plan together. The joint planning period must be monitored; to demonstrate its importance, the principal has to attend sessions. One principal believes that one of her major contributions to the school was her enforcement of joint planning. Another noted that only if the school is big enough is it possible to arrange for common planning; there is only so much you can do by using the elective areas to fill in.

Other Factors

There must be enough time provided to fairly permit both groups of students to meet the requirements of English and Spanish curriculum goals. But when scheduling classes, it's not just a matter of calculating the balance of time in English and Spanish. Because the task is complicated by such additional program components as bilingual gifted or preschool programs, the principal of a two-way school has to know how to put a schedule together. The administrator must also be sensitive to the needs of parents who do not want their children in the program. There must be a way to accommodate them, a way to aid transfer to another nearby elementary school. The logistics of scheduling can also help the school community remain an integrated whole.

Faculty Desegregation

The racial breakdown at a two-way school is similar to that of any other in the district; all schools must comply with the court order on faculty desegregation. Because bilingual teachers are needed for at least half the classrooms, racial balance is difficult to maintain as there are few bilingual teachers who are also Black. One way to solve the problem is to place monolingual teachers in special areas such as the library, the music room, or the art studio. That means the remaining teachers must be "really bilingual" and possess high levels of skill in reading and writing and an excellent knowledge of Spanish-language literature, particularly those who will be teaching at grades 4–6. The interviewer has to be adept at finding out what level of language skill the applicant possesses. The principals often ask the applicants to write a short essay in Spanish as one means of making a language assessment.

Hiring and Interviewing

"You demand commitment from the applicant before a hiring decision is made. The initial interview is critical." As another principal pointed out, "The selection of teachers is very important, the most important factor of all. You must have adequate faculty, as teachers are the key to program success." Several principals recommend telling job candidates about the workload from the first moment of the first interview. The teachers need to know what they are getting into. For this reason, they include teachers on the interview committee. "I want the applicant to hear it from me and from the teachers. I tell them, 'It's great to be a teacher here, but it's difficult. Let me tell you how it's difficult, and listen to what the teachers say. If you want to be part of this school, part of a gifted, chosen group of professionals, know that you will be working more than if you were in another school. It's great what it will do for you professionally; but using two languages can mean double duty. It helps with career development because two-way bilingual schools are really innovative; you'll go down in history as a pioneer. Your school will be mentioned in the professional literature and at conferences; you are part of a special group. If you decide to move on, your having worked here makes a difference, but not everyone can take this.'"

Participants think it important to discuss and consider the applicant's philosophy, but even more, they believe the principal must carefully check background and references. One principal made it clear that she prefers to hire only those she has observed teaching at her school, perhaps teachers who have been long-term substitutes, for example, or interns. The principal recommends that these observations take place several times a day, for as many months as possible, before a permanent contract is offered.

Although the work of the principal of a two-way school is perceived as different from that of principals in other schools, the selection process is the same for all principals. However, principals of two-way schools are often placed by direct appointment because of the importance of the position to the whole system.

Language

"The most important feature of the program is instruction in the subject areas by means of two languages. The equal status of the two languages must be reinforced. All Morning Announcements should be in both languages. With parent communications, you have to be subtle; both languages in a letter to parents must be equal. If you use one language on one side of the paper, and the other language on the reverse side, don't have one side of the letter numbered 'one' and the other side numbered 'two.' Your message to parents has to be consistent."

Teachers' language competence in the heritage language came up repeatedly, and in various contexts. Principals would like teachers to be certified in elementary education and Spanish. Even with that combination, additional staff development would be needed. Paraprofessionals need more training also. "One teacher quit in three days; she couldn't handle the Spanish language demands of the job. Younger teachers were having so much trouble with Spanish that they could not teach the program appropriately. I'd walk into the room and see errors in the Spanish language text on the blackboard. So, I arranged with one of the modern language professors to organize a school-site Spanish course. I followed up with an hourly employee who was a retired Spanish teacher with a doctorate from Spain to continue the school-site training. Now that our veteran teachers (many of them native speakers, educated in their heritage language) are beginning to retire, I want to recruit in Spain. This aspect of staffing is critical."

One school district is providing tuition reimbursement to support teacher participation in a program that addresses the teacher language gap at a local university. A graduate Spanish program for elementary school teachers of classes in Spanish for Spanish speakers, or for those who teach in a two-way school, is offered at that institution. To ensure attention to the academic use of the language and to its literature, the program features two weeks of study at universities in Spain.

Other Staff Training

One participant applies the principle of transfer to professional development activities. All her teachers attend district workshops in reading, computer literacy, writing, or math. Subjects presented to the teachers through English can be applied in their classrooms in either English or Spanish.

Several principals make it a point to take a group of teachers to conferences sponsored by the National Association for Bilingual Education (NABE). This is considered to be a necessary part of consciousness-raising. When possible, school or district funds are requested to assist with travel expenses; and at the very least, professional leave is approved. School funding is also provided for a larger group of teachers to attend the local conferences of the state affiliates of NABE and TESOL. Substitute funds are employed to support an exchange of teacher visits between two of the schools in the two-way school network.

Administrators' Training Needs

Participants also identified language-training needs for principals. This aspect of training will become more and more important as the group of principals educated abroad reaches retirement. One principal, who came to this country when she was four years old, took the time to engage in a rigorous program of self-instruction and reeducation in her native language. The ideal, she noted, would be special preparation for teachers and for administrators preparing for careers in two-way schools. Other principals believe it crucial to have an intensive training period for principals and assistant principals on the research and knowledge base for bilingual education. This is all the more important should there be a principal appointed to a two-way school who does not have previous experience as a bilingual teacher.

In times past, the principals had to try to make the two-way schools work in spite of the misconceptions of their own supervisors. Although the model is now more generally understood, there is still reason to provide opportunities for senior staff members to develop their knowledge in this area.

Budgeting

"We have the same textbook budget as the other schools, except for the years we qualify as a Title I school. But a textbook in each of the two languages is needed in each subject for our two-way program. In the other schools, you need one teacher for every twenty-five youngsters. In the two-way schools, you need *two* teachers for every twenty-five."

The principal of the two-way school must be expert at budgeting because the only extra funds these schools are allocated go to employ two bilingual aides. In a two-way program, two sets of everything must be purchased, one set for each language. There are state-adopted textbooks (and state funding) for subjects taught in English, but not for Spanish. Additional funds that provided support for start-up costs are no longer provided. The two-way schools are now funded in the same way as all other schools in the district.

Only by astute budget planning can the principals staff their programs appropriately. "The other schools get allocations for, let's say, four Spanish teachers; three ESL teachers, two visiting teachers. If those teachers are assigned correctly, they become your classroom teachers." Several principals referred to budgeting as a formidable task, for which they receive no formal preparation. "You learn that by on-the-job training; finding out how others do it. We have taught each other, from within the group of principals of two-way schools. Each of us got help from our predecessors and subsequently helped our successors. Oftentimes a key lead teacher who helped one principal with budget duties would continue to provide that assistance to the next principal."

Leadership

Participants' comments related to leadership functions are reported in the following sections, arranged according to a classification scheme inspired by Talcott Parsons's functional imperatives for organizational survival (Parsons 1956). The categories are: *pattern maintenance and integration* (functions that lead to internal unity of purpose and foster harmony), *adaptation and resource acquisition* (interaction functions with the external environment), and *goal attainment* (functions related to achievement of school objectives). Although these categories are presented as analytically distinct, the reader is reminded that they are intertwined in practice.

Pattern Maintenance and Integration

This section includes summaries of comments on vision, commitment, workload equity, and intercultural and interlingual communication. These aspects of organizational life contribute to the ability of group members to function in coordination and harmony with each other to achieve the school's language, academic, and other goals.

Vision and Commitment

You as the Principal must be convinced first, then your teachers will also be happy to be part of a school that offers the best kind of education for the future. The reward for those teachers who have been in the school many, many years is the satisfaction that flows from a huge sense of pride. Our teachers know that they are very special and very successful. We know we are successful in a number of ways, we know from the students who come back to visit us, and from comments from the middle and high school; their teachers say they can always tell which students came from our school.

Most participants stated that the principal of a two-way school has to be truly committed to the model and has to be sure her faculty and community are aware of that commitment. But mere articulation of the vision is not enough. The principals' example of dedication gives meaning to those statements. For many of the principals, it was important to spend school hours working directly with teachers and parent groups. Paperwork was postponed until the end of the day, often keeping the principal at school until 6:00 or 7:00 P.M. As stated by a principal with thirty years' experience in education, "It's the most exciting thing I've ever done in my professional life, but I never had enough time."

The ability of the principal to engage the faculty in the development of a jointly held vision of the promise of the school's model, and to constantly echo their common belief in the value of what they are doing, helps account for the stability of staff in two-way schools. Faculty members take great pride in their association with these schools. Institutional self-esteem, not often seen in other schools, leads to positive expectations that result in greater student achievement. The faculty members who originated the two-way program in a school had a strong sense of mission and pride in language and culture. Often they were from a background where bilingualism was highly valued. Veteran teachers, who take an extraordinarily active role in the orientation of teachers new to the school, have taken care to inculcate newcomers in the ethos of their special community. As part of the process of instilling pride in the school, participants advise school leaders to pay close attention to the aesthetics of the school buildings and grounds.

> The faculty is really motivated, planning activities all the time. I provide positive reinforcement. We celebrate everything: teacher appreciation day, perfect attendance, every holiday we can identify. I provided roses or apples, plaques, little notes of appreciation for what I observed in the classroom. Encouragement to keep up the good work is necessary to maintaining moral and motivation. Always focus on the positive. We had very low turnover; any vacancies were a result of enrollment increase. Those on maternity leave always wanted to come back to the school.

"They do it because they believe in it, they know it is beneficial for the kids" was the recurring explanation for why principals and teachers choose to work at two-way schools despite the complexities and rapid pace. There were also speculations that some teachers simply wanted a job or wanted to be in a bilingual school; that the two-way schools are well-known and it is prestigious to be associated with them; or that the schools' locations in areas of single-family homes were a deciding factor.

Both Hispanic and non-Hispanic principals noted that their English-language-origin teachers don't have the same degree of commitment or history of longevity at the two-way schools as the language minority teachers. They seem to need variety. Concern was expressed about the newer teachers in both language groups, many of whom are thought to accept bilingual education as business as usual and place priority on career development and personal benefit. Several principals expressed a sense that something must be done to counteract those attitudes, to "awaken these teachers' dormant sentiment of idealism, and to begin to involve them in advocacy activities."

Workload Equity

No comments were volunteered related to the topic of workload equity. Upon prompting, suggestions were provided on how to be fair to the teachers in light of their double load. At one school, an aide was used to provide an extra half hour of planning time for the teachers; at another, "Pink Slips" representing a time bonus to permit released time for research during the workday were awarded to teachers who attended PTA meetings. One of the participants summarized the experience of the group of two-way principals: "There were no special problems, not even one grievance, nor have I had to put anybody on prescription. I ask only that the teachers give the same level of effort that I do. Even when teachers are asked to participate in conferences held on the weekend, there are no protests from the teachers. I set the example with my own participation, of course."

Intercultural and Interlingual Communication

Discussion of problems or concerns in the area of intercultural or interlingual communication was not initiated by the participants. When asked if concentrated diversity in linguistic, cultural, and national-origin background created cross-cultural communication problems, the typical response was that the participants had experienced no problems. They saw diversity as a strength that permitted members of the school community to learn from each other. Further, they did not see more diversity in the two-way schools than in other schools they identified in the district. "The biggest differences are not between groups based on language or culture but between younger and older teachers. The new teachers seem to feel the older teachers are not up to date. The older teachers have concerns about the Spanish language skills of the newcomers."

One principal recalled minor conflicts related to curriculum materials and their application by teachers who protested that in their country "it was done another way." Typically, these discussions were easily resolved by administrative fiat ("These are the curriculum materials we have, so these are the curriculum materials we will use").

All other principals said there was never a problem with language and culture. Both Hispanic and non-Hispanic participants gave much of the credit for this desirable state of affairs to the Hispanic teachers. They were described as so cooperative, helpful, positive, appreciative, and energetic that it was almost impossible for teachers from other ethnic groups not to like them. "The real commitment to the program comes from the Spanish-language origin teachers. They are the leaders. They work the hardest. They don't have all the materials that are available in English, so they have to do the translating. Parents say they are the better teachers."

When pressed for reasons why the predictions of challenges related to diversity raised in the research literature did not apply, a number of possibilities were suggested:

- Multiculturalism is the norm for us in this district.
- These schools are so special that each develops an esprit de corps that overcomes any tendency to disintegration based on cultural or language differences.
- By the time teachers have been here long enough to become certified in the state, they are sufficiently acculturated to know how to avoid problems. When foreign nationals are hired, however, administrators must be alert and avoid problems based on differences in expectations for students' behavior or in conceptions of how schools should operate.
- The two-way schools have a sufficiently large number of faculty members trained as ESL or foreign-language teachers to form a critical mass of expertise and leadership in matters of language and culture.

ADAPTATION AND RESOURCE ACQUISITION

This section includes summaries of comments on image, media, public relations, communications to parents, and political duties. These factors determine the extent to which interactions with the external environment will result in acquisition of resources needed by the school.

Image, Media, Public Relations, and Communications to Parents

"I constantly look for ways to focus attention on the school. This provides reinforcement for the teachers, the parents, the children, for everybody. Nobody taught me how to do this. To maintain pride in the school I have to showcase the good things we do, and that means telling the community, the neighborhood, and extending that process through the media. That's a natural progression. It's not part of any course; that's just leadership."

Most of the principals described similar intentions, to the extent consistent with district policies that from time to time required that all media contacts be limited to designated spokespersons. They made it a point to cultivate media contacts, were aware of who in their school community was a member of the press corps, never turned away the press, and enjoyed good relations with the media representatives they worked with. Whether in times of crisis and tragedy or in times of celebration, many principals will have to work with the press from both the Spanish-language and English-language communities, and be available for interviews with the newspapers, the radio stations, and the television stations serving both language communities.

Several principals referred to their public information duties as selling: "You have to sell the idea of bilingual education to your communities. You constantly have to keep the community informed of the advantages of two-way schools. It's a hard program to sell because people don't understand it. You have to explain why or how the program is good for their children." They reported sending clippings and brief research reports to the parents to show them the academic and economic benefits their children could anticipate: "Parents have no experience with the concept so they don't know what to expect." The sales job was complicated by the need to promote the model and at the same time counteract parents' tendencies toward unrealistically high expectations for the pace of second-language acquisition.

Sometimes a real public relations campaign was needed to persuade the majority group to value the language of the minority. "Lots of parents moved to my school's neighborhood to get away from the inner city. Then the inner city came out to surround them. The frustration of the parents was evident. It's not really a problem capturing the enthusiasm of the children; good teachers make language-learning fun. Parents, however, can really resent the second language, and come to perceive the principal as a traitor."

The participants also agreed that more time is devoted to parent and community communication at a two-way school than at other types of schools. It's important to keep reminding the parent of the school mission. Parents of students about to end their elementary school experience must be reminded that "bilingual education does not end here. You must continue it at home, you must encourage continuation of bilingual studies in the secondary schools."

One peculiarity of the two-way school is that it is unlikely that parents can help their children with their homework in subjects taught through the second language. Another way to build on strength and to increase the extent to which students learn from each other is to link families across language lines so that each parent's home-language skills can be used to help with homework in the linked family's second language.

Political Duties

"Political work: You have to do it to survive. I remember hiding under a desk so I wouldn't be caught waiting to ask the mayor to speak to the board about the budget cuts."

Most of the principals clearly understood the role of politics in the distribution of resources, and belonged to community-based organizations that had resisted efforts to eliminate various parts of the bilingual program budget. During these periods of crisis, the support of elected officials, academics, parents, and community advocates who came to speak to the board in support of program continuation was crucial to winning the day. Equally persuasive were avalanches of calls and letters demonstrating the depth of support the programs enjoyed in the community. As senior staff typically frowns on such efforts to influence policy development and budget decisions by the board, only the community group members who were not school-system employees would orchestrate these communications.

The skills involved with these political successes were not learned in any course. The participants taught themselves, building on the strength of their commitment and motivated by their dedication to their students, and then taught each other. Although concern was expressed that the new group of educators does not share that history of crisis or feel the necessity for political involvement, there was also recognition that their very success had dampened if not extinguished the spirit of advocacy, which rises in response to adversity. There was commonality of understanding with the younger principals on the matter. They reported little involvement in politics, but quickly (and gratefully) added that there had been no recent crises.

GOAL ATTAINMENT

This section includes summaries of comments on covering curriculum objectives, educational reform, and institutional priorities. These topics refer to the degree to which the school staff is able to foster students' achievement and reach other institutional goals.

Coverage of Curriculum Objectives

One principal raised concerns about covering curriculum objectives. As students spend roughly half the school day learning content presented through the second language, and there is no duplicate presentation of material in the home language, some students might not master all the objectives.

No other principal raised a similar issue. When prompted on this topic, one other opined that the students had to cover the curriculum in half the time. "How do you get gun safety and AIDS education into the day when you can't squeeze things into afternoon social studies or art classes?"

The rest of the participants did not share the concern: "If teachers really focus on planning, and set up plans at grade level meetings, that should take care of any adjustments that are needed."

Educational Reform

One principal noted that issues brought to the school faculty council by the teachers at her two-way school were always of an educational nature: "It's curriculum that drives the dialog at the council meetings." Other principals reported that the process of school reform at their two-way schools was similar to that of other schools.

Institutional Priorities

When presented with the gist of the concerns stated by Valdés (1997) that the needs of students from the majority language group would be favored over those of the language minority group, one principal fully and emphatically agreed that these concerns are valid. She noted that constant monitoring was required to prevent lowering the level of home-language instruction for the Spanish-language-origin group as teachers aimed their instruction to meet the needs of the English-language-origin or English-dominant students. In one of her schools, she had to be very careful to see that it did not happen. In another, where Hispanic students were in the majority, the problem was to avoid catering to the language needs of Spanish-language-origin students at the expense of the other students.

Another principal reported that changing school demographics had changed her priorities; more and more attention went to LEP issues because there were more LEP students in the school. However, at this school, students did not study content through their second language until they had exited from their second-language sequence (ESL or Spanish as a second language). A third principal stated, "My major concern for the LEP students is their overall success in school. For English-language origin students, my priority is second-language acquisition." She believed her faculty was always looking for ways to do more for the students in relation to those two goals.

Other principals responded by restating their goals: biliteracy for all students, proficiency in two languages for the total population of the school, teaching students to read in both languages at the same time. The majority of the principals were not concerned about the issue. They reported that their teachers provided attention to both groups, so there was no problem at all.

CONCLUSION

Bilingual education models are theoretical constructs whose elements are the components described in Chapter 1. They exist in the mind and on paper. Programs, not models, are implemented by school districts. They are the end products experienced in the classroom after the models have been transformed by the impact of each district's realities, aspects of which have been described in this chapter. A variety of bilingual education models have been selected by school district officials to promote the attainment of district goals for student achievement. The potential of two-way bilingual education models for advancing these goals, both for language minority and language majority students, has been widely recognized.

REFERENCES

Association of Departments of English. 1966. Advance draft of final copy of the guidelines for the preparation of teachers of English. *ADE Bulletin* 010

(November). [Online]. Available: *http://www.ade.org/ade/bulletin/n010/010003.htm.*

Attinasi, J. 1998. English Only for California children and the aftermath of Proposition 227. *Education* 119, no. 2.

Baca, L., K. Escamilla, and P. Walton. 2000. *National study of effective teacher education for diverse student populations.* Santa Cruz, CA: University of California, CREDE Center; University of Colorado, BUENO Center.

Beeson, E., and M. Strange. August 20, 2000. *Why rural matters: The need for every state to take action on rural education.* Washington, DC: Rural School and Community Trust. [Online]. Available: *http://www.ruraledu.org/streport.html.*

Bilingual education traces its U.S. roots to the colonial era. 1987. *Education Week* 6, no. 27 (April). [Online]. Available: *http://www.edweek.org/ew/1987/27early.h06.*

Castro Feinberg, R. 1999. Administration of two-way bilingual elementary schools: Building on strength. *Bilingual Research Journal* 23, no. 1: 47–68. [Online]. Available: *http://brj.asu.edu/v231/articles/art5.html.*

Castro Feinberg, R., J. Reiss, and P. Killian. 1997. Preparation of teachers for limited English proficient students: Keep your eyes on the prize. *Sunshine State TESOL Journal* (fall).

Children's Defense Fund. 2001. *The state of America's children yearbook 2001.* Washington, DC: Author.

Council of Great City Schools. 1999. Characteristics of member districts. Washington, DC: Author. [Online] Available: *http://www.cgcs.org/about/about.htm.*

Díaz-Rico, L., and J. Smith. 1994. Recruiting and retaining bilingual teachers: A cooperative school community-university model. *Journal of Educational Issues of Language Minority Students* 14 (winter). [Online]. Available: *http://www.ncbe.gwu.edu/miscpubs/jeilms/vol14/diazrico.htm.*

Editorial Projects in Education Inc. 1999. Quality counts 99: School report cards. *Education Week on the Web.* [Online]. Available: *http://www.edweek.org/sreports/qc99/ac/tables/ac-t3.htm.*

Education Vital Signs 1998: By the numbers. *American School Board Journal.* [Online]. Available: *http://www.asbj.com/evs/98/bythenumbers.html.*

Fanselow, J. F., and R. L. Light, eds. 1977. *Bilingual, ESOL, and foreign language teacher preparation: Models, practices, issues.* Washington, DC: TESOL.

Garshick, E., ed. 1995. *Directory of professional preparation programs in TESOL in the US and Canada, 1995–1997.* Alexandria, VA: TESOL, Inc.

Kreidler, C. 1987. ESL teacher education. *ERIC Digest ED289361* (November). Washington, DC: ERIC Clearinghouse on Languages and Linguistics. [Online]. Available: *http://www.ed.gov/databases/ERIC_Digests/ed289361.html.*

Macías, R. 1998. *Summary report of the survey of the states' limited English proficient students and available educational programs and services, 1996–97.* The SEA Report. Washington, DC: National Clearinghouse for Bilingual Education.

McDonnell, L., and P. Hill. 1993. *Newcomers in American schools: Meeting the educational needs of immigrant youth.* Santa Monica, CA: RAND.

National Center for Education Statistics, U.S. Department of Education. 2000. *The condition of education 2000* (NCES 2000-602). Washington, DC: U.S. Government Printing Office.

National Center for Education Statistics (NCES). 1999. Table 136. Average number of Carnegie units earned by public high school graduates in various subject fields, by student characteristics: 1982 to 1994. *Digest of Education Statistics,* 1998 (May). NCES 1999-032. Washington, DC: Author. [Online]. Available: *http://www.nces.ed.gov/pubs99/digest98/listoftables. html.*

National Clearinghouse for Bilingual Education (NCBE). May 1995. What are the most common language groups for LEP students? [Online]. Available: *http://www.ncbe.gwu.edu/askncbe/faqs/05toplangs.htm.*

National Clearinghouse for Bilingual Education (NCBE). September 2000. Which states offer certification or endorsement in Bilingual Education or ESL? [Online]. Available: *http://www.ncbe.gwu.edu/askncbe/faqs/ 09certif.htm.*

Orfield, G. 1993. *The growth of segregation in American schools: Changing patterns of separation and poverty since 1968.* A report of the Harvard Project on School Desegregation. Alexandria, VA: National School Boards Association, NSBA/CUBE. Available: *http://www.edweek.org/sreports/qc99/ ac/tables/ac-t3.htm.*

Parsons, T. 1956. Suggestions for a sociological approach to the theory of organizations. *Administrative Science Quarterly* 63, no. 85.

Peyton, J. K. December 1997. *Professional development of foreign language teachers.* Washington, DC: ERIC Clearinghouse on Language and Linguistics. [Online]. Available: *http://www.cal.org/ericcll/digest/peyton02. html.*

President's Advisory Commission on Educational Excellence for Hispanic Americans. September 2000. *Creating the will: Hispanics achieving educational excellence.* Washington, DC: Author. [Online]. Available: *http:// www.ed.gov/offices/OIIA/Hispanic/.*

Reyhner, J. 2000. *Teaching English to American Indians.* In J. Reyhner, J. Martin, L. Lockard, and W. Sakiestewa Gilbert, eds., *Learn in beauty: Indigenous education for a new century.* Flagstaff, AZ: Northern Arizona University. [Online]. Available: *http://jan.ucc.nau.edu/~jar/LIB/LIBconts.html.*

Riley, R. W. 1999. On fixing our schools from the bottom up: State, local, and private reform initiative. Statement by the Secretary of Education before the United States House of Representatives Committee on the Budget, September 23. [Online]. Available: *http://www.ed.gov/Speeches/ 09–1999/ 990923.html.*

Ruiz-de-Velasco, J., and M. Fix, with B. Chu Clewell. December 2000. *Overlooked & Underserved: Immigrant Students in U.S. Secondary Schools.* Washington, DC: Urban Institute Press. [Online]. Available: *http://www.urban.org /immig/overlooked2001.html.*

Rumbaut, R. 1998. Transformations: The post-immigrant generation in an age of diversity. Paper presented at the American Diversity: Past, Present, and Future meeting at the annual meeting of the Eastern Sociological Society, March 21, Philadelphia, PA.

San Francisco Chronicle. 2001. 49 million kids swell U.S. schools: Most from boomer or immigrant families, March 23. [Online]. Available: *http:// www.sfgate.com/cgi-bin/article.cgi?file=/chronicle/archive/ 2001/03/23/MN148455.DTL.*

Schnaiberg, L. 1996. Verdict still out. *Education Week* (November 27). [Online]. Available: *http://www.edweek.org/ew/1996/13nside.h16.*

Siu, S. F. December 1996. *Asian American students at risk: A literature review.* Report No. 8. CRESPAR Program 5: Language Minority Studies. Baltimore: Johns Hopkins University, Center for Social Organization of Schools (CSOS). [Online]. Available: *http://scov.csos.jhu.edu/crespar/ Reports/ report08entire.html.*

Study: Hispanic students more likely to quit school. March 31, 2000. *Education News.* CNNfyi.com. [Online]. Available: *http://www.cnn.com/2000/fyi/ teacher.resources/education.news/03/27/hispanic/#r.*

Unz, R. 1999. The right kind of outreach for the GOP. *Weekly Standard,* Monday, March 1. [Online]. Available: *http://www.onenation.org/9903/030199. html.*

Valdés, G. 1997. Dual-language immersion programs: A cautionary note concerning the education of language-minority students. *Harvard Educational Review* 67, no. 3.

Zehr, M. 2000. OCR ponders ESL teacher certification in Pa. *Education Week* (December 13). [Online]. Available: *http://www.edweek.org/ew/ew_ printstory.cfm?slug=15esl.h20.*

Chapter Four

•◦ State Policies and Bilingual Education

This chapter presents an introduction to state legislation and policies that govern the provision of bilingual and second-language education. To illustrate the impact of standards-based reform on second-language learners and their programs, a panoramic view of state policies across the country is followed by an in-depth tour of two states from different regions of the nation.

OVERVIEW OF STATE ACTION IN EDUCATION

Education becomes a national priority in times of peace and plenty, when fewer issues compete for congressional consideration. Specific crises may also focus national attention on education. Concerns about U.S. military preparedness were raised, for example, by Russia's Sputnik 1, the world's first artificial satellite, launched on October 4, 1957. These concerns led to the passage of the National Defense Education Act (NDEA) to support improvements in foreign language, math, and science instruction, the areas considered crucial to ensure our security and to maintain competitive status internationally. Education, however, is a state responsibility, typically under local control. Funding for public school education reflects that division of responsibility: Approximately 92 percent of the funds received by local districts come from state and local sources. The federal government's share is generally less than 10 percent of any district's budget.

State laws and policies related to second-language learners or language-education programs are identified in the following sections. Education policies are subject to change; the reader is advised to keep up-to-date by regularly consulting the resources identified in Chapters 8 and 9.

At the state level, constitutional, statutory, or regulatory provisions may address issues of education, language, and language education. The state legislatures and citizens' initiatives can bring about changes in their constitutions and in the state codes. Delegation of responsibility for interpretation of legislative intent to state commissions (for example, a state educational standards commission or ethics commission) may be included in the provisions of a statute. Governors' offices and state education agencies participate in drafting proposed budgets and bills and in seeking legislative approval of these proposals. They may be guided in these efforts by the recommendations of state-established advisory committees, task forces, or blue-ribbon committees. Requests and recommendations from education associations, professional organizations, educators' unions, parents' associations, the media, civil rights groups, and community-based organizations may be taken into consideration in the process.

State boards of education and higher-education governing boards implement policy and establish regulations. State departments of education implement the education code and body of regulations and add further interpretation; in so doing, they add to that body of regulation. In most states, they set curriculum standards, manage fiscal and curriculum audits, and establish statewide testing programs. State officials authorize mechanisms for approval of instructional materials to be purchased with state funds, for teacher training programs, and for applications for teaching licenses. State education authorities are responsible for setting civil rights standards and monitoring compliance with those standards.

Reform

Great variability exists among the states in their application of educational reform principles to the specific circumstances of English-language learners or to the general area of language education. Two matters in particular present challenges and dilemmas: the development of language arts and other subject matter standards that are fair and reasonable when applied to LEP students, and the development of a valid means of assessing the progress of English-language learners in reaching those standards. It does not seem reasonable, for example, to expect a recently arrived student who does not speak English to be tested on the works of Shakespeare or Chaucer, an expectation found in several states' language arts curriculum frameworks. At the same time, the current process of educational reform requires that all students be held to the same high standards and that schools be held accountable for ensuring progress toward meeting those goals. Standards-based examinations provide a mechanism for monitoring progress, ensuring accountability, and providing feedback leading to improvements in the instructional process. In several states, the results of these examinations determine students' eligibility for promotion and graduation, matters that determine students' life opportunities. It is important and urgent that solutions be found to these problems.

Programs for language minority students were initiated to meet the basic educational needs of low-income non-English-speaking children. Bilingual programs that include language majority students stress the biliteracy skills needed for success in domestic or international multilingual environments. These two aspects of bilingual education have contributed to the overall school reform efforts now under way.

The original enactment of the Bilingual Education Act in 1968 was part of a series of social programs designed to win the war on poverty. As such, the act reflected concerns surrounding the dismal level of educational opportunities available to language minority students. Reauthorization of the act shifted emphasis and mirrored national concern with civil rights by increasing attention to equity issues. After publication of *A Nation at Risk* in 1983 by the National Commission on Excellence in Education, subsequent enactments of the Bilingual Education Act focused on professional development, research-based curriculum and instruction, and accountability measures linked to high content-area standards.

Many of the initiatives nurtured in bilingual education settings or with language minority students became part of educational reform options now available to all students. Examples of these innovations include:

- Development of models to operationalize alternatives to traditional classroom recitation scripts, such as the guidelines for conducting instructional conversations and joint productive activity refined by researchers affiliated with the Center for Research on Education, Diversity, and Excellence (CREDE).
- Demonstration of the value of parental and community involvement in the schooling process, such as family literacy programs, and professional development programs that train teachers to enrich classroom instruction by drawing on community funds of knowledge.
- Development of sophisticated models for high-quality language education for language minority and language majority students, including two-way bilingual, dual-language, heritage, and expanded foreign-language programs.
- Examination of and advocacy for proper use of high-stakes

tests, including the concerns expressed by the President's Advisory Commission on Educational Excellence for Hispanic Americans that state testing practices may violate federal antidiscrimination laws.

•• Utilization of interdisciplinary collaboration to improve curriculum and instruction, illustrated by school-based teacher cooperation across disciplinary lines in sheltered English programs and by university-based social science research projects carried out in the schools, such as Project AVID, Advancement Via Individual Determination, a demonstration of the feasibility of detracking the high school curriculum.

•• Elaboration of K–16 partnerships such as the International High School located on the campus of LaGuardia Community College. The New York City Board of Education and the College, which had initiated a middle-college model in 1974, established this project in 1985. There are now some thirty middle-college programs of high schools located on college campuses linked in a national network. The model functions as an alternative to the traditional comprehensive high school.

Just as legislation and the development of successful initiatives have shaped educational efforts, the courts and their decisions have had an important role. Court decisions in cases brought by advocates for language minority students, such as *Idaho Migrant Council v. Board of Education* (1981) *and Gomez v. Illinois* (1987) have established that state education agencies must ensure compliance with civil rights laws. These decisions have forced state agencies into increasing their efforts to maintain opportunity to learn standards. These standards refer to a set of conditions that schools, districts, and states must meet to assure students of an equal opportunity to meet performance expectations. Equal opportunity to meet the standards becomes increasingly important, as states require students to pass exit exams as a prerequisite to high school graduation. In *Debra P. v. Turlington* (1979), the federal district court established the importance of defining and communicating the content of high school exit exams to students well in advance of the testing; communicating the consequences of either passing or failing the exam; and ensuring that the testing is based on the content that has been taught. These cases clearly acknowledge that a systemic approach to reform requires adequate notice of requirements, instructional and curricular alignment with the standards to be assessed, teacher training, adequate funding, and access to appropriate instructional materials. To be fairly assessed, students must first be given equitable opportunity to learn the content.

Although legislation and court decisions shape educational reform, political party platforms also affect the reform agenda. In 2000, both political party platforms reflected the connections between bilingual education and the national educational reform agenda. The 2000 Democratic Party platform included positive mention of programs for English-language learners (including bilingual education and English-plus initiatives), and stated opposition to language-based discrimination in all its forms. The platform also acknowledged that multilingualism is increasingly valuable in the global economy. For the full statement, see the Democratic Party Platform at http://www.cnn.com/ELECTION/2000/conventions/democratic/features/platform.00/#7.

The Republican Party platform referred to the role of English as our common language, and the importance of mastering other languages for America's competitiveness in world markets. It advocated foreign-language training in our schools and the fostering of respect for other languages and cultures throughout our society. For the full statement, see the Republican Party platform at http://www.cnn.com/ELECTION/2000/conventions/republican/features/platform.00/.

Standards and Assessment

A survey of state education officials was conducted by the Council of Chief State School Officers (CCSSO) to describe state efforts to include LEP students in educational reform (Lara and August 1996). Their findings include:

- Thirty-eight out of forty states reported that state subject-matter standards applied to LEP students. Utah reported that none of their standards apply to LEP students. In Montana and Texas, ESL standards have been developed. Texas has also developed bilingual education standards. All subject-matter standards in Rhode Island will have sections that address the educational needs of LEP students.
- Forty-three states permit waivers for one to three years to exempt LEP students from some or all of the examinations included in the statewide assessment program.
- Twelve states and the District of Columbia provide alternative examinations in some of the students' home languages. The set of states includes Alaska, Arizona, California, Colorado, Connecticut, Delaware, Hawaii, Illinois, New Jersey,

New Mexico, New York, Texas, and Utah. Alternative examinations are available in Albanian, Amharic, Burmese, Cambodian, Chinese languages, the French, Haitian Creole, Hindi, Laotian, Serbo-Croatian, Spanish, and Thai. In five states, these alternative examinations are aligned with state standards.

- Five states reported various accommodation strategies, including application of special scoring formulas, simultaneous translation, extended time, oral administration, bilingual dictionaries, alternative settings, repeating directions, reading directions in the students' native languages, and permitting students to use native-language dictionaries or translators.

A subsequent survey of state agencies (CCSSO 1998) includes reports on reform in foreign-language education:

- Twenty-five states have developed state standards in foreign languages.
- Six additional states are developing foreign-language content standards.

According to the Education Commission of the States (2000), six states include foreign-language credit among their requirements for high school graduation:

- California: (an unspecified number) credits in foreign language or arts
- Delaware: 6.5 credits in foreign language, arts, or vocational education
- Illinois: 1 credit in foreign language, music, or art
- Maryland: 2 credits in foreign language or technology
- Oregon: 1 credit in applied arts, fine arts, or foreign language
- West Virginia: 1 credit in foreign language, performing arts, or applied arts

Three states require students to have earned foreign-language credit for high school graduation:

- District of Columbia: 2 credits
- Massachusetts: competency determination at the tenth grade level includes foreign languages
- Rhode Island: 2 credits

Eight states require students to have earned foreign-language credit for the honors diploma:

- ❧ Arkansas: 2 credits
- ❧ Georgia: 2 credits
- ❧ Hawaii: 2 credits
- ❧ Louisiana: 2 credits
- ❧ New York: 3 credits
- ❧ South Carolina: 1 credit (applicable to the graduating class of 2001 and henceforth)
- ❧ Tennessee: 2 credits
- ❧ Virginia: 3 credits

High school graduation requirements that exceed those mandated by the state may be set by district boards of education.

The American Council on the Teaching of Foreign Languages (ACTFL) reports that in 2003, the National Assessment of Educational Progress (NAEP) will administer its first foreign-language assessment of secondary school students. The 2003 NAEP will provide information on how well a sample of high school students, including native speakers of the language, can communicate in Spanish, the foreign language most often taught in grades K–12. The conceptual framework for the assessment is informed by the foreign-language profession's content standards developed in response to Goals 2000.

Teacher Training and Licensing

Educational reform cannot take place without well-qualified teachers in the classrooms. Teacher supply-and-demand projections, emphasis on the assignment of teachers to courses that correspond to their areas of preparation, and the development of models for faculty development and preservice education are among the recurring themes in the educational reform literature. Less often noted, but of prime importance, is the need for university professors in educator preparation programs and trainers in district-sponsored staff development programs to be appropriately assigned. As interest increases in training all teachers for instructional duties with English-language learners (not only specialists in ESL or bilingual education, but *all* teachers), it becomes increasingly important that their trainers are themselves prepared through graduate coursework in bilingual or second-language education and clinical experience with English-language learners. College and university faculty members are the guardians of academic quality at their institutions, but they are sometimes hampered by limitations in funding needed to bring in new faculty members to fill gaps in areas of expertise.

In sixteen states, autonomous state credentialing or standards boards have been established (Education Commission of the States 2000). In most states, departments of education establish criteria for teacher licensure in accordance with legislative mandates and state board rules. School districts require applicants for teaching positions to present documentation that shows the state has granted them permission (license) to teach. The licensing credential is often referred to as a teaching certificate. Teacher licensure standards specify everything the teacher should know to provide instruction to a given age group or in a specific content area. The credential that results from the process therefore indicates the teaching fields for which the teacher has been prepared. Teaching assignments that correspond with teaching fields specified on the teaching certificate are referred to as in-field assignments.

State certification policies for teachers in elementary and middle grades may require preservice teachers to meet state-defined standards, to be graduates of an approved teacher education program, to have earned a certain number of credits in core fields, or to have earned a specified number of credits in several fields. At the secondary level, requirements for licensing typically require the applicant for certification to have earned a specified number of course credits in a major or minor in the teaching field. Most states specify time allocations or credit hours for supervised teaching experience required of preservice teachers. Assessment of prospective teachers in basic skills, professional knowledge of teaching, knowledge of subject matter, or some combination of these is required in forty-three states (National Conference of State Legislators 2001).

Surveys of state education agencies were conducted in 1999 to identify states that offer certification in ESL and bilingual education. The full report of that study is available on the NCBE (2000) Web site at http://www.ncbe.gwu.edu/askncbe/faqs/09certif.htm and provides the following information: thirty-seven states and the District of Columbia offer ESL teacher certification or endorsement, and twenty-three states and the District of Columbia offer bilingual or dual-language teacher certification or endorsement. In addition to offering teacher certification in ESL, twenty-three states have legislative requirements that teachers placed in ESL classrooms must be certified in ESL. In addition to offering bilingual and dual-language certification, seventeen states have legislative requirements that teachers placed in bilingual and dual-language classrooms must have bilingual and dual-language certification.

The 1999 survey identifies the states that offer ESL credentials as Alabama, Arizona, Arkansas, California, Colorado, Connecticut, Delaware, District of Columbia, Florida, Georgia, Hawaii, Illinois, Indiana, Iowa, Kansas, Kentucky, Maine, Maryland, Massachusetts, Minnesota, Missouri, Montana, Nebraska, Nevada, New Hampshire, New Jersey, New Mexico, New York, North Carolina, Ohio, Oregon, Tennessee, Texas, Utah, Virginia, Washington, and Wisconsin.

NCATE and the TESOL board of directors approved ESL Standards for P–12 Teacher Education Programs in October, 2001. A draft is available online at http://www. tesol.org/assoc/p12standards/index.html. Recommendations contained in Teacher Preparation Guidelines for ESL teachers (1975) and ESL Standards for Pre-K-12 Students (1997), both developed by Teachers of English to Speakers of Other Languages (TESOL), are professional resources that have been used to develop teacher preparation programs as well as requirements for certification in ESL. The teacher preparation guidelines recommend coursework in:

- Linguistics and culture: the grammatical, phonological, and semantic systems of English
- First and second language acquisition; the role of culture in language learning
- Methods: preparation in language teaching, including courses in second language testing; methods of teaching content through ESL methods, and methods that use content-area instruction to teach the language
- Additional languages: the learning of another language, including its linguistic structure and cultural system
- Professional education: historical, philosophical, psychological, and social/anthropological foundations of education; learning theory and curriculum development
- Language teaching practicum: directed observation and progressive supervised work with students

States that offer bilingual education credentials are Alabama, Arizona, California, Colorado, Connecticut, Delaware, District of Columbia, Illinois, Indiana, Kansas, Maine, Massachusetts, Michigan, Minnesota, Nevada, New Jersey, New Mexico, New York, North Dakota, Ohio, Texas, Utah, Washington, Wisconsin, and Wyoming (NCBE 2000).

The National Association for Bilingual Education (NABE) published Professional Standards for the Preparation of Bilingual/Multicultural Teachers (1992). Although these guidelines are similar to those of TESOL, they differ in their greater emphasis on coursework in:

⚬➤ The history of bilingual and multicultural education, laws, and minority communities
⚬➤ Methods and materials for bilingual as well as ESL classes
⚬➤ Assessment issues pertinent to bilingual settings

The NABE guidelines recommend proficiency in a non-English language (and in English) as desirable recruitment criteria for preservice bilingual educators; they emphasize that the development of teachers' language proficiency in two languages is of great importance in the bilingual teacher preparation curriculum.

A recent survey conducted by the National Center of Education Statistics included teachers who are not specialists in language, but who will have English-language learners in their classrooms (Lewis et al. 1999). The teachers were asked to evaluate their ability to work effectively with English-language learners; only 20 percent reported they felt very well prepared for such assignments. However, 42 percent of all public school teachers had one or more English-language learners in their classrooms (NCES 1996).

Certification requirements for foreign-language teachers incorporate standards for knowledge of subject matter in eleven states: Alabama, California, Connecticut, Massachusetts, Minnesota, New Hampshire, New Mexico, Oklahoma, Pennsylvania, South Dakota, and West Virginia (CCSSO 1998). The percentage of public school teachers whose main assignment is foreign-language education and who also earned a major in that field ranges from 48 percent to 100 percent, with a national average of 84 percent (NCES 1996).

Foreign-Language Education

According to Dutcher (1995), foreign-language education is available in every state. Foreign-language enrollments in 1997 included 4 million elementary school students (out of a total enrollment of 27.1 million), and the percentage of elementary schools offering foreign-language instruction increased from 22 percent in 1987 to 31 percent in 1997 (Rhodes and Branaman 1998). Spanish and French, in that order, are the languages most commonly taught at the elementary school level; course enrollment in Spanish for Spanish speakers, Japanese, Italian, and Sign Language has increased during the last decade. In several states, elementary or middle schools are required to offer instruction in a foreign language, including Arizona, Arkansas, Louisiana, Montana, and Oklahoma (Lewelling and Rennie 1998). Foreign-language instruction is required in all grades, K–12, by the North Carolina Basic Education Program. A searchable database, the National Directory of Early Foreign Language Programs, provides information on nearly 1,500 public and private elementary and middle schools that start teaching foreign languages before grade 7; it may be accessed at http://www.cal.org/public/databases.htm.

The 1998 Digest of Educational Statistics provides the following information about foreign-language programs at the secondary level:

- 5,002,000, or 41 percent of all students in grades 9 to 12 in public secondary schools during the fall 1994 semester were enrolled in foreign-language courses.
- The average number of Carnegie Units earned by public high school graduates in fall 1994 was 1.76 out of a total average credit hours earned of 24.16.

According to Lewelling and Rennie (1998), by 1998, secondary schools were required to offer foreign-language instruction in the following states:

- Arizona (through grade 8)
- Arkansas (two years of one foreign language)
- California (grades 7–12)
- Connecticut (one or more foreign languages at the secondary level)
- Delaware (senior high schools must offer at least two foreign languages)
- Illinois (two years of one foreign language)
- Indiana (two years of one foreign language)
- Kansas (two years of one foreign language)
- Kentucky (three years of one foreign language)
- Maine (two years of one foreign language)
- Maryland (two years of foreign-language instruction)
- Michigan (districts must offer an uninterrupted sequence from elementary to high school to qualify for extra funding)
- Minnesota (three years of one foreign language in grades 7–12)
- Missouri (two to three years, depending on the size of the high school)
- Montana (in grades 7 and 8, and two years in high school)
- Nebraska (two years of one foreign language)
- New Hampshire (three years of one foreign language and two years of a second foreign language)

- New York (one foreign language in grades 8–12; Native American languages may be selected to meet the requirement)
- North Carolina (grades 6–12)
- Ohio (three years of one foreign language or two years of two foreign languages)
- Oklahoma (sequential foreign-language courses in grades 7–12 that build on elementary school coursework; Native American languages may be selected to meet the requirement)
- Oregon (all senior high schools)
- Pennsylvania (four-year sequence)
- South Carolina (two years of one foreign language)
- South Dakota (two years of one foreign language)
- Texas (two years of one foreign language)
- Utah (all senior high schools)
- Vermont (three years of one foreign language)
- Virginia (three years of one foreign language)
- West Virginia (two years of one foreign language)
- Wisconsin (grades 9–12).

For the 1995–1996 school year, 55,000 postsecondary students were enrolled in foreign-language courses (NCES 1999); 13,952 students with a major in foreign languages and literatures earned bachelor's degrees. Since 1977, foreign-language enrollment at the college level has ranged from 7.3 percent to 8.2 percent of the total undergraduate enrollment (Brod and Welles 2000). Credit in foreign language was required for admission to 21 percent of four-year institutions and required for graduation from those institutions by 68 percent; for two-year colleges, 3 percent have foreign-language admission requirements and 23 percent have foreign-language graduation requirements (Brod and Huber 1996). According to the National Council of Organizations of Less Commonly Taught Languages, French, German, Italian, and Spanish are the languages most often taught at any level, elementary through university, to approximately 90 percent of foreign-language students; 10 percent study the less commonly taught languages, such as Arabic, Chinese, Russian, and Indonesian.

Bilingual Education

Every state responding to the 1996–1997 survey of the states' limited English proficient (LEP) students and available educational programs and services reported an LEP student population. Among the fifty states, total

LEP enrollment reached 3,378,861, an increase of 7.5 percent from the previous school year. Of the 477,911 students served by OBEMLA-funded programs, 1,827,587 were enrolled in Title One Basic Programs, 1,059,279 participated in state-funded bilingual programs, 682,953 were in state-funded ESL programs, and 398,042 were not enrolled in any special program. Overall, 76 percent of LEP students were in public schools that provide ESL programs, and 36 percent in schools that also provide bilingual programs (Macías 1998). Twelve percent of the schools enrolling LEP students offered neither program. For 1997–1998, 15.4 percent of migrant program students received ESL services (Migrant Education 2000).

Heritage-language programs have increased at both K–12 and college levels. These programs are for students who want to maintain and develop skills in their native languages. They are the counterparts of English-language arts programs for native speakers of English. Although an annual conference on Teaching Spanish to Native Speakers has been sponsored by New Mexico State University since 1995, the first national heritage languages conference was sponsored by the Center for Applied Linguistics (CAL), the National Foreign Language Center, and the California State University at Long Beach in 1999. It was attended by over 300 pre-K to university-level educators and policymakers representing over two dozen languages. For news of developments in heritage-language education, the reader is advised to consult the Web page maintained by CAL at http://www.cal.org/public/heritage.htm.

BRIDGE PROGRAMS: FUSION IN LANGUAGE EDUCATION

Both at K–12 and postsecondary levels, rapid growth has been noted in programs that blur traditional distinctions among levels or types of foreign- or second-language education and bilingual education programs. Heritage-language programs, for example, often classified as part of a bilingual education program, are also frequently classified as components of foreign-language programs.

Innovations that eradicate barriers between high school and college levels, such as middle college and dual enrollment programs, are also multiplying: The International High School at LaGuardia Community College is an example of an application of the concept to English-language learners. Vocational English as a Second Language (VESL) and bilingual vocational programs are conducted at both district (K–12 and adult) and college levels. At the college level, offerings may include programs in English for Specific Purposes (ESP), a continuum of ESL offerings with a focus on the language-related occupational or professional needs of English-language learners. These needs exceed skills normally acquired by the average English speaker, and may range from concentration on vocabulary from the targeted domain to bilingual immersion in professional courses in such fields as medicine and management.

The parallel development in postsecondary foreign-language circles is referred to as Languages for Specific Purposes (LSP); by 1991, courses or programs in LSP were offered by 275 institutions (Grosse and Voght 1991). Time spent studying in other countries may be part of an LSP program. Access to study-abroad programs, including but not limited to those related to LSP, are offered by 75 percent of the institutions responding to the Modern Language Association's (MLA) 1987–1989 survey of foreign-language programs (Huber 1993). Study-abroad programs are also frequently featured as part of international education, multicultural education, or intercultural education programs. Venice International University, located on the island of San Servolo in Venice, illustrates these interrelationships. The university is governed by its member institutions: Università Ca' Foscari di Venezia (Venice, Italy); Universitat Autónoma de Barcelona (Barcelona, Spain); Istituto Universitario di Architettura di Venezia (Venice, Italy); Ludwig Maximilians Universität (Munich, Germany); Duke University (Durham, North Carolina); Tel Aviv University (Tel Aviv, Israel); Fondazione Cassa di Risparmio di Venezia (Venice, Italy); and Provincia di Venezia (Venice, Italy). Each academic institution sends students and faculty members to the Venice site and offers courses taken by all students. These courses, all taught in English, are accepted for credit by all participating universities. For Duke University students, the program serves international and intercultural education purposes. For students from all other participating institutions, the program serves those goals, and English-language learning goals as well.

The point of these examples is to illustrate (1) the illusory nature of program labels, and (2) the flow along a continuum of intensity in language and culture learning settings that contributes to the interrelationships among the programs. It is not so much that ESL, Foreign Language, bilingual, multicultural, intercultural, and international education programs are different as that they are subsets of one another, in configurations that depend on which area is in the foreground of attention. Teaching English to speakers of other languages is teaching a second language; the language foreign to the student happens to be English, and the language is taught with a view to the immediate need for that language by English-language learners. Inclusion of FL/SL/Bilingual Education in the curriculum can fit within several levels of multicultural education typologies, from "additive" to "reconstructionist."

Language study is a key component of international and comparative education programs, so much so that funding for national centers has been available for combined language and area studies. As a further similarity, in today's global economy, access to foreign- and heritage-language instruction has become viewed as an equity issue in cities whose economies rely on international trade and commerce.

Immersion and Two-Way Programs

Immersion, two-way bilingual, bilingual college, and language across the curriculum programs also demonstrate amorphous boundaries. According to CAL, which maintains a directory of immersion programs, 242 schools in twenty-eight states and the District of Columbia teach all or part of their curriculum through a second language to English-speaking children. CAL also maintains an online database that includes profiles on 248 two-way or dual-language programs from twenty-three states and the District of Columbia. These programs serve both language majority and language minority students, each learning for a portion of the day in and through their native languages, and another portion of the day learning in and through their second languages. Both databases may be accessed on the Internet at http://www.cal.org/public/databases.htm.

Languages Across the Curriculum (L.A.C.)

Public school bilingual immersion programs may articulate with similar postsecondary models such as Languages Across the Curriculum (L.A.C., or sometimes LxC), a college-level approach to teaching language and other disciplines in the college curriculum. The Languages Across the Curriculum Internet Clearinghouse at Brown University's Center for Language Studies, http://www.brown.edu/Departments/ CLS/, defines the innovation as the practice through which the study and use of languages take place throughout the curriculum. Options for L.A.C. programs include the development of double majors, foreign-language readings and assignments in courses otherwise taught in English, and courses taught entirely through the medium of the foreign language. Early adopters of this innovation include Agnes Scott College, Binghamton University, Brown University, Earlham College, Syracuse University, University of Connecticut, University of Minnesota, and University of Rhode Island. The Fund for the Improvement of Post Secondary Education (FIPSE) in the U.S. Department of Education has funded the University of Connecticut, for example, to develop joint German/Engineering and Spanish/Nursing programs. DePaul University was awarded FIPSE grants to develop a Bilingual Professional Preparation Program, to prepare under-graduates in DePaul's International Studies Program with Spanish/English bilingual fluency at professional levels in law and commerce. Graduate programs in DePaul's Colleges of Law and Commerce will also feature bilingual and bicultural components.

At the community college level, FIPSE funding supported Lee College's efforts to prepare Spanish-speaking ESL students for careers in petrochemical maintenance, office administration, and allied health, areas of high demand in the Baytown, Texas, area. The project aims to develop skills in three areas: technical/vocational skills; speaking, reading, and writing skills in English; and reading and writing skills in Spanish. These skills meet biliteracy educational needs of students, and the local and global workforce needs of the business community.

Bilingual Colleges

Bilingual colleges extend the concept of L.A.C. from the program to the college level. These colleges and universities may adopt postsecondary versions of dual- or transitional-language programs or augmented heritage-language models. The history of the few bilingual colleges in the United States began in the early days of the republic.

In 1787, Franklin College (now Franklin and Marshall College) was founded by Germans in Lancaster, Pennsylvania, as the first bilingual college in the United States. The Finnish community established Suomi College and Theological Seminary (now Finlandia University) in 1896 in Hancock, Michigan. More recently established examples include Eugenio María de Hostos Community College and Boricua College, both in New York City; St. Augustine College in Chicago; and the Hawaiian Language College, one of three colleges at the University of Hawaii at Hilo. The Hawaiian Language College was recently renamed Ka Haka 'Ula O Ke'elikolani (The Venerable Standard of Ke'elikolani) in honor of Ke'elikolani, the nineteenth-century Hawaiian queen and advocate for the Hawaiian language.

Examples in other countries include the University of Ottawa (Canada), the University of Helsinki (Finland), the University of the Americas (Mexico), and St. Mary's University College Irish-Medium Pathway (Northern Ireland). In Spain's autonomous communities, professors may choose to use either the national language (Spanish) or the regional co-official language (Catalonian, Galician, Valencian, and Basque), or both. At the University of Fribourg in Switzerland, students can choose to take courses held in either or both of the two university languages: French and German. Students who combine the two may be awarded a bilingual degree. In South Africa, courses up to the doctoral level are presented in Afrikaans and English at Rand Afrikaans University in Johannesburg. The University of Port Elizabeth is phasing in Xhosa along with the university's traditional languages of English and Afrikaans.

During the past two decades, elected officials and educators at district, college, and university levels in Miami-Dade County have held informal discussions about the feasibility of a K-Ph.D. Spanish/English Bilingual Delivery System. Such an institutional arrangement could link programs such as the K–12 biliteracy programs, bilingual vocational programs at the community college, bilingual teacher-training programs, and modern-language programs at several universities in the area, and the Spanish-language master's program in journalism at the state university. Although south Florida has the critical mass of bilingual professionals needed for this type of extension of the bilingual college model, the synergistic union of the elements already in place along the lines of a bilingual college model has yet to be realized.

STATE PROFILES

Language education programs differ from state to state in ways that reflect each state's geographic location, population attributes, economic base, history, and language politics. These factors were used as the basis for selecting the two states profiled in this section, Illinois (which has enacted an Official English law) and Hawaii (an officially bilingual state).

Illinois

Illinois is a north-central state and has the country's fifth largest population. According to Census 2000 figures, 75 percent of its population of 12,419,293 residents are European in origin. Illinois ranks third among all states in total cash receipts from crops and fifth in agricultural exports; it ranks among the top states in several measures of manufacturing, transportation, and finance. As noted by the Illinois Department of Commerce and Community Affairs, its $36.5 billion in exports placed the state in the sixth position among the fifty states in value of overseas sales. See Illinois state Web sites for additional information on its economic base at http://www.state.il.us/budget/Book/Summary_EDInfo.pdf and http://www.commerce.state.il.us/doingbusiness/research/illinois.htm. For additional demographic information, see Census 2000, USATODAY.com at http://www.ncbe.gwu.edu/states/census.htm.

The American Local History Network (ALHN) provides the etymology of the word *Illinois*. It comes from the French word meaning "Illini" or "Land of Illini," based on an Algonquin word meaning "men" or "warriors." Illinois originally referred to a confederacy of Native American peoples (including the Kaskaskia, Cahokia, Michigamea, and Tamaroa) formerly inhabiting northern Illinois, or to the Algonquian language of the Illinois. For additional information about the Illinois, visit http://www.alhn.org/.

The area was claimed at various times by Spain, France, and England. It came under the authority of Virginia as a consequence of a battle in the Revolutionary War. In 1787, the Congress of the Confederation passed the Northwest Ordinance (An Ordinance for the Government of the Territory of The United States Northwest of the River Ohio) to establish the process for incorporation of the area that would eventually become six states (including Illinois). Article 3 of the ordinance included a promise that the utmost good faith would always be observed toward the Indians and that their lands and property would never be taken from them without their consent. A series of treaties with the Indian peoples of the area resulted in ceding their land to the United States. In 1803, for example, the Kaskaskia signed a treaty ceding all their Illinois lands (except for about 1,500 acres for the permanent use of the tribes) for $1,000 and a subsidy for the construction costs for a few buildings. The boundaries of the ceded land were established as:

> Beginning at the confluence of the Ohio and the Mississippi, thence up the Ohio to the mouth of the Saline creek, about twelve miles below the mouth of the Wabash, thence along the dividing ridge between the said creek and the Wabash until it comes to the general dividing ridge between the waters which fall into the Wabash, and those which fall into the Kaskaskia river; and thence along the said ridge until it reaches the waters which fall into the Illinois river, thence in a direct course to the mouth of the Illinois river, and thence down the Mississippi to the beginning. (Kappler 1904, 67–68)

After Illinois joined the union as the twenty-first state in 1818, the Illinois tribes were relocated several times. Their descendants now reside in Oklahoma.

Constitution

Article X, Section 1 of the constitution of the state of Illinois declares education a fundamental goal. High-quality public educational institutions and services are to be provided through the secondary level.

Legislation and Regulations

The State Designations Act, in Chapter 5, names English as the official language of the state. The 1969 official English amendment replaces the prior 1923 law declaring "American" as the official state language: "Be it enacted by the People of the State of Illinois, represented in the General Assembly: The official language of the State of Illinois shall be known hereafter as the 'American' language and not as the 'English' language" (Crawford 1992).

Chapter 775 of the Illinois Compiled Statutes, the Illinois Human Rights Act, guarantees freedom from discrimination against any individual because of his or her race, color, religion, sex, national origin, ancestry, age, marital status, physical or mental handicap, military status, or unfavorable discharge from military service in connection with employment, real estate transactions, access to financial credit, and the availability of public accommodations; from discrimination based on citizenship status in employment; and from sexual harassment in employment and higher education. It also establishes equal opportunity and affirmative action as policies of the state and describes a complaint procedure.

Chapter 105 contains the school code, which includes Article 14C, the state's Transitional Bilingual Education (TBE) Act. The act requires a full program, including all subjects required by the district or the state, to be taught in the native language and in English by teachers who have speaking, reading, and writing skills in their home language and communicative abilities in English. The curriculum is to address literacy skills in both languages and provide for instruction in the history and culture of the United States and of the home culture. A program is to be offered in all schools where twenty or more eligible children from the same language background are enrolled. A program of TBE may be offered to students from language groups with fewer than twenty students, or a Transitional Program of Instruction (TPI) may be offered instead. TPI programs provide instruction in subject matter in a language other than English to the extent necessary to aid the student's transition into the regular school curriculum. Parents are informed about program placement, invited to visit the classes, and advised of their rights to choose an alternative program. Annual examinations of English-language skills must be administered to provide a basis for program exit decisions. Program students will participate in the regular classroom setting with their English-speaking peers in courses such as art, music, and physical education, and shall be entitled to take part in extracurricular activities. Districts are authorized to offer supplementary preschool or summer programs.

School districts must establish parent advisory councils. A state advisory council must also be established to advise the state superintendent on bilingual education policy.

Standards and Accountability

At the direction of the General Assembly in 1997, learning standards were developed in English-language arts, physical development and health, science, social science, mathematics, foreign languages, and fine arts. The state assessment program is aligned to these standards and measures performance in six of the seven areas. The foreign-language standards are advisory, not required, and are not part of the assessment program. The Illinois Standards Achievement Test (ISAT) results are reported in English-language arts, science, social science, and mathematics. Administrative rules require that these reports be disaggregated by race, income, attendance, and LEP status, made available to the press, and mailed to parents (CCSSO 1999).

Waivers from the ISAT are provided for students during their first three years in a transitional bilingual education program. The alternative assessment instrument for English-language learners, the Illinois Measure of Annual Growth in English (IMAGE), is also aligned with the Illinois Learning Standards, and measures growth in acquisition of English-language reading and writing skills.

Teacher Certification

The state Teacher Certification Board administers basic skills and area tests that all applicants for Illinois teaching certificates must take and pass. Area tests are required for Spanish, French, German, Italian, Latin, Russian, and ESL. ESL teachers must hold a certificate in Early Childhood, Elementary, or Secondary Education; complete 100 clock hours of ESL clinical experience or three months of ESL teaching; and earn eighteen semester hours of credit from Linguistics, Theoretical Foundations of Teaching ESL, Assessment of Bilingual Students, Methods & Materials for Teaching ESL, and Cross-cultural Studies for Teaching LEP Students.

Teachers seeking certification for TBE may complete a state-approved program or submit transcripts for evaluation. They must be tested in the program and the English languages to assess their speaking, reading, writing, and grammar skills, effective July 1, 2001, as per 105 ILCS 5/14C-8A.

Completion of a thirty-semester-hour major in the academic

field is required for certification in foreign-language education. In Illinois, 90 percent of public school teachers in grades 7–12 assigned to teach foreign language have a major in that field.

Population and Program Data

Spanish, Arabic, Korean, Cantonese, Vietnamese, Russian, Tagalog, Japanese, Cambodian, and Laotian are the languages most commonly spoken by English-language learners in Illinois (NCBE 1999). Total school enrollment of LEP students in Illinois in 1996–1997 was 118,246, an increase of 3.8 percent from the previous year's enrollment of 113,899. Funds administered by OBEMLA programs served 67,622 students, including 1,593 students in foreign-language programs; 71,771 LEP students were served by federal programs other than Title VII, 105,567 participated in state-funded bilingual programs, and 28,248 in state-funded ESL programs. All LEP students in Illinois were enrolled in a special program (Macías 1998). In 1997–1998, 57 percent of Illinois migrant students received ESL services (Kindler 1996).

The state reimburses each district for the amount by which the costs of providing required K–12 TBE or TPI programs exceed the average per pupil expenditure in the district. The state also funds optional pre-K bilingual programs. For fiscal year 2000, the state received $9,508,779 in federal Emergency Immigrant Education Funds from OBEMLA (USDE 1999).

Two years of one foreign language must be offered by senior high schools (Lewelling and Rennie 1998). One unit in foreign languages or art is required for high school graduation. Credit in a foreign language is an admission requirement at 8 percent of the four-year institutions in Illinois and a graduation requirement at 58 percent of those institutions (Brod and Huber 1996). The National Directory of Early Foreign Language Programs maintained by CAL and the ERIC Clearinghouse on Languages and Linguistics includes ten public school foreign-language programs in operation in elementary or middle school grades (grades K–8).

St. Augustine College in Chicago, a bilingual institution of higher education, was granted operating authority on October 7, 1980, by the Illinois State Board of Higher Education.

Public School Programs

The Chicago Public School (CPS) System is the largest in Illinois and the nation's third-largest school district. It manages 559 schools and serves

430,000 students, from 103 language backgrounds, representing 87 percent of the 118 languages spoken by students in Illinois schools.

The district's Office of Language and Cultural Education provides support to programs that help students to develop proficiency in English while continuing to progress in academic areas. Those programs reflect the premise that developing proficiencies in the native language of English-language learners aids their acquisition of literacy and competency in English. Accomplishments listed by that office for the 1999 school year include the alignment of bilingual programs with the School Code of Illinois, the development of ESL goals and standards for pre-K through grade 12, the adoption of strengthened and standardized measures of accountability for bilingual programs, and the creation of a multilingual and multiethnic parent advisory council that reflects the CPS bilingual student population.

Funding from the state for LEP students is provided for three years of bilingual education services. In CPS, a fourth-year extension is granted automatically if a student does not meet established exit criteria. Fifth-year extensions are granted case by case.

Bilingual programs in the CPS include:

- A high school Newcomer Center for new immigrants with significant gaps in their education to assist students and their families
- Dual-language pre-K and kindergarten programs
- The Chicago Bilingual Showcase Project Bilingual literacy program, implemented in fifteen schools, for 5,000 students, to assist in the transition from reading in the native language to reading in English
- Thirty-three world language programs, including twenty-five in Spanish, one in Polish, two in German, two in French, one in Mandarin (Chinese), and two in Japanese
- Saturday Foreign Language Exposure programs in two schools where no bilingual or world language programs exist
- Twelve International Language and Career Academies in High Schools (ILCAHS)

Additional information about bilingual programs in CPS is available at http://www.cps.k12.il.us/AboutCPS/Departments/langculture/langculture.html.

Hawaii

Hawaii was once a kingdom, ruled by its own native royalty, governed by its own constitution, legislature, and courts. The Hawaiian kingdom lasted for nearly a century.

Hawaii is composed of a group of eight major islands and numerous islets in the Pacific Ocean. It ranks in forty-second place among the states in the size of its population. According to Census 2000 data, its population of 1,211,537 residents is 42 percent Asian; 15 percent Native Hawaiian, partly Native Hawaiian, or other Pacific Islander; and 24 percent White.

The Department of Business, Economic Development & Tourism (DBEDT) 1999 State of Hawaii Data Book identified the income derived from the state's major industries:

- ➡ Visitor expenditures (1997): $10.8 billion
- ➡ Federal defense spending (1998): $4.1 billion
- ➡ Sugar and pineapple (1997): $269.2 million

For additional information about Hawaii's economy, see the DBEDT Web site at http://www.hawaii.gov/dbedt/db99/index.html. For additional demographic information about the state, see Census 2000, USATODAY.com at http://www.ncbe.gwu.edu/states/census.htm.

According to the Hawaiian state government Web site's section on the history of the state, Polynesian explorers migrated to the Hawaiian Islands in the first century A.D. In 1778, the British mariner Captain James Cook arrived in Hawaii. King Kamehameha the Great completed the work of uniting the Islands into one internationally recognized kingdom. In 1820, the first missionary families arrived on the Islands. By 1835, commercial production of sugarcane was under way. Laborers were imported to work in the sugar fields, primarily from Asia. Their descendants contribute to the multicultural diversity of present-day Hawaii.

Although economic investment in the Islands was primarily from the United States, political control belonged to the government of the Hawaiian Kingdom. Conflicts ensued. The investors formed a Committee of Safety in 1893, and declared an end to the government of Hawaii. Within two years, the Republic of Hawaii was established. In two more years, the government of the Republic entered into a treaty of annexation to become a territory of the United States. Hawaii became the fiftieth state of the union on August 21, 1959.

The Office of Hawaiian Affairs (OHA) provides additional information and interpretation of the events summarized above. According to this version, the end of the monarchy came about because the White business community believed the only way to avoid tariffs and protect profits on Hawaiian sugar sold to the United States was for Hawaii to become part of the United States. Also described are the roles of the United States Minister to Hawaii and of the United States Marine Corps in the annexation.

The OHA account describes Queen Lili'uokalani's attempts to restore the government's authority and to reinstate voting rights for the Hawaiian people, who had been disenfranchised by the terms of the constitution urged upon the previous head of state by the White business community. The Committee of Safety prevailed against the queen with the support of U.S. troops acting without congressional authorization. To avoid bloodshed, the queen yielded her throne on January 17, 1893. Sanford Dole was proclaimed president of the Republic of Hawaii. On July 7, 1898, President William McKinley signed the Resolution annexing Hawaii to the United States. English became the language of instruction in the schools and use of the Hawaiian language was forbidden.

The OHA pages also include an article prepared by attorney J. Van Dyke on the political status of Native Hawaiians; Dyke makes the following observations:

- Although Native Hawaiians controlled the land in the Hawaiian Islands in communal land tenure when the nineteenth century began, almost all of it came under control of non-Hawaiians by the beginning of the twentieth century.
- Native Hawaiians, now 200,000 in number, constitute the only native group in the United States that has never been allowed to utilize a claims commission or other mechanism to seek redress for its losses from the federal government.
- In 1993, Congress enacted an Apology Resolution, which acknowledges the illegality of the 1893 overthrow and recognizes that 1,800,000 acres of lands were acquired by the United States without the consent of, and without compensation paid to, the Native Hawaiian people. This public law urges the president to seek a reconciliation with the Hawaiian people.
- The Native Hawaiians' lands and sovereign autonomy were taken from them, attempts were made to destroy their culture, their population declined dramatically, and they occupy the bottom of the socioeconomic scale in their own islands.

The political status of Native Hawaiians and of the OHA has been contested in the courts. The OHA administers programs that benefit Native Hawaiians. Harold "Freddy" Rice, whose family has been in Hawaii for over 100 years but who is not "Hawaiian," sued after being denied the opportunity to vote in an OHA election. Rice initially lost his challenge in both the trial court and the court of appeals, which held that OHA's voting rules were not primarily racial but legal or political. The United States Supreme Court decision in *Rice v. Cayetano* (2000) rejected the definition of Native Hawaiians as a political group, and ruled that state-sponsored election of the OHA trustees could not be limited to the racial category of Native Hawaiians on whose behalf they administer programs. The full decision of the majority and of the dissenting justices is available in full text online at http://caselaw.lp.findlaw.com/scripts/getcase.pl?navby=search&court=US&case=/us/000/98%2D818.html.

Two bills are pending to begin the process of reconciliation urged in the Apology Resolution, H.R. 617 and S. 746. The proposed legislation provides for a process within the framework of federal law for the Native Hawaiian people to exercise their rights as a distinct aboriginal, indigenous, native community to reorganize a Native Hawaiian governing entity to express their rights as native people to self-determination and self-governance.

For additional information about the controversies surrounding the annexation of Hawaii, see the state of Hawaii's Web site at http://www.state.hi.us/about/history.htm and the state's Office of Hawaiian Affairs sites at http://hoohana.aloha.net/~oha/ and http://www.nativehawaiians.com/rvc_articles.html. For the full text of the 1993 Apology Resolution (Public Law 103-150, a joint resolution to acknowledge the 100th anniversary of the January 17, 1893, overthrow of the Kingdom of Hawaii, and to offer an apology to Native Hawaiians on behalf of the United States for the overthrow of the Kingdom of Hawaii) see the United States House of Representatives Web site at http://resourcescommittee.house.gov/105cong/laws103.htm.

Constitution

Article XV, Section 4 established in 1978 that English and Hawaiian were the official languages of Hawaii, with Hawaiian required for public acts and transactions only as provided by law. Article X, Section 4 included requirements that the state promote the study of Hawaiian culture, history, and language, and provide for a Hawaiian education program consisting of language, culture, and history in the public schools.

Legislation and Regulations

Several provisions related to language appear in the Hawaii Revised Code (HRC). The HRC specifies that the Hawaiian language is the native language of Hawaii and may be used on all emblems representative of the state. Diacritical markings needed for spelling in the Hawaiian language may be used in documents prepared by or for state or county government agencies. Translators may be employed to translate documents such as titles to real estate, and circuit and district judges are authorized to appoint court interpreters. All legislative proceedings, however, are to be conducted, and tax records kept, in the English language.

The HRC education code contains requirements for the promotion of Hawaiian culture, history, and language in the public schools and encourages the use of community expertise in furtherance of the Hawaiian education program. Section 304-69 of the revised code mandates the establishment of a Hawaiian-language college at the University of Hawaii at Hilo to provide a Hawaiian liberal education program taught primarily in the Hawaiian language. Language-related teacher training and research activities to be carried out by the college are specified.

Chapter 41 of the Department of Education Administrative Rules includes a civil rights policy and complaint procedure. Discrimination on the basis of race, color, religion, sex, age, national origin, ancestry, or disability is prohibited in the public school system of the state.

Standards and Accountability

Hawaii has a legislative mandate to develop a comprehensive system of accountability, including a student-assessment system explicitly aligned with Hawaiian content and performance standards that embody high expectations for the attainment of all students. An annual school profile, including information on student achievement and other indicators of school success, is made available to parents, the general public, and government agencies. Schools may grant waivers from state assessments participating in school-based management plans, but the results of alternate assessments must be included in the published annual report. Both the standards and the assessment systems are currently under review.

Teacher Certification

All persons are required to obtain a teaching credential according to the rules established by the Department of Education as a prerequisite to teaching in department schools. The Department of Education also has approval authority for teacher training programs. The state approves ESL teacher education programs and issues teaching licenses to graduates of approved programs. All candidates for licensure in Hawaii are required to take competency tests administered by the Educational Testing Service Praxis Series: Professional Assessments for Beginning Teachers. The Department of Education requires tests for basic skills and teaching principles, and an assessment of subject matter. Licensure areas included in the subject-matter assessments include French, German, Spanish, and Teaching English as a Second Language.

Population and Program Data

Ilokano, Tagalog, Samoan, Marshallese, Cantonese, Vietnamese, Korean, Tongan, Japanese, and Spanish are the languages most commonly spoken by LEP students in Hawaii (NCBE 1999). Total enrollment of LEP students in Hawaii's schools in 1996–1997 was 12,500, a slight decrease of 0.9 percent from the previous year's enrollment of 12,611. Funds administered by OBEMLA programs served 1,349 students, including 265 students in foreign-language programs; 4,311 LEP students were served by federal programs other than Title VII, 4,649 participated in state-funded bilingual programs, and 7,700 in state-funded ESL programs. All LEP students in Hawaii were enrolled in a special program (Macías 1998). Currently, 6.7 percent of Hawaii's students speak a first language other than English (Pablo, Ongteco, and Koki 1999). The state's compensatory education program is the source of funding for bilingual programs. For fiscal year 2000, the state received $381,718 in federal Emergency Immigrant Education Funds (USDE 1999).

Approximately 50 percent of the state's 180 elementary schools include instruction in foreign languages in grades 4 through 8. The study of world languages is required by state Board of Education policy and by Act 309 of the 1998 Hawaii legislature. Act 309 requires "a course of study for the first twelve grades to enable all students to meet progressive standards of competency in a language in addition to English." Credit in foreign language is a graduation requirement at 86 percent of the four-year institutions in Hawaii (Brod and Huber 1996). The National Directory of Early Foreign Language Programs maintained by CAL and the ERIC Clearinghouse on Languages and Linguistics includes profiles of four public school foreign-language programs in operation in elementary or middle school grades (grades K–8).

Public School Programs

Hawaii is unusual in that the state and the school district are coterminous. In Hawaii, all schools in the state are part of one statewide district.

ESL and Bilingual Education Programs

Since 1985, the goal for bilingual education in Hawaii has been to provide equal access to education and equity for language minority students who speak a language other than English by institutionalizing
bilingual multicultural education. The ESL program is the overall umbrella for educational services to language minority students. Program
features include newcomer or learner centers and sheltered English
programs. Program funding continues for at least five years to build
commitment and capacity for schools and districts to continue providing educational services to students of limited English proficiency without reliance on federal dollars (Pablo, Ongteco, and Koki 1999).

Speakers of Hawaiian Creole are also able to receive bilingual
and ESL services through Title VII projects that are not available
through the state-funded ESL program. The Hawaiian Language Center
of the University of Hawaii reports that in 1898, the Hawaiian language
was supplanted when English became the official language for all government offices and transactions. Within a few years, a Hawaiian Creole
language developed as a result of the Hawaiians' sudden attempt to
adapt to English and the influence of the Pidgin Hawaiian that was spoken by immigrants.

Foreign-Language Programs

According to the online National Directory of Early Foreign Language
Programs maintained by the Center for Applied Linguistics at http://
www.cal.org/ericcll/earlyfl/earlyfldb/FMPro?-db=earlyfl.fp5&
format=detail.html&-lay=webdetails&-sortfield=State&-sortfield=
School&state=HI&SchoolType=public&-recid=33745&-find=, elementary and middle school world language programs are offered in French
(one program), Ilokano (one program), Hawaiian (four programs), Japanese (five programs), Tagalog (one program), and Spanish (two programs).
The University of Hawaii was granted funds authorized by Section 603,
Title VI, of the Higher Education Act to develop the National Foreign Language Resource Center (NFLRC), one of nine such centers in the country.
The NFLRC undertakes projects that focus primarily on the less commonly taught languages of East Asia, Southeast Asia, and the Pacific.

Hawaiian Immersion Programs

According to Hawaii's Department of Education, Hawaiian-language
immersion programs serve students seeking to learn through the first

language of the islands, Hawaiian, and contribute to reviving the Hawaiian language. These programs were started in 1987 in two elementary schools. For the 2000–2001 school year, total enrollment in the Hawaiian immersion program reached 1,636 students in grades K–12. The total number of teachers participating in the program was 101.

The model calls for a full-immersion program up to grade 5. That means that all skills and subjects are learned using the Hawaiian language. In grade 5, English-language arts are introduced for approximately one hour a day. The majority of the students do not speak Hawaiian prior to their entrance into kindergarten. Enrollment in the program is by parental request. Parents are encouraged to take classes in Hawaiian so they can support their children's language learning at home.

Immersion schools are responsible for ensuring that all students meet state achievement standards; the content and means of delivery, however, are based on Hawaiian traditional knowledge and a Hawaiian perspective. Because students in Hawaiian immersion programs do not receive formal instruction in English until grade 5, they are exempt from the state's testing requirements until grade 7. At that grade, immersion students generally do as well as their English-only peers on SAT tests.

Under the terms of the settlement agreement entered into by the OHA and the Department of Education, Hawaiian-language immersion programs in the public schools receive up to $7.5 million in additional funding over five years. For additional information about Hawaiian immersion programs, see the Department of Education Web site at http://www.k12.hi.us/~kaiapuni/welcome.html.

CONCLUSIONS

The following conclusions are drawn from this chapter's review of provisions for language education established by the various states:

- State action exerts major influence on education within each state.
- The influence of crosscutting themes is felt in all states; for example, emphasis on educational reform and accountability. Programs for second-language learners must conform to state initiatives for standards and accountability. Nevertheless, education policies among the states, including those affecting language education, differ from state to state.
- Both in an official English state (Illinois) and in an officially bilingual state (Hawaii), bilingual programs have been

adopted as a means of teaching English and other content areas of the curriculum. In both states, the establishment of bilingual colleges has been authorized.

⟶ In both states, historic, demographic, economic, and political factors influenced the choice of languages to be taught.

School programs reflect the needs and resources of their student populations and the concerns of their communities. These factors may differ from state to state, and indeed, from district to district. Hawaii's language education programming would not make sense in Illinois, and Illinois's programs would not adequately respond to Hawaii's circumstances. Flexibility in guidelines governing program development and funding permits appropriately different responses to vastly different circumstances. Flexibility in guidelines governing the duration of program services permits appropriate responses to individual differences among students.

REFERENCES

Brod, R., and B. Huber. 1996. The MLA survey of foreign language entrance and degree requirements. *ADFL Bulletin* 28, no. 1 (fall). [Online]. Available: *http://www.ade.org/adfl/bulletin/v28n1/281035.htm*.

Brod, R., and B. Welles. 2000. Foreign language enrollments in United States institutions of higher education, fall, 1998. *ADFL Bulletin* 31, no. 2 (winter). [Online]. Available: *http://www.adfl.org/resources/enroll.htm*.

Council of Chief School Officers (CCSSO) State Education Assessment Center. December 1998. *Key state education policies on K–12 education: Standards, graduation, assessment, teacher licensure, time and attendance: A 50-state report.* Washington, DC: Author. [Online]. Available: *http://www.ccsso.org/pdfs/keystate98.pdf001-1431*.

Council of Chief School Officers (CCSSO). 1999. *State education accountability systems: Illinois.* Washington, DC: Author. [Online]. Available:*http://www.ccsso.org/ILprofile.html#5*.

Council of Great City Schools. 1999. Characteristics of member districts. Washington, DC: Author. [Online]. Available: *http://www.cgcs.org/about/about.htm*.

Crawford, J. 1992. *Hold your tongue: Bilingualism and the politics of English Only.* Reading, MA: Addison-Wesley.

Dutcher, D. 1995. *Overview of foreign language education in the United States.* Washington, DC: Center for Applied Linguistics.

Education Commission of the States. 2000. *Teaching quality: Licensure, evalua-*

tion & accountability. [Online]. Available: *http://www.ecs.org/html/ IssueSection.asp?issueid=126&s=What+States+Are+Doing*.

Grosse, C. U., and G. M. Voght. 1991. The evolution of languages for specific purposes in the United States. *Modern Language Journal* 75.

Huber, B. J. 1993. Characteristics of college and university foreign language curricula: Findings from the MLA's 1987–1989 survey. *ADFL Bulletin* 24, no. 3 (spring).

Kappler, C. J., ed. 1904. *Indian affairs: Laws and treaties.* Vol. I, *Laws* (compiled to December 1, 1902). Washington, DC: Government Printing Office. [Online]. Available: *http://digital.library.okstate.edu/kappler/Vol2/treaties/ kas0067.htm*.

Kindler, A. February 1996. Section on migrant education. In Kris Anstrom, ed., *Federal policy, legislation, and education reform: The promise and the challenge for language minority students.* NCBE Resource Collection Series No. 5. Washington, DC: National Clearinghouse for Bilingual Education. Available: *http://www.ncbe.gwu.edu/ncbepubs/resource/fedpol.htm*.

Lara, J., and D. August. February 1996. *Systemic reform & limited English proficient students.* Washington, DC: CCSSO and Stanford Working Group. [Online]. Available: *http://publications.ccsso.org/ccsso/publication_ detail.cfm?PID=155*.

Lewelling, V., and J. Rennie. 1998. State initiatives for foreign language instruction. *The ERIC Review: K–12 Foreign Language Education* 6, no. 1 (fall).

Lewis, L., B. Parsad, N. Carey, N. Bartfai, E. Farris, and B. Smerdon. 1999. *Executive summary: Teacher quality: A report on the preparation and qualifications of public school teachers.* Statistical Analysis Report, NCES 1999-080. Washington, DC: National Center for Education Statistics, U.S. Department of Education. [Online]. Available: *http://nces.ed.gov/pubs99/ 1999080.htm*.

Macías, R. 1998. *Summary report of the survey of the states' limited English proficient students and available educational programs and services, 1996–97.* The SEA Report. Washington, DC: National Clearinghouse for Bilingual Education.

Migrant Education. 2000. *Migrant national summary reports.* [Online]. Available: *http://www.migranted.org/*.

National Center for Education Statistics (NCES). September 1996. Table 3.9. Percentage of public school foreign language teachers (grades 7–12 only) with a major in field, by state: 1993–1994. *1993–1994 SASS by State: Schools and Staffing Survey: Selected Results* (NCES 96-312). [Online]. Available: *http://nces.ed.gov/pubs/96312.html*.

National Center for Education Statistics (NCES). May 1999. Table 136. Average number of Carnegie units earned by public high school graduates in various subject fields, by student characteristics: 1982 to 1994. *Digest of Ed-*

ucation Statistics, 1998. NCES 1999-032. Washington, DC: Author. [Online]. Available: *http://www.nces.ed.gov/pubs99/digest98/listoftables.html.*

National Center for ESL Literacy Education (NCLE). 1997. The waiting game. *NCLEnotes* 6, no. 1 (summer).

National Clearinghouse for Bilingual Education (NCBE). 1999. State K–12 LEP enrollment and top languages 1989–1997. [Online]. Available: *http://www.ncbe.gwu.edu/ncbepubs/reports/state-data/index.htm.*

National Clearinghouse for Bilingual Education (NCBE). September 2000. Which states offer certification or endorsement in bilingual education or ESL? [Online]. Available: *http://www.ncbe.gwu.edu/askncbe/faqs/09certif. htm.*

National Conference of State Legislators. 2001. *Education program: Teacher licensure.* [Online]. Available: *http://www.ncsl.org/programs/educ/TOverV. htm.*

Pablo, J., B. Ongteco, and S. Koki. January 1999. *Title VII bilingual education in Hawaii: Lessons learned.* Honolulu: Pacific Resources for Education and Learning. [Online]. Available: *http://www.prel.org/products/products/ TitleVII-bilingual.pdf.*

Rhodes, N. C., and L. E. Branaman. 1998. *Foreign language instruction in the United States: A national survey of elementary and secondary schools.* Washington, DC: Cal/Delta Systems. [Online]. Available: *http://www. cal.org/public/results.htm.*

U.S. Department of Education (USDE). 1999. Guide to U.S. Department of Education programs and resources. Web99 home page. [Online]. Available: *http://web99.ed.gov/.*

Chapter Five

Bilingual Education and Federal Law

Descriptions of federal legislation, policies, and court decisions that govern the provision of bilingual education are presented in this chapter. See Chapter 2 for a chronology of related social, legal, and political developments.

Authorization, incentives, requirements, or prohibitions related to language education in grades K–12 can be established at the federal, state, and local levels by the judicial, executive, or legislative branch of government. This body of law may affect native speakers of English, native speakers of languages other than English, or both groups. The emphasis may be on the promotion of civic virtues, academic excellence, compensatory education and dropout prevention, access to equal educational opportunity, support of family values, or enhancement of the country's diplomatic or military preparedness and competitive posture in a global economy. The goal may be assimilation (total replacement of the language minority cultural and linguistic heritage) or acculturation (expansion of linguistic and cultural repertoire to include additional languages and associated cultural skills). Significant initiatives presented in chronological order are summarized in the following sections.

FEDERAL AUTHORIZATION

No education or language rights are stated in the constitution. However, the First Amendment of the Bill of Rights guarantees freedom of speech, and the Fourteenth Amendment guarantees that no state shall deprive any person of life, liberty, or property without due process of law. As the constitution neither requires nor prohibits bilingual education, states and districts have established policies on language education.

Language minority students' protection from discrimination is based on the concept of national origin. Persons whose home language, native language, or most frequently used language is other than English are included in the group defined as National Origin Minority (NOM). Although no federal law requires districts to adopt bilingual programs, many states and districts have selected bilingual education programs as a mean of complying simultaneously with their dual responsibility to teach English and other content area to English-language learners. Districts that choose a sequential approach by focusing first on the development of English-language skills must later provide students with compensatory and supplemental education to remedy curricular deficiencies in other areas that may develop during the time devoted to English-language instruction.

The practice of providing instruction in languages other than English in schools on the North American continent began in precolonial times and became widespread in the nineteenth century. During World War I, anti-immigrant and anti-German sentiments resulted in laws enacted by thirty-five states prohibiting instruction in or through a language other than English.

In Nebraska, for example, state law prohibited any person from teaching any subject to any person in any language other than the English language; the state permitted teaching languages other than English only to students who had attained and successfully passed the eighth grade. An instructor in a private religious institution, Zion Parochial School, was tried and convicted for teaching a ten-year-old boy to read in German. The U.S. Supreme Court reversed the conviction, observing that the Nebraska legislature had attempted to interfere with the calling of modern-language teachers, with the opportunities of pupils to acquire knowledge, and with the power of parents to control the education of their own children, in ways not in keeping with the Fourteenth Amendment protection against deprivation of liberty without due process. Parents' right to select a private school education for their children that includes the study of foreign languages was upheld on substantive due process grounds by the United States Supreme Court in *Meyer v. Nebraska* in 1923. Teachers' discretion in professional decisions regarding language study was also supported by this decision.

CURRENT FEDERAL LANGUAGE GOALS

Secretary of Education Richard W. Riley articulated the policy preferences of the executive branch of government on language learning on March 15, 2000, during a presentation at Bell Multicultural High School in Washington, D.C., when he stated that we need to encourage all young people to acquire proficiency in English and one other language. He went on to highlight the growth and promise of dual-language bilingual programs that challenge young people with high standards, high expectations, and a curriculum in two languages as the wave of the future. On April 19, in a statement delivered at La Maison Française in Washington, D.C., on "The Growing Importance of International Education," he reiterated his strong support for high-quality dual-immersion schools that help children develop biliteracy in English and another language, an approach he referred to as English + One. On that same date, then president William J. Clinton issued a statement of general policy directing the secretaries of state and education to support the efforts of state and local governments and educational institutions to promote international awareness and skills in the classroom and on campuses, and to strengthen foreign-language learning at all levels.

The administration's proposal for reauthorization of the Elementary and Secondary Education Act, the "Educational Excellence for All Children Act of 1999," would intensify foreign-language instruction in elementary schools. The bill includes as a national goal that 25 percent of all public elementary schools offer high-quality, standards-based foreign-language programs by the year 2005, rising to 50 percent by 2010. Funds from the newly authorized act would provide for the development of standards, the preparation of teachers, and applications of technology in support of the foreign-language education goals.

According to comments from then–president-elect George W. Bush and nominee for secretary of education Rod Paige, the incoming administration was also supportive of bilingual education ("Bilingual Program . . . ," 1998).

In the early 1990s, the legislative branch of government stated its purposes related to language or to language minority students in several key legislative acts, including the Native American Languages Act of 1990, Goals 2000: Educate America Act, the School-To-Work Opportunities Act of 1994, and Improving America's Schools Act (IASA).

The Native American Languages Act of 1990
(Public Law 101-477, 25 USC 2901)

In Section 104 of the act, Congress declared that the policy of the United States is to preserve, protect, and promote the rights of Native Americans (Indians, Native Hawaiians, and Native American Pacific Islanders) to use Native American languages and to encourage and support the use of Native American languages as means of instruction (the term *Indian* is defined in Section 7881(4) of Title XX and includes Alaska Natives).

Several aspects of this support are enumerated; they include encouraging the recognition of proficiency in Native American languages by institutions of higher education as fulfilling foreign-language entrance or degree requirements, and granting the same academic credit for the study of Native American languages as is granted for comparable proficiency achieved through coursework in a language of wider communication. All institutions of elementary, secondary, and higher education are encouraged to include Native American languages in the curriculum in the same manner as foreign languages and to grant proficiency in Native American languages the same full academic credit as proficiency in foreign languages. In Section 107, express authorization is provided for the continued use of federal funds to teach English to Native Americans. These provisions demonstrate the evolution in congressional policy on Indian education from previous assimilationist goals to current goals of acculturation and additive bilingualism. Current policy, in other words, encourages students to add the English language to their linguistic repertoire and to develop skill in both languages, not to substitute English for their home languages.

The following three measures are examples of congressionally authorized education reform efforts in Congress, ultimately traceable to the effects of the 1983 *Nation at Risk* report. They contain notable provisions for language education and for the education of language minority students.

Goals 2000: Educate America Act
(Public Law 103-227, 20 USC 5801)

The overall purpose of the legislation is to improve learning and teaching by providing a national framework for standards-based education reform and by promoting the research, consensus building, standard setting, curriculum and assessment alignment, professional development, and systemic changes needed to ensure equitable educational opportunities and high levels of educational achievement for all students. The term *all students* includes disadvantaged students and children; students or children with diverse racial, ethnic, and cultural backgrounds; American Indians; Alaska Natives; Native Hawaiians; students and children with disabilities; students and children with limited English proficiency (LEP); school-aged students and children who have dropped out of school; migratory students and children; and academically talented students. The extent to which congressional intent to include all students has been met with respect to LEP students is uncertain. What is certain is that the extent and manner of compliance vary from program to program and by jurisdiction. The inclusion of LEP students in Title I programs, for example, may take place with or without programs to train teachers to provide assistance with second-language acquisition or to use a language other than English. See Chapter 3 for additional information on teacher training and on district policies.

Section 102 of Title I of this act states national education goals, a series of policies first agreed to by the National Association of Governors and the president of the United States in 1989. They include student goals for demonstrating competence in a set of core subjects, specifically including foreign languages. Related objectives include a substantial increase in the percentage of all students competent in more than one language and a universal objective for all students to become knowledgeable about the diverse cultural heritage of our country and of the world. Parent involvement goals are set for all schools; parents of children who are bilingual are identified as part of the parent group to be included.

These provisions demonstrate (1) congressional recognition of a role for foreign-, second-, or heritage-language learning equal to that of other academic subjects, and (2) determination to extend the benefits of educational reform and high standards to language minority students.

The School-To-Work Opportunities Act of 1994 (Public Law 103-239, 20 USC 6101)

The major purpose of this act is to establish a national framework to enable states to help all students attain high academic and occupational standards that prepare them for first jobs in high-skill, high-wage careers and increase their opportunities for further education, including education in a four-year college or university. The activities funded under this act are to be integrated with the systems developed under the Goals 2000: Educate America Act and the National Skill Standards Act of 1994. The term *all students* in this act, as in Goals 2000, includes LEP students, migrant children, school dropouts, academically talented students, and all students who enter the workforce without a college degree, a group that includes three-fourths of all high school students. For language minority students, the importance of these provisions depends on realization of their potential for helping students to surmount gender, race, ethnic, disability, language, or socioeconomic impediments to career options.

Improving America's Schools Act (IASA)

The Improving America's Schools Act (IASA) reauthorized the Elementary and Secondary Education Act (ESEA). This act is the most comprehensive example of federal support for K–12 education. Originally designed as part of President Lyndon Johnson's War on Poverty, it currently provides $12 billion in grants a year to increase access to educational opportunity and the quality of education.

The 1994 ESEA reauthorization, like Goals 2000, stresses the education reform resolution that all students, including those disadvantaged or at risk, should be held to the same rigorous academic standards. The underlying premise of this objective is that elementary and secondary school organizations and students will meet the expectations set for them. To increase achievement, first raise the standards.

Several sections of IASA directly address bilingual programs or language minority students, including Title I, Helping Disadvantaged Children Meet High Standards; Education of Migratory Children; Federal Evaluations Demonstrations and Transition Projects; the Dwight D. Eisenhower Professional Development Program; the Star Schools program; Magnet School Assistance; Women's Educational Equity; and the Bilingual Education Act.

TITLE I: HELPING DISADVANTAGED CHILDREN MEET HIGH STANDARDS

Funding from this $7.7 billion program is directed to raising the achievement levels of some 11 million students in more than 45,000 high-poverty schools in 13,000 school districts (Macías 1998). The amount of funding for each agency is determined by application of a formula based on how many eligible children reside in each jurisdiction. The 1994 reauthorization carried forward stipulations that focus on educational improvement in schools with high concentrations of children from low-income families. In addition, new IASA provisions helped LEP children to participate, waived certain employment criteria for instructional aides who are proficient in a language other than English, and established requirements for:

- Translation of school-wide plans into the primary language of the parents of participating children
- Evaluation of student achievement based in part on assessments conducted in the language and form most appropriate for LEP students, with reasonable accommodation procedures, and aligned with rigorous state standards
- Reports of LEP assessment results disaggregated by racial and ethnic group, English-proficiency status, migrant status, disability status, and economic status

- ☞ Evaluations of parental involvement policies, giving particular attention to special populations of parents, including those who have limited English proficiency, and parental involvement in the development of state plans
- ☞ Translation of school information sent to the homes of participating children to the language used in such homes
- ☞ Coordination of plans with those funded under other IASA programs, such as the Bilingual Education Act
- ☞ Development of professional development plans, which must include instruction in ways to teach special-needs children

Seventeen percent of those served by Title I–funded programs in the 1996–1997 school year were LEP students.

TITLE VII: BILINGUAL EDUCATION, LANGUAGE ENHANCEMENT, AND LANGUAGE ACQUISITION PROGRAMS

The purpose of Title VII, as described in Section 7102(a)(8), is "to help ensure that limited English proficient students master English and develop high levels of academic attainment in content areas." Among the means identified in the act for meeting this purpose are the development and implementation of exemplary programs that help students develop English skills, native language skills, and multicultural understanding.

Funds authorized by the Bilingual Education Act are administered by the Office for Bilingual Education and Minority Language Affairs (OBEMLA) in the Department of Education. With the exception of the Emergency Immigrant Education Program, OBEMLA funding is awarded competitively to eligible applicants whose proposals meet preestablished criteria and pass the scrutiny of peer review. The Emergency Immigrant Education Program, a formula grant program, provides funding to states who in turn pass through funds to districts with over 500 immigrants aged three to twenty-one who have not attended schools in the United States for more than three years. It is temporary assistance intended to assist school districts that experience large increases in their student population due to immigration in meeting their responsibilities related to the arrival of the newcomers.

OBEMLA's discretionary grant-award program began as a small seed-money and demonstration grant program funding fewer than eighty programs for disadvantaged students. After several reauthorizations of the Bilingual Education Act, these programs have changed to reflect emerging research findings and prevalent educational priorities and added provisions to support additional equity and excellence goals. Initially, the focus was on compensatory and transitional bilingual programs. Later, English-speaking children were permitted to participate in bilingual education programs; heritage-language maintenance was accepted; district requests for funding for programs conducted entirely in English were honored; and professional development objectives were stressed. During the 1990s, as part of a systemic approach to capacity building, there has been increased stress on parental involvement and family literacy, professional development, services to LEP students who also have special needs or talents, research and development, and coordination with state agencies and resources.

Currently, the Bilingual Education Act reflects the education reform emphasis of IASA and Goals 2000 on high academic standards, highly qualified teachers, and rigorous accountability measures. The influence of concern about the nation's academic and economic competitive status in a global economy can be noted in the act's expanded attention to heritage, foreign- and second-language education, and in the competitive priority accorded to applications that propose to develop skills in English and another language for all participating students.

Funding for OBEMLA programs has grown apace with the enlarged scope of its assigned responsibilities. The Foreign Language Assistance Program (FLAP), for example, is now administered by this office. Even more students are to be served: 3.5 million LEP students were identified in 1996–1997. The current authorization for the Bilingual Education Act in Fiscal Year 2000 was $406 million.

Grants awarded from these funds include those to:

- All states and over 1,200 local education agencies and schools, for direct service to second-language learners and associated faculty development
- State education agencies, for technical assistance and training functions
- Postsecondary institutions and consortia for preparation programs for teachers, paraprofessionals, administrators, and other education personnel, and for scholarships and fellowships
- Nonprofit organizations, colleges, and universities for support services such as technical assistance, research, analysis, and disseminating information

According to a survey conducted by Fleischman and Hopstock (1993), the ten most common language groups among LEP students are Spanish, Vietnamese, Hmong, Cantonese, Cambodian, Korean, Laotian, Navajo, Tagalog, and Russian. Creole (French), Arabic, Portuguese, Japanese, Armenian, Mandarin and other Chinese languages, Farsi, Hindi, and Polish are among the top twenty.

TITLE X: PROGRAMS OF NATIONAL SIGNIFICANCE, PART C—PUBLIC CHARTER SCHOOLS

This legislation is designed to support the development and implementation of charter schools. Typically, charter schools are theme-based or have a special focus selected by the school community that is to carry out the plans. Charter schools apply for approval of these plans by submitting a charter (a performance-based contract) to the state or district education agency specifying what the school hopes to accomplish. Charter schools, though semiautonomous public schools, must nevertheless adhere to health, safety, disability rights, and civil rights regulations applied to any other school, but may waive many other requirements as needed to carry forward their charter-approved plans. The overall aims of the funding program are to encourage creativity in educational reform, and demonstrate and evaluate the results of the new approaches. This process is intended to increase parental choice within the public school system, and to function as a catalyst for change in public education by piloting models for improving low-performing schools.

Because California's charter schools are exempt from the majority of state education regulations, more schools in that state are focusing on bilingual education. By September 1998, Lynn Schnaiberg reported in *Education Week* (1998) that five applications for conversions of two-way bilingual programs to charter schools (such as the Edison Elementary School in the Santa Monica–Malibu district) were received and approved by the California Department of Education; similar applications from nine additional bilingual programs were under review. These applications were submitted by parent groups who wanted their children to continue to participate in the bilingual programs jeopardized by passage in June of that year of Proposition 227, a voter initiative that restricts services to English-language learners. Other California public schools with two-way bilingual programs converted to charter school status in 1998, including the Alianza School, Watsonville, California; the Cali Calmecac Charter School, Windsor, California; and the Language Acquisition Magnet Program Charter School, Temecula, California. In many other California schools, such as Paradise Charter Middle School in Paradise Unified School District, the English Only restriction is adhered to.

Several charter schools offer bilingual programs in English and American Sign Language, including the Dimensions Academy, Scottsdale, Arizona; the Magnet School of the Deaf, Jefferson County, Colorado; and Metro Deaf School, St. Paul, Minnesota.

U.S. Charter Schools' list of schools focusing on bilingual education includes the Kanu o ka 'Aina New Century Public Charter School, Kamuela, Hawaii (a Hawaiian and English bilingual bicultural program); the Dearborn Academy, Dearborn, Michigan (an English and Arabic program of comprehensive study in literary and language arts); and the Kansas City Foreign Language Charter School, Kansas City, Missouri (a French-language total immersion program). See the U.S. Charter Schools Web site at http://www.uscharterschools.org/.

According to the Center for Education Reform, over 400,000 students in thirty-one states are enrolled in charter schools. See the Web site at http://edreform.com/pubs/chglance.htm.

FEDERAL INCENTIVES: FUNDING SOURCES

School districts may seek support for programs serving linguistically and culturally diverse students and for education programs in second languages, foreign languages, or heritage languages by competing for funding from programs such as the following:

Magnet Schools Assistance

(Elementary and Secondary Education Act of 1965, Title V, Part A as amended, 20 USC 7201-7213, Office of Elementary and Secondary Education [OESE], CFDA # 84.165A)

The Magnet Schools program provides funding for public school districts implementing desegregation plans that include schools with a distinctive theme or approach designed to attract and enroll students from a variety of ethnic backgrounds, attendance zones, and neighborhoods. Hispanics, the largest group of language minority students in the public schools, are far more likely than other students to attend predominantly minority schools. By supporting the elimination, reduction, and prevention of minority group isolation in elementary and secondary schools attended by substantial numbers of minority group students, implementing magnet school programs helps districts to comply with court-ordered or federally approved desegregation plans. These funds are intended to support innovations in education that lead to students' knowledge of academic subjects and their mastery of vocational skills. To be eligible for federal funding, these schools must also participate in a systemic reform process that provides opportunities to master challenging content and uphold performance standards for all students.

The challenging option selected may include language study, as illustrated in the magnet programs at Thomas Jefferson High School for World Languages and International Governmental Studies in Richmond, Virginia. The school teaches seven languages: Spanish, French, Italian, German, Japanese, Russian, and Latin. Students participate in student exchange programs that provide opportunities for travel to many of the countries associated with the languages they study. Another example of Magnet Program funding applied to language study is found in the Miami-Dade County Public Schools. The Coral Gables Feeder Pattern includes the International Studies Programs at Sunset Elementary School and Carver Middle School and the International Baccalaureate and International Education Programs initiated at Coral Gables Senior High School and now housed at Coral Reef High School. In these schools, each target language is studied as a separate subject and also used as the language of instruction for several periods of the school day.

The appropriation for Magnet Programs for fiscal year 2000 was $103,800,000.

Academic Excellence Awards

(Elementary and Secondary Education Act of 1965, Title VII, Part A, Subpart 2, as amended, 20 USC 7453, Office of Bilingual Education and Minority Languages Affairs [OBEMLA], CFDA # 84.194G)

The Academic Excellence Awards Program is one of several grants administered by OBEMLA that provide competitive funding opportunities to school districts. In 1997–1998, 480,405 English-language learners were served by district programs funded by this agency, or 14 percent of the total reported LEP student population of 3,452,073 for that academic year. The purpose of the Academic Excellence Awards Program grants is to promote the adoption and implementation of exemplary bilingual education, ESL and other special alternative instructional programs, and professional development programs. The focus is on the dissemination and replication of exemplary programs. To be eligible for funding under this program, applicants must present valid and verifiable data to demonstrate their success in developing English-language skills among linguistically and culturally diverse students, and potential for dissemination and replication of the applicant's model in a variety of school settings. Recent grantees include Glendale Unified School District's Project SEA (Sheltered English Approach) and New York City's Project EXCELL at Seward Park High School.

Project SEA in Glendale Unified School District is in its thirteenth year of operation. Project materials have been disseminated to over ten districts throughout the nation. Project SEA provides specialized instructional services and support in the content areas of social science and science to English-language learners in grades 4, 5, and 6. Specially Designed Academic Instruction in English (SDAIE) is the approach used in the classroom and the focus of training efforts in staff development sessions. This approach is supplemented with primary language support materials in Armenian, Spanish, and Korean.

New York City's Project EXCELL at Seward Park High School is based on a Chinese bilingual education program at that school, now in its twentieth year. The program serves Chinese-speaking students, grades 9–12, who require ESL and bilingual instruction, by providing bilingual instruction in content area and career/vocational education and Native Language Arts and ESL components. EXCELL also develops Chinese bilingual curriculum and informational materials, and directs staff development and parental involvement activities.

The appropriation for this program for fiscal year 2000 was $1,000,000.

Foreign Language Assistance Program (FLAP)

(Elementary and Secondary Education Act of 1965, Title VII, Part B, as amended, 20 U.S.C. 7511–7516, Office of Elementary and Secondary Education [OESE], CFDA #84.293B)

FLAP provides grants to pay half the costs incurred by school districts in establishing, improving, or expanding study in foreign languages. Priority is given to expanding elementary school programs in foreign languages. Funding requirements include systemic reform, innovation, capacity building, and replication. Recent recipients of these grant funds include the Tacoma Public Schools Elementary and Middle School Language Immersion Program, and the Colorado Implements Foreign Language Standards Program administered by the Colorado Department of Education.

The Tacoma program offers students a choice of French or Japanese dual-language immersion programs at Sheridan Elementary School that lead to participation in a previously established middle school program. The program also funds a sixth grade extension of the Korean as a Second Language program in grades 7–8 at Baker Middle School.

The Colorado program expands instruction in foreign languages at the elementary school level and teaches six languages: Chinese, French, German, Japanese, Russian, and Spanish. In cooperation with the United States Air Force Academy in Colorado Springs, the project aims to develop and implement an Internet-accessible, electronic media, foreign-language resource library of instructional and assessment materials for language teachers. Associated teacher training activities focus on methodology for standards implementation, FLES, and the use of technology in language education.

The appropriation for this program for fiscal year 2000 was $8,000,000.

FEDERAL REQUIREMENTS OR PROHIBITIONS

Major federal legislative measures and court decisions protecting the rights of second-language learners and governing the provision of bilingual education are summarized in this section.

Rehabilitation Act of 1973, as Amended
(29 USC 794, Public Law 93-112)

Section 504 of this act prohibits discrimination on the basis of disability in any program or activity receiving federal financial assistance. Consequently, LEP students who are also disabled are included among those protected by the provisions of this act.

Title VI, Civil Rights Act of 1964
(20 USC 1701, Public Law 93-380)

The Civil Rights Act of 1964 forbids federally funded discrimination. Title VI of this act prohibits discrimination or exclusion from participation or benefits on the ground of race, color, or national origin under any program or activity receiving federal financial assistance. Under Title VI regulations, school districts must provide English-language learners with alternative language services to enable them to acquire proficiency in English, and to provide them with meaningful access to the content of the educational curriculum available to all students, including special education and related services. Districts must not merely refrain from discrimination; they must also take affirmative steps to give special training to non-English-speaking pupils. Failure to do so can result in the district's losing all federal funds.

May 25, 1970, Memorandum

The May 25, 1970, Memorandum from the director of the Office for Civil Rights (OCR) in the Department of Health, Education, and Welfare to the chief state school officer of every state was a policy clarification stating that Title VI regulations are applicable to National Origin Minority (NOM) students. It identified three major areas of concern:

1. Unequal access to participation in school programs because of language
2. Segregation by tracking, ability grouping, and assignment to special education programs
3. Failure to provide language minority parents with school information provided to other parents

According to those guidelines, it is inappropriate, for example, to assign LEP students to special-education programs on the basis of procedures or tests that essentially measure and evaluate English-language skills. The OCR cites the May 25 Memorandum, subsequently affirmed in the *Lau* decision, as part of its Title VI enforcement policy concerning discrimination on the basis of national origin.

Lau v. Nichols *(1974)*

In *Lau,* nine of the United States Supreme Court justices unanimously found that the San Francisco school district had violated the rights of 1,800 Chinese students represented in the class action by failing to provide these students with special instruction designed to overcome their English-language deficiency. The Court held that merely providing the same instruction offered to other students does not provide access to the benefits of schooling because students who do not understand English are effectively foreclosed from meaningful education. The Court based its decision on Title IV regulations, upholding OCR's authority to promulgate them.

Equal Educational Opportunity (EEO) Act of 1974 (20 USC 1701, Public Law 93-380)

Section 1703(f) of the Equal Educational Opportunity Act of 1974 states, "No state shall deny equal educational opportunity to an individual on account of his or her race, color, sex, or national origin, by . . . (f) the failure by an educational agency to take appropriate action to overcome language barriers that impede equal participation by its students in its instructional program."

Under this act, both states and school districts are charged with civil rights compliance responsibilities. The decisions in *Idaho Migrant Council v. Board of Education* (9th Circuit, 1981) and *Gomez v. Illinois State Board of Education* (7th Circuit, 1987) are among those that specify the obligations of Section 1703(f) are shared by local and state educational agencies. The state role, at a minimum, is to supervise the local school districts to ensure compliance with equal educational opportunity mandates. Such supervision requires state education agencies to establish and enforce adequate and uniform standards for compliance.

Castaneda v. Pickard *(1981)*

In *Castaneda v. Pickard,* the Appeals Court for the Fifth Circuit set forth criteria that define the "appropriate action" required by the Equal Educational Opportunity Act of 1974. According to the court's criteria, to be considered in compliance with that act, school district plans for alternative programs for LEP students must:

1. Implement a program based on an education theory recognized as sound or, at least, as a legitimate experimental strategy, by experts in the field of providing services to LEP students
2. Allocate sufficient resources to the program (including those earmarked for teacher training and program evaluation) so that it can reasonably be expected to implement the selected theory
3. Evaluate the program after it has been used for enough time to constitute a legitimate trial, and revise it as needed, to ensure that it has proven effective in teaching English (including English literacy skills comparable to those of average native speakers) and other content areas (which may be assessed through standardized tests in the students' home language)

According to the *Castaneda* decision, effective programs lead LEP students to parity with their English-speaking peers. The *Castaneda* three-part test has been adopted by OCR as the standard used to determine whether districts' programs for LEP students are in compliance with Title VI regulations.

The decision in *Keyes v. School District No. 1* (1983) is an example of a decision that applied the requirements of the Equal Educational

Opportunity Act and the *Castaneda* criteria. In applying the test to Denver's Transitional Bilingual Education Program, the court found that the district did not meet the requirements for the allocation of resources and program evaluation. The district was ordered to hire bilingual teachers and institute teacher training and standardized testing to ensure that teachers have bilingual and biliteracy skills as needed for understandable instruction to take place.

The court dismissed arguments that only small numbers of students were involved, noting that under the Equal Educational Opportunity Act, any individual denied an equal educational opportunity as defined in the act may institute a civil action for private relief. It also dismissed arguments affirming lack of discriminatory intent by school officials. According to the *Keyes* court, good faith must be joined by a reasonably effective effort to produce the intended result of removing language barriers to participation in the instructional programs offered by the district.

Plyler v. Doe *(1982)*

The United States Supreme Court ruled that states and public schools are prohibited from excluding undocumented students solely on the basis of their immigration status. The right to education is based on residence, not status as a citizen. In the opinion of the majority of the Court, the alien plaintiffs in these cases may claim the benefit of the Fourteenth Amendment's guarantee of equal protection. The opinion also notes that regulation of immigration is an exclusively federal function.

As states have no authority with respect to the classification of aliens, immigration classification matters are rarely relevant to legislation by a state, or to policy set by school districts, which are established through state law.

The Individuals with Disabilities Education Act of 1997 (IDEA 97) (20 USC 1400, Public Law 105-117)

Several directives for the provision of services to language minority students are presented in IDEA 97 and its associated regulations. For example, as disabled English-language learners are entitled to access to all aspects of the curriculum, including special education, Individual Education Plans (IEP) must state whether the special education and related services will be provided in a language other than English. Reasonable efforts must be taken to ensure that parents understand, and are able to participate in, all group decisions relating to the educational placement of their children; this includes providing an interpreter for parents whose native language is other than English.

DEVELOPMENTS IN THE TWENTY-FIRST CENTURY

As of this writing, ESEA is scheduled for reauthorization, which may result in changes to provisions noted above. The reader is advised to consult the Department of Education Web site at http://www.ed.gov for news about revised legislation.

The preceding sections summarized congressional and judicial action in the area of language education. Although these measures generally support linguistic pluralism, several bills whose purpose is to establish English as the nation's official language, or as the sole language of government, have also been considered (though not enacted) at the congressional level during the last two decades. Several English Only laws have been enacted at the state level. The reader is advised to consult the Web sites of James Crawford at http://ourworld.compuserve.com/homepages/jwcrawford/langleg.htm, or U.S. English, at http://www.us-english.org/inc/official/states.asp, for ongoing information about Official English and English Only legislation. See Chapter 6 for additional information about the politics of language.

REFERENCES

Bilingual program gets $221,168: Bush, Paige support efforts. 1998. *Sam Houston State University News* (August 6).

Fleischman, H. L., and P. J. Hopstock. 1993. *Descriptive study of services to limited English proficient students.* Vol. 1, *Summary of findings and conclusions.* Arlington, VA: Development Associates. [Online]. Available: *http://www.ncbe.gwu.edu/miscpubs/siac/descript/index.htm.*

Macías, R. 1998. *Summary report of the survey of the states' limited English proficient students and available educational programs and services, 1996–1997.* The SEA Report. Washington, DC: National Clearinghouse for Bilingual Education.

Schnaiberg, L. 1998. Some Calif. schools finding ways around Prop. 227. *Education Week* (September 30). [Online]. Available: *http://www.edweek.org/ew/ewstory.cfm?slug=04biling.h18&keywords=Schnaiberg.*

Chapter Six

✎ Politics and the Challenge of Linguistic Diversity

Government activities related to language, policies that guide those actions, and factors influencing their development and affecting public opinions about them are described in this chapter. The broad topic of language politics is closely related to unresolved contradictions in such important civic matters as immigration, the definition of what it means to be an American, and benefits assumed to flow from expansion or contraction of civil rights protections. Those contradictions give rise to many questions. For example:

- ✎ Do immigrants revitalize or drain the economy?
- ✎ Is diversity in language enriching or divisive?
- ✎ Should policies in language education aim for monolingualism, bilingualism, or multilingualism?
- ✎ Is the experience of immigrants of color, many from former colonies or conquered nations, similar to, or different from, that of earlier immigrants from Europe?
- ✎ Should the policies of the United States be color-blind? Should the blinds be lifted for benign purposes, such as affirmative action? Should race be a criterion for admission and citizenship?
- ✎ Are civil rights measures examples of unwarranted special privilege for minority group members, misguided efforts that end up subordinating minority populations, or the means by which the goals of American democracy are reached?
- ✎ Are language and culture wars the result of a phantom polarization created by pollsters, politicians, and the media? Are they nothing more than camouflaged manipulations of public opinion about conflicts waged over access to cheap land and labor and control of government?

Although information presented in this volume relates to many of these questions, they are raised primarily as a guide to the reader, to help make sense of the information provided, and to encourage further research. The overall purpose of this chapter is to review selected political issues related to linguistic diversity and to summarize associated bodies of knowledge. The first section of this chapter consists of a status report on immigration and immigrant students. The second section describes politics as the distribution of resources. The discussion in the third section turns from the effects of the political process on education funding to identity politics. A summary of salient issues in debates about language legislation and language rights constitutes the fourth section.

IMMIGRATION

In 2000, 28.4 million persons in the United States, or 10 percent of the population, were foreign-born (Lollock 2001). The immigrant population today comes primarily from Latin America and Asia. From 1860 to 1920, the percentage of immigrants was approximately 15 percent, with the foreign-born arriving primarily from Europe (Gibson and Lennon 1999). By 1920, one-third of the population were either immigrants or the children of immigrants (Daniels 1990).

From 1970 to 1990, immigrants constituted 5 to 6 percent of our population. Among residents of African descent, a group that includes over 2 million immigrants, the percentage of foreign-born was higher than the comparable figure for the U.S. population as a whole (Levine and Levine 1997).

The U.S. Immigration and Naturalization Service (INS) reports (based on 1980 data from the U.N. Demographic Yearbook, Table 31) that immigrants were:

- 42 percent of the population of Israel
- 41 percent of the population of Hong Kong
- 16 percent of the population of Canada
- 11 percent of the population of the Bahamas
- 9 percent of the population of Belgium
- 7 percent of the population of Venezuela

In other words, the percentage of immigrants in the United States in recent times was exceeded by the comparable percentage of immigrants in other countries. In the United States, immigration was at its height almost a century ago. From 1990 to 2000, the average annual number of immigrants admitted was 5.0 per thousand U.S. residents; the annual rate during 1900 to 1910 was 11.0 (Smith and Edmonston 1997). The percentage of immigrants in the United States is currently less than half of that during the beginning of the twentieth century.

The INS defines an immigrant as a foreign national who has been authorized to live and work permanently in the United States. In 1993, undocumented immigrants comprised 1 percent of the population. Documented residents include from 100,000 to 150,000 refugees each year (who seek permission to enter the country because they fear persecution in their homelands because of their race, religion, or political views) and asylees (who apply for asylum after arriving in this country) (Schwartz 1996). In 1996, immediate relatives of U.S. citizens and those admitted through a system that accords preference to family-sponsored or employment-based immigrants accounted for 78 percent of all admissions. For additional information on characteristics of current and past immigrants, see the Statistical Yearbook (U.S. Immigration and Naturalization Service [INS] 1997) and the INS Web site at http://www.ins.usdoj.gov/graphics/index.htm.

ATTITUDES TOWARD IMMIGRATION AND IMMIGRANTS

Various organizations aim to reduce or eliminate immigration. One of the oldest is the Federation for American Immigration Reform (FAIR). FAIR describes itself as a national, nonprofit, public-interest organization of concerned citizens who share a common belief that unforeseen mass immigration has occurred over the last thirty years and should not continue. FAIR advocates a moratorium on all immigration (except for that of spouses and minor children of U.S. citizens and a limited number of refugees) to allow time for consideration of the impact of immigration. The organization considers immigration's impact to include the following problems:

- Low-skilled immigrants from underdeveloped nations are admitted who are not suited for integration into the United States.
- Immigrant labor depresses wages and blocks native low-skilled workers from entry-level positions.
- Immigrants need welfare and constitute a tax burden.
- Immigrants increase crime rates and cause ethnic separatism and strife.

- Immigration increases the population, adversely affecting the environment.
- Immigrants create traffic congestion, urban sprawl, and scarce housing.
- Immigration increases the risk of terrorist attacks.
- Immigrants spread disease and constitute a public health hazard.

FAIR has been taken to task for misleading statements and extreme associates, for accepting $600,000 from the Pioneer Foundation (a group that has promoted the discredited science of eugenics), and for sponsoring alarmist and exaggerated newspaper ads. See "Is FAIR Unfair?" on the Anti-Defamation League's Web site at http://www.adl.org/Civil_Rights/Is_Fair_Unfair.pdf.

However, the organization's statements of principles, available at http://www.fairus.org/, includes a declaration that there should be no favoritism toward or discrimination against any person on the basis of race, color, or national origin in the immigration laws of the United States. FAIR's opposition to favoritism is illustrated by its recommendations to repeal laws granting special immigration treatment for Cubans.

ProjectUSA believes that too many immigrants have arrived in the United States, that legal immigration in the United States must be reduced to levels that will enable the population to stabilize, and that this situation deserves the attention of the American people, who are misinformed about immigration. Their lack of information, states ProjectUSA, is preventing adoption of wise public policy based on rational discussion of the issue. To correct the state of misinformation, they plan to educate the American people with billboards to stir public debate. See http://www.projectusa.org/press/index.html for additional information and accounts of reactions to "Billboard Democracy." This organization is also concerned with controlling illegal immigration, and believes the best way to end it is to call on the military to defend the borders. ProjectUSA maintains that legal and illegal immigration is destroying the environment and that multiculturalism is destroying our multiethnic but monocultural society by leading to separatism.

Linda Chávez (1995), president of the Center for Equal Opportunity, who describes herself as an immigration enthusiast, expresses concern that immigration will change what it means to be an American unless assimilation takes place. She believes the obligation to assimilate immigrants is owed to immigrants and American society. To reach that goal, she states, requires abolishing bilingual education in favor of

English-immersion programs in the public schools. Her views are available in full text at the CEO Web site, http://www.ceousa.org/.

Brimelow (1996) is also concerned with the political impact of immigration and asserts that national identity must be defined in explicitly racial and ethnic terms. He believes that immigration causes massive demographic transformations leading to a radical shift in the racial balance of the United States. Whites, who constituted nearly 90 percent of the population in 1960, in 1995 made up only 75 percent of the population. He views Census Bureau predictions that by 2050, Whites will be a minority in the United States (and that the Hispanic population will increase to 25 percent), a dispossession that White persons have every right to oppose. As part of this expression of racial consciousness, he offers a reminder that the first naturalization law, passed in 1790, permitted only "free white persons" to become U.S. citizens. Elected officials can and should, he asserts, establish a moratorium on all immigration to this country while its effects are considered.

Still another view is held by Ranch Rescue, an organization whose major stated concern is to protect private property. Ranch Rescue describes itself on its Web site at http://ranchrescue.com/texas.htm as a volunteer organization helping along state borders to repair private property destroyed by multiple incidents of criminal trespass. It provides volunteer security for affected landowners, their homes, and their property. Its Web site features a photograph of two men standing next to a roadside sign that reads "We are being invaded . . . something must be done now." A recruitment notice inviting others to become volunteers states that all Ranch Rescue members will be permitted to carry firearms if they so choose.

These volunteers, while appreciated by many of the ranchers and local law enforcement agents, are described by the Intelligence Analysis Branch at the U.S. Immigration and Naturalization Service (Ibarra, November 16, 2000) as a threat to undocumented immigrants and U.S. Border Patrol agents alike. A warning was issued on October 27–29, 2000, that up to thirty members of anti-immigration hate-crime organizations planned to meet in Douglas, Arizona. The intelligence report concluded that the involvement of known racial supremacy hate groups created an opportunity for acts of violence. The document listed organizations expected to participate, including the Federation for American Immigration Reform, the California Coalition for Immigration Reform, Arizonans for Immigration Reform, the National Grass Roots Alliance, the National Organization for European American Rights, the Ku Klux Klan, and the Foundation for Optimal Planetary Survival.

Violent hostility against immigrants is not limited to border towns or to Hispanic victims. Some examples: Bias crimes against immigrants include 481 anti-Asian incidents reported for 1997 (National APA Legal Consortium 1997). Vietnamese, who make up only 1 percent of the population of Boston, represent 15 percent of the victims of hate crimes in that city. Bombings and other violent attacks on Asian and Latino immigrants or their advocates have been repeatedly reported in California, where 40 percent of those who immigrate to the U.S. settle. The Council on American-Islamic Relations publishes an annual summary of anti-Muslim discrimination (see http://www.arabmedia.com/ 98sepcair.html for a detailed report). Amnesty International USA's report on police brutality identified the majority of victims as unarmed, not criminal suspects, and from African, Asian, and Hispanic immigrant communities and ethnic minority groups (Amnesty International 1996).

The Voice of Citizens Together maintains a Web site devoted to text and graphics related to fears that immigration, especially from Mexico, has reached unprecedented levels and strains the bonds of our union. The organization's Web site attributes separatism as the goal of immigrants, who intend to reconquer the southwestern states; see http://www.americanpatrol.com/.

According to Joseph L. Daleiden, failure to cut mass immigration will destroy the unique and bountiful country we have inherited from our forebears. This position is set forth in "Selling Our Birthright," a thirty-nine page tract sold by the American Immigration Control Foundation and described on the foundation's Web site at http://www.aicfoundation.com/booklets.htm. The increased use of benefits, such as public education and emergency medical care, and competing with American citizens for low-wage jobs are among the problems attributed to immigration.

Nonetheless, data contained in a report prepared by the United Nations Population Division (2000) titled *Replacement Migration: Is It a Solution to the Declining and Aging Population?*, available online at http://www.un.org/esa/population/unpop.htm, lead one to conclude that more immigration is needed to maintain our economic birthright. The authors of this report examined demographic trends in eight countries: France, Germany, Italy, Japan, Russia, South Korea, Britain, and the United States. The population in these industrialized countries is predicted to become smaller and older, thereby changing the ratio of the working-age population (persons fifteen to sixty-four) to the old-age population (persons sixty-five and older). If retirement ages in these countries remain essentially where they are today, vastly increased levels of international migration will be needed to increase the size of the working-age population and reduce declines in the potential support ratio. The alternative, in most cases, would be to increase the upper limit of the working-age population to seventy-five. In the United States, such a change would require redefining the normal retirement age for eligibility for social security and other retirement benefits.

The views of the business community on immigration are summarized in the April 24, 2000, edition of *Businessweek Online* at http://www.businessweek.com/careers/content/jan1990/b3678102.htm. According to this perspective, immigration is beneficial. Immigrants are filling jobs at every level that might otherwise be left unfilled or transferred to other countries. Immigrant labor provides a critical boost to the economy through the multiplier effects of consumer spending, taxes paid, and small-business generation. Accordingly, Federal Reserve Chairman Alan Greenspan suggested that more immigrants may be needed to cope with a shrinking pool of available workers in the United States.

By October 2000, Philadelphia City Councilman James Kenney had held hearings on ways to attract immigrants to offset the city's declining population. Arizona's governor, Jane Hull, expressed interest in reviving an agricultural guest-worker system. In December 2000, Iowa's Governor Tom Vilsack tentatively proposed that his state become an immigrant enterprise zone, open to more foreign-born labor through exemption from federally established immigration limits (Ginsberg 2000).

The current positions of business and organized labor are similar on many immigration issues. In 1994, unions campaigned against Proposition 187 in California, a voter initiative that would have denied undocumented children the right to attend school and reduced health care services available to immigrants. Subsequently, the AFL-CIO persuaded the Department of Labor to stop inspecting workers' immigration papers when examining complaints of labor-standards abuses, and led the fight against efforts to blame immigrant workers for economic problems. In 2000, the Executive Council of the AFL-CIO adopted a position supporting the rights of all immigrant workers regardless of their immigration status.

The union resolution proposed revised legislation to grant amnesty and eligibility for permanent status and naturalization for illegal immigrants now living in the United States, and to grant full workplace rights to all workers, legal or illegal, to protect illegal workers from intimidation and exploitation. It recommended an end to the Employers Sanctions program, which penalizes employers who hire illegal immigrants; instead, criminal penalties should be imposed against employers who knowingly hire an illegal immigrant and then use the worker's legal status with the INS as a weapon for imposing substandard wages or working conditions.

In "Recognizing Our Common Bonds," available in full text at
http://www.aflcio.org/articles/commonbonds/, the AFL-CIO policy
statement noted that many immigrants have no choice but to leave impoverished countries whose poverty is exacerbated by the government
and business policies of the United States. Multinational corporations
seeking the lowest wages and least regulation locate their enterprises in
foreign countries. Foreign workers end up with employment that yields
minuscule salaries. At the same time, the repayment terms on massive
debt foisted on foreign governments by institutions such as the World
Bank and the International Monetary Fund leave developing countries
with no way to meet the basic needs of their populations. Recognizing
that exploitation of poorly paid foreign workers negatively affects workers everywhere, and that immigrants are not to blame for the conditions
that drive them from their countries, the executive council of the labor
group launched a Campaign for Global Fairness to insist on protection
for foreign and domestic workers' rights in all trade and loan agreements. The council also pledged to work to cancel the debts that can
never be repaid, as part of the Jubilee 2000/USA Campaign, a coalition
of national environmental, labor, religious, and social justice groups
calling for definitive cancellation of the crushing debts owed by impoverished nations.

Immigrant Students

Attitudes toward immigration and immigrants inevitably affect attitudes toward immigrant children, their languages, and their school programs. Bilingual education programs serve native-born as well as immigrant children. Nevertheless, the programs are closely associated with
the phenomenon of immigration. Whatever the outcome of debates on
the policies that should govern immigration, the children who are here
must be educated.

One-fifth of all children in the country are immigrants; they constitute the fastest growing segment of the child population in the United
States. This group includes 3 million foreign-born children under eighteen, and over 10 million U.S.-born children under eighteen living with
at least one foreign-born parent (Rumbaut 1998). Of the immigrant students arriving in this country since 1960, 52 percent have come from
Latin America and the Caribbean, and another 29 percent have come
from Asia and the Middle East.

Third-generation students (native-born children of native-born
parents) constitute 10 percent of the LEP population. The LEP population also includes 40 percent of the students who are foreign-born.

Among the foreign-born, child poverty rates reach 39 percent, three times the non-Hispanic White rate (Ruiz-de-Velasco, Fix, and Chu Clewell 2000). Asian and White immigrants, like their native-born ethnic counterparts, were least likely to live in families having incomes in the lowest quartile and to have parents with less than twelve years of schooling (Schwartz 1996).

The Urban Institute reports that immigrant students represent 3.5 percent of the elementary school student population, and 5.7 percent of the high school population. Although program funding for English-language learners is greater at the elementary school levels, foreign-born and recently arrived students are more likely to be enrolled at secondary levels (Ruiz-de-Velasco, Fix, and Chu Clewell 2000). However, LEP students must prepare to meet high school graduation requirements and pass state high school completion examinations presented in the English language. Given the compressed time frame of the high school years, this requirement imposes great challenges for districts with students who arrive in this country as teenagers, or with interrupted prior schooling.

Research on Immigrant Children

Recent research on the experiences and adaptation processes of immigrant children was summarized by Zhou (1997). Included in her summary are studies of the roles language and culture play in the education of immigrant students. Her conclusions:

- English-language acquisition and use are not entirely matters of individual preference (or of patterns of instruction), but are constrained by contextual factors, such as residential isolation from English speakers, ethnic concentration in school and community settings, and proximity or ease of access to the country of origin.
- A growing body of empirical evidence indicates that both cognitive abilities and scholastic achievement are positively associated with bilingualism.
- Pre-immigration class standing and education exert a persistent and substantial effect on occupational mobility. Children of highly educated immigrants consistently fare better in school than do fourth- or fifth-generation descendants of poorly educated ancestors.
- Command of the home language allows immigrant children to tap the social capital resident in the ethnic minority group,

such as support and control from non-English-speaking family and community members. This guidance is crucially important for immigrant children who begin their lives in the United States as part of the most underprivileged segments in the socioeconomic structure. Under these circumstances, the major force for assimilation will come from peers who have experienced long-term economic inequality and developed in response an "oppositional culture" conducive to school failure. This oppositional stance among native-born immigrant and minority students bereft of hope for the future is characterized by rebellion against authority and rejection of the goals of achievement and upward mobility. Rejection of middle-class mores is a strategy for psychological survival and a means of protecting self-esteem. Although it is an adaptive response to a gap between socially approved goals and socially approved means of achieving them, it leads to permanent confinement in the underclass.

➤ Assimilation may be advantageous for immigrant children whose parents enter mainstream labor markets and suburban middle-class communities immediately or shortly after arriving in the United States.

HISTORY OF IMMIGRANT SCHOOLING

Instruction through the medium of the home language has been part of the immigrant experience since colonial days, according to *Education Week* (1987). Using languages other than English as subjects and as the languages of instruction is associated with the times and places of concentration of immigrant populations from the same language group who had sufficient economic and political influence to affect policy development.

In San Antonio, for example, the population was one-third German in 1860. By 1870, official state notices were published in English, Spanish, and German (see Legio Patria Nostra at http://www.ktc.com/personal/texaswas/GermTexPen.htm for additional information about German influence in Texas). In the mid-1800s, Colorado, Illinois, Indiana, Iowa, Kentucky, Louisiana, Maryland, Minnesota, Missouri, Nebraska, the Territory of New Mexico, Pennsylvania, Ohio, Oregon, and Wisconsin had passed legislation authorizing instruction through various home languages. Instruction through native languages was available for Chinese, Japanese, German, Italian, and French immigrants in the San Francisco schools. By 1892, one-fourth of Chicago's public school enrollment was instructed in German-language schools. Seven Czech-language schools were publicly funded in Texas (*Education Week* 1987; Rothstein 1998). In 1852, the German-American Union School (also known as the Comal Union School) was incorporated in Comal, Texas (Comal Union School 1999). The New Braunfels Academy, in New Braunfels, Texas, was established in 1856 as the first tax-supported Texas school. As Rothstein points out, although support for bilingual education was rarely unanimous or consistent, it has been part of American education for some time.

Until relatively recently, however, not all children went to school, whatever the language of instruction. Although in the 1800s various jurisdictions passed laws restricting child labor, they were widely ignored, and in many cases were not applied to immigrants. Prompted in part by the campaign of the National Child Labor Committee, and influenced by the photographs taken by Lewis W. Hine of children who worked seventy-hour weeks in hazardous occupations, Congress passed the Fair Labor Standards Act in 1938. This act prohibited child labor under the age of sixteen in nonagricultural occupations. Additional information on the history of child labor and views of selected photographs taken by Hine are available at http://www.historyplace.com/unitedstates/childlabor/about.htm.

Of the children who did go to school during the height of the last wave of immigration, few succeeded in attending long enough to complete graduation requirements. Rothstein (1998) reports that as of 1930, half of all fourteen- to seventeen-year-olds enrolled in schools in the United States did not complete high school. From 1880 to 1924, Italian Americans, Polish Americans, Jewish Americans, and other immigrant groups were largely expected to amputate their former culture, language, and customs as soon as possible; this process of immigrant assimilation was commonly referred to as Americanization (Leonor 1996). Rothstein (1998) summarized the results of the English-only process:

- In Boston, Chicago, and New York, 80 percent of native-born children, but only 58 percent of southern Italian children, 62 percent of Polish children, and 74 percent of Russian Jewish children, continued to attend school after the seventh grade.
- Those who continued to attend school after the eighth grade included 58 percent of native-born children but only 23 percent of southern Italians.
- In New York, 54 percent of native-born children compared to 34 percent of foreign-born children began the ninth grade.

Although the overall high school graduation rate was 40 percent, only 11 percent of Italian students graduated.

•➤ In 1910, only 6,000 of the 191,000 Jewish children enrolled in New York schools were in high school. The majority of the students dropped out before graduating.

•➤ In a survey of retarded students (students who were three years or more over-age for grade), 19 percent of those identified were native-born, compared to 50 percent who were children of Italian fathers.

Pascucci (1984) described the educational experience of immigrant Italians and Poles in Schenectady, New York, from 1880 to 1930. The conclusions of his report are consistent with Rothstein's: many immigrant students experienced grade retardation while becoming proficient in English and dropped out of school. An interesting contrast of monolingual and bilingual schooling resulted from the preference of the Poles for bilingual instruction (as a way of preserving their cultural traditions) available in the parochial schools. Pascucci surmises that the bilingual instruction the Polish children received in the parochial schools enabled them to progress more rapidly than Polish and Italian students in the public schools. Nevertheless, only a small percentage of either group of immigrant children completed high school throughout the period.

Language Loss

The propensity for language loss, a shift in use from the home language to another, is accelerating among immigrant families. The current trend is to loss of home-language use among children of immigrants, a phenomenon that previously took three generations (Schwartz 1996). As Rumbaut points out, this trend is evident even in Miami (with the highest percentage of foreign-born in the country) and San Diego (with the busiest international border crossing in the world). In 1995–1996, for example, 79 percent of San Diego's high school seniors who were immigrants or children of immigrants preferred to use English; the comparable figure for Miami was 95 percent (Rumbaut 1998). Immigrant children are learning English, but may be losing their home languages.

DISTRIBUTIVE POLITICS: RESOURCE
DISTRIBUTION AND LANGUAGE ECONOMICS

Public funds are distributed as a result of political processes. They are earmarked for bilingual programs, or withheld from them, in accord with the general availability of dollars for education, the presumed costs and benefits of the programs, the nature of competing priorities, and the importance attached to educating immigrant and other language minority populations.

Funds to support public education, and for the operation of schools and programs (including bilingual programs), come from tax dollars collected at the local, state, or national level. The collection and distribution of these funds are authorized by elected officials. Their identity as elected officials and their decisions on priorities for the allocation of resources both result from political processes.

Education is a state function. At most, only from 8 to 10 percent or so of the total budget for a school system will come from the federal government. The remaining costs of schooling are shared by the other two levels of government according to education funding formulas that differ from state to state. State revenues provide a significant portion of the funding for public schools. The local portion is generated through taxation by local boards of education on the value of property in the district. The characteristics of the funding formulas and the resulting distribution of funds are determined through political processes at each of the levels of government, within the area of permissible or required activity established by their constitutions. In addition to generic political factors, the knowledge base and attitudes of elected officials toward immigrants, minority groups, and language education affect their decisions to channel resources to or away from bilingual education. A variety of actors and agents try to influence the process, with varying degrees of success.

Influence

Unions, business interests, and their political action committees (PACs) have more influence on the final determination of legislative funding decisions than professional education associations, civil rights organizations, or minority groups. According to a survey of executive directors of state school board associations conducted by the Rural Trust Policy Program (1999), the degree of influence on statewide education decisionmaking wielded by fifteen lobbying groups ranked as follows:

➡ Teachers unions (perceived as most active and influential)

- Business groups
- Superintendents' associations
- Higher education
- Special education groups
- Disability rights groups
- Child advocacy groups
- Chambers of commerce
- Parent-teacher associations
- Principals' associations
- Right-wing groups
- Rural education organizations
- Ethnic and minority groups
- NAACP
- ACLU (perceived as least active and influential)

The full report of survey results is available online at http://www. ruraledu.org/sb_survey3_99.html.

As an additional complication in the legislative process, elected leaders must balance the needs of children (who are not eligible to vote) against the equally compelling needs of 35 million persons over the age of sixty-five (who are eligible to vote). Further, these funding decisions take place at a time when, according to the U.S. Census Bureau's 1997 National Data Chart for Total Occupied Housing Units, 63 percent of households in the United States do not include children under the age of eighteen. For additional information on demographic trends affecting children and youth, see the U.S. Census Bureau American Housing Survey data online at http://www.census.gov/hhes/www/housing/ahs/ 97dtchrt/ahs97.html, and America's Children 2000 site at http://www. childstats.gov/ac2000/detail.asp.

In many states, education finance systems have been enacted that were considered unfair. Through school finance-reform litigation, school boards, civic associations, and community groups (including advocates for language and other minority students) in almost every state in the union have sought relief from the courts for inequities in school funding.

SCHOOL FINANCE REFORM

States raise money primarily through taxation based on sales, income, or property. School districts are authorized to levy taxes on property. When disparities occur in property wealth from district to district, the variance is reflected in the amount of money available for the schools. Even in low-wealth districts whose voters choose to tax themselves at a higher level than required, their additional effort may not suffice to reduce inequality in educational resources. These inequities result in children having more or less instructional material, equipment, or supplies such as chalk, pencils, toilet paper, and paper towels, or higher or lower teacher/pupil ratios, than their neighbors in other districts in the state. The first wave of school finance-reform cases sought to realize the promise of equal protection of the laws by bringing about greater equalization in funding between school districts in the same state.

Serrano v. Priest *(1971)*

In a California Supreme Court case, *Serrano v. Priest* (1971), the system of local funding based primarily on local property taxes was successfully challenged under the equal protection clauses of the Fourteenth Amendment to the United States Constitution and of the state constitution. School district records reviewed by the *Serrano* court revealed extensive disparity among districts in the same state. The Baldwin Park Unified School District, for example, spent $577.49 to educate each of its pupils. During the same year, the Pasadena Unified School District spent $840.19 on every student, and the Beverly Hills Unified School District paid out $1,231.72 per child (Slayton 1997). By 1976, the final decision in a protracted series of stages in this case supported the contention that funding disparities based on property wealth and tax-rate differences among districts was fundamentally unfair and constitutionally impermissible, based on the equal-protection provisions in the state's constitution.

San Antonio Independent School District v. Rodriguez *(1973)*

While *Serrano* was in progress (1973), *San Antonio Independent School District v. Rodriguez* was filed in the District Court for the Western District of Texas (a federal court). The plaintiffs challenged the constitutionality of using property tax in each district to supplement educational funds. The three-judge district court agreed with the plaintiffs. On direct appeal, the United States Supreme Court reversed the decision of the lower court, reasoning that while strict scrutiny under the equal protection clause was appropriate when state action impinged on a fundamental right or operated to the disadvantage of a suspect class, wealth did not constitute a suspect class and education was not a fundamental right.

Subsequent efforts in school finance reform took place at state courts, relying on equal protection or education clauses in state constitutions. According to the online "Boxscore" maintained by G. Alan Hickrod, Larry McNeal, Robert Lenz, Paul Minorini, and Linda Grady at http://www.coe.ilstu.edu/boxscore.htm, between 1973 and 1994, state supreme courts in eleven states declared that education was not a fundamental constitutional right. During the same period, state supreme courts declared that education was a fundamental constitutional right in thirteen states.

Edgewood ISD v. Kirby *(1984)*

An example of a statewide school finance reform case is *Edgewood ISD v. Kirby,* filed in 1984 by the Mexican American Legal Defense and Education Fund (MALDEF) and Multicultural Education, Training, and Advocacy, Inc. (META) on behalf of the Edgewood Independent School District in San Antonio, seven additional school districts, and twenty-one parents. Eventually, sixty-seven additional school districts and many parents and students joined in the suit. In contesting the state's reliance on property taxes, discrimination against students in poor school districts was alleged, in violation of the state constitution that obligated the state legislature to provide an efficient and free public school system (Comal Union School 1999). Many of the petitioners were from poor districts from the rural border areas and from the barrios in urban centers. Evidence presented in the case included the extra costs of educating English-language learners. During the next ten years, the case was appealed, amended, retried, postponed, and finally decided by the Texas Supreme Court in 1989.

The court's unanimous decision upheld the plaintiffs' claims and ordered the state legislature to come up with a plan by the next school year that met constitutional requirements. Between 1989 and 1993, the legislature presented several plans that were found wanting. The fifty-seven wealthy school districts in the state tried unsuccessfully to intervene, protesting that they would lose money under the new plans. Not until January 1995, five years after the legislature had been directed to devise and adopt an equitable system, did Texas Supreme Court Judge Scott McCown rule that a constitutional plan had been presented, although he noted that additional equalization was still needed throughout the state. The final plan capped the amount of money that districts can raise locally through property tax, and redistributed funds from some high-wealth school districts to low-wealth school districts. By 2001, eighty-four districts were required to share their tax revenue.

Rodriguez v. Los Angeles Unified School District *(1992)*

Although *Serrano* and *Edgewood* are examples of court-ordered statewide equalization among districts, *Rodriguez v. Los Angeles Unified School District* is the first instance of a court order in the United States requiring equalization among schools within a district (Slayton 1997). Petitioners, represented by META, the Legal Aid Foundation of Los Angeles, and others, challenged greater per-pupil expenditure for students in suburban nonminority schools (such as those in the west side of Los Angeles) than for students in urban and minority schools (such as those in East Los Angeles). The Los Angeles Superior Court found that, compared to predominantly majority schools, predominantly minority schools were larger, and had more inexperienced, undercredentialed teachers, resulting in lower expenditures of up to $400 a year less per pupil in predominantly minority elementary schools. Much of the funding differences resulted from the higher salaries paid to teachers with seniority and advanced degrees, who often elected to leave the city schools to teach in suburban settings.

The terms of the settlement agreement greatly expanded resources to schools in low-income and immigrant communities. Beginning with the 1992–1993 school year, the district equalized resources among all its schools, taking teacher training and experience into account. In light of the opposition of the school employees' unions, however, anything akin to a controlled staffing plan based on teachers' credentials proved difficult to implement. The district made an agreement with the teachers' union that no teachers would be forced to transfer schools and allocated $10 million a year to train new teachers. Since that year, funding levels have varied, but have been as high as $16 million, targeted on the schools with the lowest per-pupil expenditures.

In the 1970s, courts were asked to fashion remedies for financial disparities that emphasized dollar equity. Since 1978, petitioners have asked for funding adequate to allow all students a fair chance at achieving desired educational outcomes, emphasizing programs and services for students most in need (Minorini and Sugarman 1999). The strategy of equalization of dollar-for-dollar funding did not take into account the effects of municipal overburdens related to differences in cost of living in different parts of a state. It also did not take into account the disproportionately higher percentages of children with special needs (for example, children who are English-language learners and therefore require specially trained bilingual teachers and linguistically and culturally appropriate materials) in certain districts within a state. Equality in the distribution of funds did not result in a distribution sufficient to adequately support desired educational outcomes for all students. Rather than asking that every student be given the same resources, more recent requests have asked that students receive appropriately different amounts of resources, in each case in amounts sufficient to bring about a stated purpose, depending on what each group of students needs.

This evolution in the concept of equity can be noted in the history of school finance reform in New Jersey. The New Jersey Supreme Court decision in *Robinson v. Cahil* (1973) held that the state's school finance system violated the education clause in the state's constitution, which guaranteed an equal opportunity to receive a thorough and efficient system of public education. The court held that the state was constitutionally obliged to ensure this opportunity, whatever the condition of local taxing policy or district funding decisions. Although the concept of adequacy was an element in the decision, it was an undefined element.

Some twenty years later, *Abbott v. Burke* (1994) extended the decision in *Robinson,* ruling that all children must have an equal opportunity to receive a level of educational opportunity that equips children for their roles as citizens and competitors in the contemporary labor market. This ruling provided a definition of adequacy and established a rationale for requirements that New Jersey provide for the educational needs of disadvantaged students by providing additional funding for supplemental remedial measures for the poorer districts in the state (Long 1999).

McDuffy v. Secretary of the Executive Office of Education *(1993)*

McDuffy is another example of a statewide case that focused on the inadequacy of educational opportunities, and was initially filed under the caption *Webby v. Dukakis* in 1978. Plaintiffs from sixteen low-wealth districts in Massachusetts alleged that their schools were insufficiently funded and that the education provided with those resources was inadequate by any reasonable standard of adequacy. The group of plaintiffs was subsequently expanded and joined with other pending cases. An amicus brief on funding transitional bilingual education programs in Holyoke, Chelsea, and Lawrence, all with 70 percent Hispanic populations, was submitted by META. A declaratory judgment that the constitution of the Commonwealth of Massachusetts requires the state to provide every young person in the Commonwealth with equal access to an adequate education was requested by the plaintiffs.

The Supreme Judicial Court of Massachusetts reviewed at great length the history of public education in Massachusetts; the court concluded that the language in the education clause of the constitution

(Part II, c. 5, 2) was not merely aspirational or hortatory, but obligatory. The state has a duty to provide an education for all its children, whether rich or poor, and without regard to the fiscal capacity of the community or district in which such children live. This obligation is intended not only to serve the interests of the children but to prepare them for their roles as citizens. The court declared that the Commonwealth was not currently fulfilling this constitutional duty. The state was directed to devise a plan with sources of funds sufficient to meet the constitutional mandate, and the court of entry was authorized to determine whether, within a reasonable time, appropriate legislative action had been taken.

Leandro v. State of North Carolina *(1997)*

An adequacy case with several provisions having potential application to bilingual education was decided by North Carolina Supreme Court Chief Justice Burley Mitchell in 1997 in *Leandro v. State of North Carolina.* The original set of plaintiffs included two parents and two students from each of five low-wealth counties (Cumberland, Halifax, Hoke, Robeson, and Vance) and the school boards of those counties. They alleged that the education finance system in the state was to blame for the physical deterioration of their schools, a lack of basic supplies and essential teaching equipment, and an inability to attract high-quality teachers. These conditions deprived children in their districts of equal or adequate, or even a minimum, education as promised by various provisions in the state constitution. The plaintiffs further alleged that these conditions had led directly to their students' diminished academic performance, whether measured by end-of-year state proficiency tests, college admissions, or remedial college coursework among local students who gained entry to North Carolina's public colleges and universities.

A set of large high-wealth districts gained status as plaintiff-intervenors. Their school districts had many special-needs students who required special education services, special English instruction, and programs for the academically gifted. They alleged that providing these services required them to divert substantial resources from their regular education programs. The intervenors agreed with the original plaintiffs that the state was not properly funding the public schools, but asked that the remedy not be at the expense of urban districts that were also underfunded in light of their greater expenses.

The court held that North Carolina's children have a right to a sound basic education as a minimum standard of quality and that the state's obligation to provide a sound basic education applied equally to children in every North Carolina school district. The decision made it clear that districts may spend local money to provide an education that is even better than the required minimum.

The court specified the indispensable requisites of a sound basic education by identifying what students must be able to do as a result of a minimum standard of schooling. Students should have sufficient ability and knowledge of subject areas to function in a complex society, make informed choices on issues of personal or community importance, successfully engage in postsecondary education or vocational training, or compete equally with others in seeking formal education or gainful employment in contemporary society. This emphasis on educational outcomes gave rise to speculations that districts would henceforth be required to provide college preparatory courses such as advanced science or foreign languages, and that such a requirement would apply even to districts presently too poor to offer them (Boger 1998). To extend Boger's argument, the requirement that students be sufficiently well educated to do well on standardized achievement tests, gain entrance to the state's public colleges, and succeed academically in the postsecondary environment may lead districts to greater reliance on those bilingual education components best suited to foster simultaneous achievement in English and other content areas.

The case was remanded to the trial court to determine whether the constitutional right to a sound basic education was being denied public school children in North Carolina, and if so, to grant appropriate relief and to supervise remedies to be devised by the legislative branch of government. Judge Howard Manning of the Wake County Superior Court in *Hoke County Board of Education v. State of North Carolina* (formerly the *Leandro* case) has issued two Memoranda of Decision in the case. In April, the state's attorney general announced the state's intention to appeal the ruling that North Carolina must spend whatever is needed to equalize educational opportunities for its neediest children. As of this writing, that case is still in progress.

Although educational adequacy is still being contested, the next significant phase in school finance-reform litigation was a greater focus on the adverse impact of state education financing arrangements on racial and ethnic minorities, in violation of Title VI of the Civil Rights Act of 1964 or of the Equal Educational Opportunities Act (Long 1999).

Flores v. Arizona *(2000)*

Edgewood indirectly included LEP students because of their enrollment in low-wealth districts. *McDuffy* and *Leandro* specifically included LEP students and data about bilingual program costs as part of a set of issues presented for the courts' review. *Flores,* however, focused exclusively on the adequacy of funding for LEP students. This case is interesting because of its relationship to Proposition 203, an initiative to restrict bilingual education passed by Arizona voters in November 2000.

In 1992, an action was filed in the United States District Court against the state of Arizona. The plaintiffs, represented by the Arizona Center for Law in the Public Interest, alleged that state funding was insufficient to ensure that LEP students overcame language barriers, and that the state of Arizona was therefore in violation of the Equal Educational Opportunity (EEO) Act of 1974. Evidence was presented in the case to demonstrate that LEP students were placed in overcrowded classrooms, not provided with appropriate or sufficient ESL and bilingual instructional materials, and that teachers and paraprofessionals assigned to work with LEP students did not have the training and experience needed to qualify them for that assignment.

The decision, issued by Judge Alfredo Marquez in January 2000, upheld these claims of the plaintiffs (but not a related claim challenging the state's testing program), describing the current per-student funding amount of $157.00 as arbitrary and capricious, not reflecting the amount needed to enable LEP students to overcome the language barrier and master necessary academic skills.

In an earlier order, the court had ordered the state to conduct a cost study to determine how much was needed to fund language education programs adequately. In January 2001, a report prepared by Senate Democrats estimated that it would cost an additional $170 million a year to reach the standard established by the court. The state, still under court order despite voters' approval of Proposition 203, now spends approximately $20 million on programs for LEP students. The state had to comply with the order in 2001 to avoid loss of all federal funding for state programs.

Campaign for Fiscal Equity, et al. v. State of New York, et al. *(1993)*

The Campaign for Fiscal Equity (CFE) filed suit in 1993 on behalf of the New York City schoolchildren for whom they advocated. The plaintiffs alleged:

- ⦿ The state failed to provide students with a sound basic education as required by the state constitution.
- ⦿ The bulk of state education aid from a $13 billion education budget was directed to suburban, wealthy, and mostly White

school districts according to their political influence, not according to an analysis of each district's needs.

•• Black and Hispanic students comprised 80 percent of the students enrolled in New York City's schools.

•• The aid formula provided lower-than-average funding, and thereby discriminated against minority students, who are disproportionately affected by the funding pattern.

•• The city should be receiving more than its proportional share of aid because of its high proportions of poor children and of students who speak English as a second language in the city schools.

•• Results of the first administration of the state's high school exit examinations (which high school students must pass before graduating) showed that city students did not meet the state's own standards for an adequate education.

•• The funding pattern violated the state constitution's education article and the implementing regulations of Title VI of the federal Civil Rights Act of 1964.

On January 10, 2001, New York State Supreme Court Justice Leland DeGrasse issued a decision in favor of the plaintiffs. The court found the state financing system did not comply with education provisions in the state constitution and did not allow New York City public schools to enable students to acquire the skills they need to obtain productive employment or to pursue higher education. This pattern resulted from the consistent manipulation of education funding formulas during the state's annual budget negotiations by state officials. The court also supported the plaintiffs' charge that minority students suffered an adverse and disparate impact from the state education finance system not justified by any reason related to education in violation of federal antidiscrimination laws and regulations.

In January 2001, the state of New York appealed the decision. Whatever the outcome of the appeal, attorney Michael A. Rebell of the Campaign for Fiscal Equity noted that this was the first case to link standards reform to adequate funding (Goodnough 2001).

Next Phases in School Finance Reform

Experts in school finance identify three overlapping predictions for future litigation in this area. According to Hess (1995), requests will continue for vertical equity, which treats pupils with different needs in an appropriately different manner, coupled with a new emphasis on equitable and adequate funding to each school in a state. Clune (1994) agrees, observing that this focus on school-level funding combines well with the current emphasis on individual school accountability for student achievement. Verstegen and Whitney (1997) expect the broad movement under way to secure the rights of poor children to equal opportunity and nondiscrimination will continue as a replay of former civil rights activities on behalf of linguistic minorities and children with disabilities.

Recap: Political deal-making affects the development of formulas for distributing state education dollars. When the legislative process, based on majority rule, results in the unjust distribution of public funds, the courts have demonstrated that they can and will enforce appropriate remedial action to protect minority rights. Enhancements in programs for English-language and other second-language learners, and greater application of opportunity-to-learn standards by states and school districts, can be expected to flow from corrections in funding formulas affecting districts with bilingual education programs.

COSTS AND BENEFITS
OF BILINGUAL EDUCATION

Although there are various cost analyses of bilingual education, few systematically take into consideration the benefit side of the equation. The conclusions of the cost studies vary considerably. This might be expected, because the costs of providing an education program can vary from district to district and from state to state. They can also vary within one district, greater costs associated with program start-up expenses than with program continuation. Nevertheless, the litigation described above suggests that it is safe to conclude that the costs of providing bilingual education are greater than funding for that purpose allocated by the states. After carefully examining the evidence provided in each case, courts in Arizona, Massachusetts, North Carolina, and New York have reached the same conclusion: Provisions for state education funding did not adequately cover the cost of providing education, including the costs involved in providing bilingual education. This conclusion may set to rest the fear that bilingual education programs are perpetuated merely to continue a lucrative flow of cash from the state coffers.

Costs

School districts receive funding from several sources. State education finance formulas take into account how many children are enrolled in each district, each student in attendance generating funds for the district as determined by the state funding formula. Categorical or weighted formula funding from the states is often targeted to the needs of LEP students in states with bilingual education acts, ESL funding provisions, or dropout prevention programs. Districts are eligible for formula-based federal funding for immigrant children during their first three years of schooling in the United States through the Emergency Immigrant Education Program, and for low-income children through Title I of the Improving America's School Act (IASA). Additional funding is available for districts serving American Indian students, and for districts in federally impacted areas. Funding through the Bilingual Education Act provides support for ESL, bilingual education, and foreign-language programs. Funding from this source is available to districts that choose to apply for these funds and whose proposals for funding are successful. Current information about Department of Education funding is available online at http://ocfo.ed.gov/grntinfo/forecast/forecast.htm#Chart%202. In addition, major foundation funding programs have addressed the needs of public school systems.

Concerns regarding the costs of language education typically focus on two issues: the level of government that should pay for educating undocumented students, and the amount of funding required to provide bilingual education.

The first of these questions is not precisely related to bilingual education because the group that includes undocumented students overlaps with but is not identical to the group that includes students in bilingual education programs. Nevertheless, the two issues are joined in public debate. By tradition and law, public education in the United States is a local responsibility; however, cash-strapped education officials have sought to draw on other than local sources to comply with the U.S. Supreme Court decision in *Plyler v. Doe* prohibiting the denial of access to public education to undocumented students. Several state and local officials have asked for reparations since the 1994 Office of Management and Budget published a study estimating that in the seven states most affected by immigration, it cost $3.1 billion to educate 641,000 undocumented children (Schnaiberg 1994a). In California, for example, the Anaheim Union High School District board approved a plan to bill foreign countries or the federal government for the cost of educating undocumented children. The proposal was not well received. Opponents of the measure started a recall drive, and the Justice Department declined to honor the request.

The Intercultural Development Research Association (IDRA) (1996) pointed out that it is important to distinguish the cost of providing bilingual education for a set of students from the basic costs of educating those same students, no matter how they are taught. Crawford (1998b) summarized a 1992 study commissioned by the California legislature that found "the incremental cost was about the same each year ($175–$214) for bilingual and English immersion programs, as compared with $1,198 for English as a Second Language (ESL) "pullout" programs. In *Class Notes* (1996), IDRA cited studies concluding that, except for minor costs such as materials and testing, bilingual instruction costs little more than monolingual instruction. In Texas, for example, an additional $230 was spent in 1995 for each child in a bilingual program. The result of a 1994 cost analysis of bilingual education programs in Connecticut found that differential costs were approximately $680 per pupil (Prince and Hubert 1994).

According to calculations by the Massachusetts Department of Education (MDOE), average statewide per-pupil expenditures for transitional bilingual education in 1993–1994 were $5,539 for transitional bilingual education, compared with a statewide average of $5,235 for all-day programs; see the online reports at http://www.doe.mass.edu/ doedocs/ ppebil.html and http://www.doe.mass.edu/doedocs/ppesum.html.

The modest difference between programs identified in 1993–1994 stands in startling contrast to the results of similar MDOE calculations for the fiscal 1999 school year, with $5,487 as the average statewide cost for regular day programs compared with an average statewide cost of $7,495 for bilingual programs (see http://finance1. doe.mass.edu/ for district-by-district comparisons). A similar anomaly occurred in New York City. In a statement presented by Mayor Rudolph W. Giuliani's office, the average per-pupil spending on bilingual education students was reported to be $7,289, compared with $5,149 for other students. At the same time, the "board of education's budget office estimates that it costs an average of $974 more than it does for other students to provide services for LEP students in elementary and middle schools and $1,215 more in high schools" (Schnaiberg 1994b).

The wide variance in the results among studies attempting to measure the costs of bilingual education in the same jurisdiction may be caused by inconsistencies in criteria for costs attributable to language education programs. Further, a common standard is needed to account for the higher expenses associated with programs that include a pullout ESL option. As Crawford (1998b) noted, this option (removing a student from an assigned class and teacher to provide ESL instruction in a second classroom with another teacher) increases expenditures because it requires additional budget allocations for supplemental teachers and for classroom space.

In a World Bank–sponsored international review of first- and second-language use in education, a feature identified as common to successful programs was approximately equal costs to traditional programs. Additional start-up costs were offset by enhanced earning potential for the students and increased efficiency and effectiveness (fewer dropouts, for example, and more graduates) for the educational institution.

Benefits

The concept that bilingual education should be considered an investment goes well beyond the anticipated outcome of increasing the schools' holding power and thereby increasing the number of students who graduate from high school. An investment in the types of bilingual education programs that support bilingualism and biliteracy can also result in individual and regional economic benefit.

Using 1990 Census figures, Boswell (1998) investigated the relationship between bilingualism and income in south Florida. He found that Hispanics who reported speaking English very well earned incomes that averaged $8,034 more than those who did not speak English at all. In addition, Hispanics who reported they spoke Spanish at home and functioned very well in English earned even higher incomes; they had annual median and mean incomes of about $2,000 higher than incomes for Hispanics who speak only English. Similar advantages were identified for Hispanics in three of the ten metropolitan areas included in a study conducted by Fradd and Boswell (1999). The authors point out that the findings of higher earnings for bilingual than for English monolingual Hispanics occurred with three demographic groups: primarily Cuban with a high percentage of recent immigrants (Miami, Florida), primarily U.S.-born Mexican Americans (San Antonio, Texas), and primarily recent immigrants from Caribbean, Central, and South American countries (Jersey City, New Jersey).

In Miami-Dade County, Florida, since the mid-1990s, prestigious civic and chamber organizations in Miami have vigorously pressed for school programs that help develop the bilingual workforce needed to fill positions in international trade and tourism. An economic basis for the school district's preference for bilingual-education programs is clearly stated in the Year 2000 State of the School System address by Miami-Dade Public Schools Board Chairperson Perla Tabares Hantman. She summarized the board's position and goals for bilingual education as follows:

With the backing of the Greater Miami Chamber of Commerce and its English Plus One campaign, we have made great strides in this regard. Since the 1997–1998 school year, the number of schools offering tracks in which the academics are taught 60 percent of the day in English and 40 percent in Spanish has grown from six to forty-two. Our objective is to eventually offer every student in every part of the county the opportunity for a continuous bilingual education, from Kindergarten through high school graduation.

Her full statement is available online at http://www.dade.k12.fl. us/board/sssaddress/index.htm.

Language and Economics Theory

It is widely accepted that in a global economy, employees with skills in more than one language and culture are needed. Studies on the extent to which a bilingual workforce helps create business activity, however, have not been widely reported. This topic is included in studies from the discipline of the economics of language. Grin (1996) and Grin and Vaillancourt (1999) summarized studies in this emerging field. They include but are not limited to empirical analysis using the concepts and tools of economics to investigate the relationship between language and labor earnings, language and economic activity, communication between linguistic groups, and language planning.

Investigations into the relationship between the earnings of individuals and their language attributes and studies explaining salary differentials among members of separate linguistic communities have examined the impact of Hispanics' ethnic origin and their language skills in English on earnings. Most of the investigations along these lines have taken place in North America. In these studies, language may be defined as an ethnic identity marker, an element of human capital, or both, in trying to assess the effect of individuals' linguistic attributes on their earnings. Results of these studies confirm that linguistic skills contribute significantly to labor earnings among men. Different market rewards, however, accrue to different levels and types of skills in different languages, and under conditions of discrimination on the part of employers against minority-language speakers.

Garcia and Otheguy (1994) pointed out that when an ethnolinguistic group has been deprived of easy access to economic integration, English-language skills are not associated with much economic gain and English-language instruction meets with uneven success. DeVoretz and Werner (2000), after a review of the social forces affecting immigrants in Canada, Germany, Israel, and the United States, reached a similar conclusion. In their view, the labor market was the primary determinant of language-learning outcomes. Further, for the majority of immigrants in these countries, a minimal level of second-language acquisition was the optimal outcome, given the incentive structure.

Chorney (1998) surveyed the leading 250 companies in Canada. The sample was drawn principally from the Department of Industry's Business Opportunities Sourcing System (BOSS) list of top exporting companies. The BOSS list identifies firms whose exports were in excess of $50 million per year. According to Chorney, the study represents one of the largest surveys of its kind to test the economic impact of bilingualism and, in particular, the relationship between bilingualism and employment. Chorney concluded that the study yielded overwhelming evidence that bilingualism increases an applicant's chances of finding employment.

Analysis of the reciprocal relationship between language and economic activity is considered a specialty of European scholarship in language economics. In a study of Scottish Gaelic, for example, it was determined that levels of production, domestic income, and employment benefited from public spending for the promotion of the minority language. Calculation of the ratio of public investment to demand for goods and services yielded a multiplier effect of 2.22, considered by Grin (1996) to be a respectable positive effect.

Additional support for the position that language can be a source of regional economic growth is provided by Beaudin (1998), who analyzed the factors leading to remarkable economic vitality in southeast New Brunswick, often described as "the Moncton Miracle." New Brunswick has a population of 700,000 (including 250,000 speakers of French (Francophones). The Francophone minority makes up one-third of the population in metropolitan Moncton and has easy access to the Université de Moncton, the only Francophone university outside Quebec. Beaudin credits a skilled bilingual labor force, the location of the Francophone university—which acted as an economic catalyst for the region—and a positive climate between the two linguistic communities as major factors leading to the economic boom caused by relocation of firms to Moncton.

Bilingualism contributes to economic growth resulting not only in new businesses within an area but also in increased trade with other areas. Bilateral merchandise trade flows are higher between pairs of countries that share a common language. Helliwell (2000) analyzed bilateral trade among twenty-two countries for 1988 through 1992. He found that sharing a common language has a large and significant effect on trade intensity, resulting in trade flows more than 1.7 times as large as those between two otherwise similar countries. The positive effect on trade holds true for countries who share the same national language and for countries who share a common language spoken by a minority of the population for either or both of the trading partners. He also determined that countries trade more with each other than with other countries because of shared language and not because of factors such as adjacent location.

Changes in trade and immigration patterns are associated with changes in national language policies, as illustrated by the examples of England and Australia. England became concerned with increasing the teaching of foreign languages for trade purposes when its share of world exports of manufactured goods slipped from nearly 25 percent in 1950 to less than 10 percent in the late 1970s. In 1950, 75 percent of Australia's trade was with England. By the 1990s, that same proportion had shifted to Asian countries. The Australian government adopted the policy of Productive Diversity, which emphasizes the economic asset derived from the country's multicultural and multilingual population, and stresses the development of competence in the languages of its export markets (Bodi 1994).

Specific business interests were addressed through Grin's model for determining the optimal point at which a firm that operates in a bilingual market should switch from monolingual to bilingual advertising. In a broader examination of communication between language groups, the efficiency of translation compared to generalized bilingualism has been undertaken. Grin (1996) reports that as long as an area has no more than five linguistic communities, the generalized teaching of a second language is more economically efficient than the development of generalized translation services. This result continues to hold true for up to ten languages if all residents know not one but two languages in addition to their mother tongues. Although fluency in three languages may seem unusual to residents of the United States, it is quite common among Africans; many regularly speak a home language, a national language, and a language of wider communication. Fluency in three languages is strongly encouraged in Israel, Australia, and Europe. According to Shipman (1992), European employers increasingly seek candidates who speak up to three languages.

Grin (1996) and Grin and Vaillancourt (1999) highlight the potential of an economic perspective on policy problems to justify and calibrate expenditures by public authorities on language policy, including those for the protection and promotion of threatened languages. They do not believe that economic analysis is the only factor to consider, but they do suggest that such analysis addresses issues often ignored, and suggest it as an ingredient to be considered in the development of language policy. As a demonstration, Grin and Vaillancourt (1999) applied economic analysis to determine a desirable degree of multilingualism and arrived at the following generic conclusions:

➥ Moving from monolingualism to bilingualism is likely to create benefits for society as a whole without causing prohibitive expense.
➥ Adding one official language in a country that already recognizes ten may yield benefits smaller than the associated costs of the move.
➥ Consequently, in most cases, optimal multilingualism is neither zero nor infinite.

These conclusions are based on the analysis of a theoretical model rather than on its application to a given time and place. Nevertheless, the conclusions do not support the belief that the costs of societal bilingualism are always greater than the benefits. In evenhanded fashion, the model rejects the English Only position, and also rejects the assumptions that the optimal degree of multilingualism tends to infinity and that the benefits of multilingualism always exceed the costs. Grin and Vaillancourt attribute the latter positions to authors fond of using the metaphor of language-as-resource.

Recap: The extent to which political factors lead to inequities in school funding and affect districts offering programs in bilingual education was illustrated with an overview of trends in school finance reform in the United States. Bilingual education is not a cash cow for school districts and neither is it free of expense; its real costs can be evaluated only in relation to its consequences. Bilingual education helps students learn English and thereby improves their chances for success in the United States. The types of bilingual education that lead to bilingualism foster economic benefits that flow to individuals with skills in English and in another language. Bilingualism is also a factor in economic development for regions whose bilingual workforce meets the staffing needs of existing enterprises or stimulates the creation of new domestic or international economic activity.

IDENTITY POLITICS

Why do bilingual education advocates think language minority groups are entitled to policies that make exceptions to the general rule of

English-only instruction in the public schools and in dealings with government agencies? What is the justification for this special treatment? What is the nature of public opinion about these matters?

Identity Politics and Linguistic Diversity

Fundamentally, the rationale for government-funded multilingual services rests on the democratic tradition that all persons in the United States are entitled to the equal protection of the laws, and on the laws that uphold that tradition. One aspect of the claim to legitimacy for policies that give language minority populations access to government services is that they are taxpayers. Their taxes contribute to the support of government agencies; their services should be accessible to all. But access to the same benefit provided to others does not necessarily constitute access to equal benefit. The concept of identity politics helps clarify that distinction.

White (2000), in a presentation celebrating the benefits of Canadian nonterritorial federalism, provided a concise definition of identity politics and many useful insights about its application. He notes that when it is determined that rights should be granted on the basis of important personal characteristics other than mere place of residence, the characteristics used to justify such rights are always essential elements of a person's identity. Accordingly, such political rights are called identity-based rights; claiming or implementing such rights is called identity politics.

These rights are claimed when minority group members within a territory, with personal characteristics different from those of the majority, discover that the laws do not meet their needs. In these circumstances, identity-based rights may be useful, justified, and necessary, preferable by far to the alternative of creating splinter territories governed by a separate set of laws.

Rights don't exist when they are claimed, but when a majority of the legislators vote to create entitlements. It is difficult to gain this approval, because the law that grants those rights benefits only a minority of the electorate; the majority may believe the law is unjust precisely because it fails to treat every person equally, but it is not impossible to achieve the goal. White provides examples of widespread recognition that the only way to achieve true equality and justice in modern society may be through granting those special rights. By way of illustration, he notes the widespread acceptance in Canada of the need to modify public buildings and sidewalks so that they are accessible to people in wheelchairs. He also mentions with approval Canadian arrangements for the effective provisions of government services, especially in education, to minority language groups.

Identity Politics and Religious Diversity

To foster the dispassionate consideration of the potentially volatile subject of language rights, the topic of discussion turns briefly to another aspect of identity: religion. The following observations on religious rights apply the previous discussion about identity politics to policies of religious tolerance in the United States.

Former Secretary of State Madeleine K. Albright, speaking in 1997 in support of the policies of the United States on religious freedom, identified freedom of religion as central to the history and identity of the United States. She quoted President Clinton's declaration in his proclamation of Religious Freedom Day on January 16, 1997: "America's commitment to religious tolerance has empowered us to achieve an atmosphere of understanding, trust, and respect in a society of diverse cultures and religious traditions. And today, much of the world still looks to the United States as the champion of religious liberty." Her full statement is available online at http://www.state.gov/www/global/human_rights/970722.

Intolerance sparked by religious diversity has led to strife, and at times to violence, in the United States and in other countries. Our country's early history is marred by incidents such as the hanging of Margate Jones for witchcraft in 1648 and the beating, imprisonment, and banishment of Quakers by Massachusetts in 1656. The establishment of the Catholic parochial school system in 1874 was a reaction to Protestant influence in the supposedly nondenominational public schools. In contemporary times, the Anti-Defamation League's (ADL) annual Audit of Anti-Semitic Incidents for the year 2000 recorded 1,606 anti-Semitic incidents in forty-four states and the District of Columbia (ADL 2000). In other countries, violent confrontation or states of war between religious groups are reported between Muslims and Orthodox Christians in Kosovo; among Jews, Muslims, and Christians in the Middle East; between Protestants and Catholics in Northern Ireland; between Buddhists and Hindus in Sri Lanka; and among Animists, Christians, and Muslims in Sudan. Nevertheless, no one in the United States is suggesting that the way to ensure harmony is to curtail religious freedom or eradicate religions.

The courts have acknowledged the legitimacy of claims for exemptions from various laws on the basis of religious identity. During World War II, for example, the United States Supreme Court decision in *West Virginia State Board of Education v. Barnette* (1943) exempted children who were Jehovah's Witnesses from the penalties imposed on all others for failure to salute the flag. Their religious beliefs include a literal version of Exodus 20:4 and 5, which says: "Thou shalt not make unto thee any graven image, or any likeness of anything that is in heaven above, or that is in the earth beneath, or that is in the water under the earth; thou shalt not bow down thyself to them nor serve them." They consider that the flag is an "image" within this command. For this reason they refuse to salute it.

In *Wisconsin v. Yoder* (1972), members of the Old Order Amish religion and the Conservative Amish Mennonite Church were convicted of violating Wisconsin's compulsory school-attendance law. Because the Amish sincerely believe that high school attendance is contrary to the Amish religion and way of life and that they would endanger their own salvation and that of their children by complying with the law, they provide their children continuing informal vocational education designed to prepare them for life in the rural Amish community. The United States Supreme Court exempted members of the Amish community from complying with the compulsory attendance laws of the state of Wisconsin.

This brief account of religious liberty as an aspect of personal and national identity in the United States leads to the following conclusions:

- Although religious diversity may at times generate hostility, it is nevertheless valued.
- Protection extended by the Bill of Rights guaranteeing freedom of religion requires that all religious denominations be treated in the same way. However, within the category of religious denominations, certain classes (such as the Amish) must be treated differently to obtain the same goal of just treatment accorded others in the category.
- Even with respect to freedom of religion, a deeply entrenched aspect of national identity, minority rights are still in need of protection.
- Religious liberty is granted on the basis of a particular personal characteristic: religion. That characteristic is not immutable, but can be a central aspect of personal identity.

Analogy

Were the conclusions stated above to be reworded by replacing such terms as *freedom of religion* and *religious diversity* with those pertinent to the discussion on linguistic diversity, would the statements be any less sound? If diversity in religion is desirable, why not diversity in language or culture?

Consider the following revised version of those conclusions:

- Although *linguistic* diversity may at times generate hostility, it is nevertheless *valuable.*
- Protection extended by the Bill of Rights guaranteeing freedom of *speech* requires that all *speech* be treated in the same way. However, within the category of *speakers,* certain classes (such as *language minority groups*) must be treated differently to obtain the same goal of just treatment accorded others in the category.
- Even with respect to freedom of *speech and equal protection of the laws,* a deeply entrenched aspect of national identity, minority rights are still in need of protection.
- *Language liberties* are granted on the basis of a particular personal characteristic: *language.* That characteristic is not immutable, but can be a central aspect of personal identity.

Recap: Language is an important personal characteristic. Identity politics is a process by which language minority groups have sought recognition of their language-related needs for effective access to education and other government services.

PUBLIC OPINION

Even for those who accept identity-based claims for language rights as legitimate, questions may remain about the type of response that would be effective. The following parts of this chapter address these questions:

- Does bilingual education work?
- Is the public adequately informed about language issues?

RESEARCH

The National Academy of Sciences (NAS) was established by an Act of Congress in 1863 to investigate and report on scientific and technical matters whenever called upon to advise any department within the government. Election to membership in this nonprofit society is a high honor awarded only to scientists with distinguished records of accomplishment as researchers. The NAS includes the National Academy of Engineering (NAE), the Institute of Medicine (IOM), and the National Research Council (NRC).

The National Research Council and the Institute of Medicine established a committee to make recommendations regarding research related to the education of English-language learners. The resulting publication (August and Hakuta 1997) summarizes thirty years of bilingual education research and is available in full text online at http://books.nap.edu/books/0309054974/html/13.html#pagetop.

To understand this research, it is important to consider definition of terms, particularly those used to describe the programs being compared and those used to define success. Failure to do so may result in significant error. For example, in an evaluation of the effect of home-language instruction in the content areas on the educational achievement of English-language learners (Rothfarb, Ariza, and Urrutia 1987), the evaluators concluded from the achievement data presented that no significant difference existed in the achievement of students who received home-language instruction in bilingual curriculum content (BCC) and those who did not. In the face of this conclusion, the school board was urged to eliminate the program by those of its members historically opposed to home-language instruction. A significant error was discovered, however: There was no consistency among BCC classes in the amount of time allocated to instruction in the home language or the extent to which home-language materials were used in those classes; indeed, some BCC classes provided no home-language instruction at all. As a result, the comparison was not between a treatment group and a control group that differed primarily in the use of home-language instruction. It was therefore impossible to compare across programs because the terms used to label the programs did not accurately describe them. Terms and definitions were not consistent with program activities.

Just as terms used to describe programs may vary from school to school, the criteria for determining the success of instructional approaches may also vary from study to study.

For example, in highly influential reports on Canada's bilingual immersion model (Lambert and Tucker 1972), programs in which children were taught content through a second language while they maintained grade-level achievement levels in nonlanguage subjects were considered successful. The children's considerable accomplishment in gaining second-language proficiency (in French) without erosion of achievement as measured in their first language (English) was celebrated. In other studies (Rossell and Baker 1996), the issue was whether home-language approaches to teaching English were *better* than those that relied solely on English to teach English. The students' achievement in the other content areas was not part of the criteria for success.

Changing criteria across studies affect the interpretation of success. Even when the coverage of content areas and languages is considered in the definition of success across studies, some investigators may consider only progress in increasing proficiency in the English language. Other investigators also measure degrees of success in advancing the academic achievement of students in one or all of the content areas required for grade-to-grade promotion and high school graduation. Measurement of achievement in the content areas may take place in the English language or in the home language, or in both languages, further confounding the interpretation of the results. In addition, many researchers feel that a full measure of accountability requires the assessment of students' progress in heritage-language arts or, in the case of language majority students, of progress in the acquisition of the language other than English; and for these the determination of researchers' success depends on an examination of all these variables.

Although the NRC, under the chairmanship of Kenji Hakuta, reviewed studies on a broad range of linguistic, cognitive, and social processes involved in the education of English-language learners, the sections of the report comparing educational outcomes related to home-language instruction received the most attention. Charles L. Glenn prepared a review of the National Research Council report for the READ Institute (an advocacy group directed by Rosalie Pedalino Porter); this report was filed by her with the California State Board of Education in support of a request by the Orange County Unified School District for a waiver from requirements for use of the home language in instructional programs. Under deposition in that matter, Hakuta (1998a) corrected misconceptions in Porter's statements and the READ review.

RESEARCH FINDINGS

These corrections also serve as a succinct synthesis of thirty years of research in bilingual education. Dr. Hakuta's sworn statement affirmed:

- ➡ Initial reading instruction in the English language does have negative consequences for LEP students. Although under optimal circumstances children instructed in their second language can learn to read, English-language learners are often concentrated in schools characterized by numerous risk factors that increase the likelihood of negative consequences.

➼ Children are not more likely to acquire English-language reading skills if provided an ESL-based program rather than a bilingual one.

➼ Ample evidence shows that native-language instruction is helpful in the education of LEP students.

The full statement is available online at http://www.stanford. edu/~hakuta/OrangeDeclaration.html. The READ Institute review is available at http://www.ceousa.org/READ/nrc.html.

Analysis of the impact of Proposition 227 on student achievement is the focus of ongoing research. The release of students' test scores from Oceanside School District in California on June 16, 1999, led to claims widely circulated and celebrated by the mass media that gains in the test scores of LEP students should be attributed to the effects of English-only instruction as required by Proposition 227. See the Web site maintained by English for the Children at http://www.onenation.org/9906/ pr061699. html for additional information about these assertions.

These claims are countered by researcher Kenji Hakuta, whose analyses dispute the claims of success for structured English immersion. Hakuta reported overall gains in scores across the state for all students: Scores increased for LEP students and non-LEP students alike, for LEP students in English-only programs, and for LEP students in bilingual programs. Increased scores, therefore, could not be attributed to the effect of English-only programs implemented under the requirements of Proposition 227. The analysis is available at http://www.stanford. edu/~hakuta/SAT9/index.htm.

A study released on December 5, 2000, by California Tomorrow reported that sixty-three schools with bilingual education programs did better on tests of academic achievement in English than over 1,000 similar schools providing instruction to most students only in English. Hakuta's analysis of this report verified the study's conclusion, but cautioned that variability in scores from school to school makes clear the limitations of SAT-9 data for drawing conclusions about the effects of Proposition 227. See Kenji Hakuta's Web page at http://www. stanford.edu/~hakuta/SAT9/SAT9_2000/analysis2000.htm for additional information about the methodology employed in conducting the analyses.

For statistically rigorous meta-analyses of bilingual education research, see Greene (1997) and Willig (1985). For a comparison of structured immersion strategy, early-exit, and late-exit transitional bilingual education, see Ramírez et al. (1991). For other recent research reviews, see Cummins (1999) and (Rossell and Baker 1996). To stay abreast of ongoing research in the field of language education, refer to the Center for Applied Linguistics (CAL) at http://www.cal.org, the Center for Research in Excellence and Diversity in Education (CREDE) at http://www.cal.org/crede/, the network of National Language Resource Centers at http://carla.acad.umn.edu/NLRClinks.html, and the National Clearinghouse for Bilingual Education (NCBE) at http://www. ncbe.gwu.edu/.

Media

Research in social science has often had an impact on court decisions affecting education, as it did, for example, in the *Brown v. Board of Education of Topeka* and *Mendez v. Westminster* decisions on race desegregation. To cite a recent example of impact at the legislative level, the work of anthropologist Alex Stepick and his associates has influenced policymaking locally and nationally. His finding that there was a 25 to 30 percent undercount of Haitians in Miami-Dade figured in congressional testimony and led to Census Bureau funding for Haitian community groups to conduct a campaign for census education in preparation for the year 2000 census. A more accurate count is expected to result in better targeting of social and educational services.

Although research is vital to the continued improvement of curriculum and instruction, to well-informed policy development, and to influencing school district decisions concerning bilingual programs, there is no disputing the influence of the mass media on the formation of public opinion and on policy. Reutzel (1996), for example, reports the results of a survey of 1,500 state legislators from twelve states regarding their perceptions and knowledge of issues in reading instruction. Newspaper articles, magazine articles, radio and television broadcasts, and personal contacts with specialists in the field were reported by more than 70 percent of those surveyed as principal sources of information.

State legislative research agencies provide reviews of studies pertinent to pending legislation to the members of their state delegations. Hy (1995) found that legislative research agencies in forty-seven states did not rely on college and university personnel in relation to this task. Although the creation and dissemination of knowledge are among the principal functions of universities, the impact of research conducted at those institutions on policymaking is limited. For the general public and for policymakers, the mass media is a major source of information.

McQuillan and Tse (1996) examined the extent to which newspaper and magazine opinion pieces from five national newspapers and three national news magazines over eleven years (1984–1994) employed scientific research findings in making their arguments in support of or opposition to bilingual education. As part of their examination, articles from educational research journals, newspaper editorials, signed opinion pieces, and letters to the editor were reviewed. It was found that less than half of all persuasive newspaper articles examined mentioned social science research and nearly a third relied on personal or anecdotal accounts. In contrast to research reviews where 82 percent of empirical studies and research reviews reported favorable findings on the effectiveness of bilingual programs, less than half (45 percent) of persuasive newspaper articles took a position favorable to bilingual education.

McQuillan and Tse speculated about this anomaly, and suggested that (1) the style of academic writing may limit the readership for research reports, or (2) the negative emphasis may reflect societal and media attitudes toward immigration and therefore to the language of immigrants and bilingualism. They raised thought-provoking questions about the extent to which university public information officers, whose work contributes to setting the media's news coverage agendas, might be constrained in publicizing faculty research on controversial topics by their relationship to university fund-raising campaigns.

Other critics of the media have noted that its profits depend on advertising revenues; this creates a vulnerability that can affect accuracy and objectivity. In addition, the products of well-funded policy centers and think tanks affect news sources. According to a special report from the National Committee for Responsive Philanthropy (1995), there are over 100 well-funded and closely linked conservative public policy institutes (the Heritage Foundation, for example, had a 1994 budget of $25 million). They outspent progressive counterparts by four to one. The network funds activist groups and conducts public relations campaigns; their efforts contribute to shaping public opinion. Media analysts fear that the cumulative effect of these pressures on the media industry can lead to a blurring of the lines between news and propaganda.

Press Coverage of Proposition 227

James Crawford (1998a), a former Washington editor of *Education Week,* added an insider's perspective to his criticisms of the English-language newspapers' coverage of the Proposition 227 campaign. He explained that controversies surrounding bilingual education led to its being treated as a political story by the press. Journalists' standards of fairness applied to political stories (as contrasted with the treatment of an education story or a science story) are satisfied if all charges and countercharges of the major players are accurately quoted for the readers' benefit. This perspective, said Crawford, resulted in presenting the views of political activists as though they were the conclusions of experts on research into bilingual education, and overreliance on anecdotes rather than on research findings. He concluded that these reporting errors left readers with little more than slogans to rely on as they decided how to vote.

Media reports after the conclusion of the Proposition 227 campaign were also distorted, as noted by Latinolink, a news service featuring news of interest to the Hispanic community; for more information, see the Web site at http://www.latinolink.com/opinion/opinion98/0614hils.HTM. Newspapers across the country continued to publish reports of a majority Latino vote in support of Proposition 227 well after CNN exit poll results showed that Hispanics had voted *against* Proposition 227 by 63 percent.

Ethnicity and Language

Characteristics attributed to the press corps may offer some explanation for skewed coverage by journalists, who have been described as more conservative (Croteau 1998) and less ethnically diverse than the general public. Few journalists are members of language minority groups or sufficiently bilingual to have direct knowledge about issues of concern to language minority communities by virtue of their participation in those communities. According to the American Society of Newspaper Editors (ASNE) Annual Newsroom Census for 1998, 42 percent of all newspapers had no journalist of color in their newsrooms; 91 percent of supervisors and 89.8 percent of copy/layout editors were White. Given these characteristics, the misinterpretation of socially and culturally rooted information is not surprising.

Anders, writing for the *American Journalism Review,* describes the growing need for Spanish-speaking skills as a crucial tool for newsrooms in the United States as the nation's Hispanic population continues to grow: "Because no newsroom has enough native speakers and writers, editors compensate by sending people to learn Spanish, getting them up to at least conversational speed, and paying for it" (2000a).

The Orange County (California) *Register* has begun to address these issues by inaugurating an Asian Task Force to cover Orange County's Little Saigon and its growing population of Vietnamese, Chinese, Japanese, Filipinos, Indonesians, and Koreans. Vietnamese is used every day by the reporter who covers the Little Saigon beat (Anders 2000b). Another point of view is expressed by those editors who report good experiences with translators. They argue that being empathetic and enterprising is more important than being capable in any given language (Anders 2000c).

On April 4, 2001, Ted Kissell, associate editor, Broward-Palm Beach (Florida) *New Times,* confirmed Anders' report of a publisher-sponsored foreign-language study by noting that as a matter of company-wide policy applicable to its newspapers in twelve cities, New Times, Inc., will subsidize any course that contributes to enhanced work-related performance, including language study. He also notes that at the *Miami New Times,* one of the three editors is bilingual, as are six of the thirteen staff writers. Three of those six are of Hispanic descent.

Network News

A lack of diversity in network news staff and coverage is also notable. The National Association of Hispanic Journalists (NAHJ) prepares an annual "Network Brownout" report of network coverage of Latinos and issues affecting the nation's Latino community (Carveth and Alverio 1998). The report is jointly funded by the NAHJ and the National Council of La Raza. Highlights from the fifth annual report for 1998 include:

- ➡ Hispanics, more than 10 percent of the nation's population in 1997, were represented in just less than 1 percent of the country's network news stories.
- ➡ Hispanics appeared as experts in stories related to Hispanics five times.
- ➡ Of 12,000 news stories, only 112 focused on Latinos or Latino issues. The majority of this coverage was devoted to crime, immigration, and affirmative action.

A detailed summary of the report is available at the NAHJ Web site at http://www.nahj.org/noticias/brownout.htm.

Recap: The *Washington Post* online at http://www.washingtonpost.com/wp-dyn/articles/A24802–2001Apr16.html reports on the Pulitzer Prizes awarded in April 2001, and identifies two newspapers honored for their coverage of immigration-related themes. The *Portland Oregonian* won two Pulitzer Prizes and the public service medal for a series on abuses against undocumented immigrants. The *Miami Herald* won the breaking-news award for its coverage of the events leading to the removal of Elián González from the González home. These award winners demonstrate in their coverage of complex and controversial issues the standard that could be applied to articles regarding the education of language minority students, but rarely is.

A sound-bite approach to the presentation of news is not a form amenable to the exposition of complicated technical matters and not a fair way to inform the public on complicated matters of public policy. Access to information is a prerequisite to the rational discussion needed to identify facts, distinguish them from value orientations, and consider alternatives and consequences.

Although the media bears responsibility for bringing the coverage of language issues up to its high standards in other areas, the public could do much to correct the situation by demanding more thoughtful coverage. In this regard, educators and academics must also shoulder the responsibility for expanding their teaching beyond the confines of their classrooms and lecture halls and into the public forum.

BILINGUAL EDUCATION MYTHS

Given the limited access to comprehensive information about the complexities of bilingual education described in this chapter, it is understandable that many people might be confused about the topic. For that reason, several collections of "myths" have been developed over the years. Those collections are identified in Chapter 8.

To identify additional misperceptions surrounding language education currently in need of clarification, two samples of convenience were drawn. The members of each survey group were asked to write two statements about bilingual education. The first group surveyed included undergraduate and graduate preservice teachers enrolled in university courses during the fall 2001 semester. The second group was composed of in-service high school teachers. Members of both groups are residents of Florida, where a wide range of bilingual education programs have been institutionalized in the public schools over the past forty years, and frequently featured in the media. Since 1990, all teachers in the state have participated in training programs to prepare them for teaching duties with English-language learners as required by the consent decree in *LULAC v. Florida Board of Education.*

As expected, preservice and in-service teachers who have had firsthand contact with bilingual education were knowledgeable about it. Nevertheless, many misunderstandings occurred. Frequently, the respondents' misstatements either mistook the part for the whole or consisted of negative or positive overgeneralizations. The areas of confusion identified in the survey results follow, with a statement of clarification following each set of the respondents' comments.

Respondents' Comments Regarding Students

Respondents
Bilingual education is only for students who do not speak English; bilin-gual education is only for students who want to learn another language.

Clarification
Bilingual education programs have been developed to serve the needs of language minority students, or of language majority students, or to serve both sets of needs simultaneously. Bilingual education includes but is not limited to either of the circumstances cited above.

Respondents
Bilingual education is provided only for students in the United States; bilingual education is only for students in south Florida; bilingual edu-cation is only offered in big cities; bilingual education is only for immi-grant students.

Clarification
The respondents' statements in the preceding section would be more accurate if the word *only* were deleted from each sentence. Bilingual ed-ucation includes but is not limited to the categories cited above.

Respondents
As soon as a student learns English, he must transfer to an all-English-language program; the purpose of ESL programs is to mainstream the child as soon as possible; bilingual education is a temporary process; bilingual education is a way to assimilate immigrant children.

Clarification
Some districts have adopted assimilation goals and employed programs that often result in replacing the home language with the second lan-guage (English). In these districts, programs such as transitional bilin-gual education or ESL are implemented, and students do transfer from these programs when they meet the program exit criteria established by the district.

In other districts, acculturation and biliteracy goals are adopted. In these districts, the goal is for students to learn English and other con-tent areas; the addition goal is continued development of their home languages. Often, language majority students are also participants in this type of bilingual program. Although the allocation of time for study in the home or target language may change from year to year, continued study in and through that language is not contingent on the students' level of English-language proficiency.

Respondents
Bilingual education is better than ESL; it leads to mastery of two languages; bilingual education is the best way to teach students whose second language is English.

Clarification
In the United States, bilingual education programs for language minority students always include ESL components, and sometimes consist entirely of ESL components.

Several types of bilingual education (such as developmental, two-way, and bilingual immersion) can lead to the mastery of two languages if they are properly administered and adequately funded, employ appropriately trained teachers, and use linguistically and culturally appropriate instructional materials at grade level for a duration of time commensurate with the goal.

Respondents' Comments Regarding Teachers

Respondents
An ESL teacher must be bilingual; Hispanic teachers get all the jobs in bilingual education programs, even though not all English-language learners speak Spanish as the first language; many teachers are unwilling to participate in bilingual education programs.

Clarification
Bilingualism is an asset for the ESL teacher because it leads to greater understanding of second-language acquisition and aids communication with students and parents who speak the same languages as those spoken by the teacher. Demonstration of competence in a second language is often a requirement in doctoral programs in applied linguistics fields; however, it is rarely a prerequisite established by school districts for employment as an ESL teacher.

Hispanic and other teachers who are proficient in the Spanish language and trained in bilingual education may be employed in Spanish-English bilingual education programs. Hispanic and other teachers who are proficient in the English language and trained in ESL may be employed in ESL programs serving any language group. Hispanic and other teachers who are proficient in a language other than English and trained in bilingual education may be employed in bilingual education programs that correspond to their second (or third) language.

California's public schools enroll the most English-language learners and have the largest concentration of Hispanic children in the country. According to the California Department of Education Spring 1997 Language Census and CBEDS Reports, only 10.6 percent of California's teachers in 1996–1997 were Hispanic. More than 16,000 teachers reported that they use English-language learners' home languages to offer content instruction bilingually, but fewer than 11,000 were certified to do so in the 1998–1999 school year. Bilingual education teachers in that state could be on "interim assignment" while they worked toward a full bilingual credential. However, if they had not passed the language test as required for full certification, the district was required to place a bilingual aide in the class. In the 1996–1997 school year, 7,414 bilingual paraprofessionals were teamed with teachers in training. It seems likely, therefore, that 50 percent of the state's 14,410 bilingual education teachers were neither native speakers of students' home languages, including Spanish, nor proficient in those home languages.

The enthusiasm of bilingual education teachers for their work can be noted from such indicators as their participation at the annual conferences of NABE; more than 7,000 members attended the February 2001 conference. The critical shortage of bilingual education teachers is evidence that too few have acquired levels of bilingualism sufficient for instructional purposes. In the case of language minority teachers, the shortage of bilingual education teachers corresponds to the underrepresentation of language minority students in higher education.

The W. K. Kellogg Foundation's Engaging Latino Communities for Education (ENLACE) program, a six-year, $28 million effort to promote more educational opportunities for Latino youth, is an example of a national effort to graduate more Hispanics from college. See the Kellogg Web site for additional information on this project at http://www.wkkf.org/Initiatives/Initiative.asp?ID=25, and on its Native American Higher Education Initiative.

Respondents
The teacher should speak more loudly and more slowly to English-language learners; the teacher should assign a bilingual student to sit next to a new student from the same home-language group; bilingual education makes use of paraphrasing, modeling, pantomime, peer tutoring, and visuals to convey meaning to the students.

Clarification
Paraphrasing, modeling, pantomime, peer tutoring, adaptation of instructional materials, and use of visuals to convey meaning to the students are among the techniques used in ESL, foreign-language, or sheltered content classes. The crucial task for the teacher is not mere mastery of the techniques, but the acquisition of sufficient knowledge about the target and home languages and cultures to use these strategies appropriately. In content courses taught through the home language (bilingual education classes), meaning is conveyed directly, through that home language.

Speaking more loudly and slowly than is normal for conversational purposes distorts the language. Consider the difference between hearing the artificially articulated "Do-you-want-to-go?" compared with the typical enunciation of that phrase, "Dya wanna go?" If students learn only the artificial form, they will have difficulty understanding the authentic form. For additional information about recommended procedures in bilingual or ESL instruction, consult a second-language methods textbook, available in most university and commercial bookstores.

Respondents' Comments Regarding Programs

Respondents
Bilingual education was eliminated in California; bilingual education is funded by the state; bilingual education is federally mandated; bilingual education is offered by all schools in the United States.

Clarification
Prior to California voters' approval of Proposition 227 in 1998, 409,879 (29 percent) of the state's English-language learners received instruction in English Language Development (ELD) and Academic Subjects Through the Primary Language classes. An additional 305,764 received ELD and SDAIE with Primary Language Support classes in the 1997–1998 school year. According to reports available on the California Department of Education Web site at http://data1.cde.ca.gov/ dataquest/ ELPart2_ 1.asp, 169,929 (12 percent) of the students continue to receive instruction in ELD and Academic Subjects Through the Primary Language, and an additional 427,720 received ELD and SDAIE with Primary Language Support during the 1999–2000 school year. There are limited provisions under Proposition 227 regulations for parents to request waivers for their children from requirements for instruction delivered solely in English. Although enrollment in programs offering instruction in the home-language programs was reduced, bilingual education was not eliminated by California's Proposition 227.

Although some federal funding is available for bilingual education, those funds support only a few of the many programs in the country. In the United States, education is a state responsibility. Local school boards are established by authority of the state, which may delegate taxing authority to the boards. School boards typically have authority to approve budgets, and responsibility to provide public education in accordance with the laws of the state. States establish funding formulas to provide funds to school districts. Bilingual education acts have been passed in some states. In those states, and in states that have established a category in the school finance code for LEP students, state funds may be earmarked for those students and used to supplement district resources.

At the federal level, formula-based funding has been established to direct resources to low-income students. English-language learners in schools that meet the eligibility requirements may participate in programs such as Title I. Funding from the Bilingual Education Act is available through a competitive grant process for districts that choose to compete for such funding.

Federal antidiscrimination law requires school districts to take steps to provide LEP students with access to equal educational opportunity. This requirement means that school districts must provide English-language learners with instruction designed to teach English, and must provide access to other parts of the curriculum. Districts may comply with this requirement with a bilingual education program or with some other program that is based on a sound theory, receives adequate funding, and is properly evaluated. A court may require bilingual education in a specific situation, or state or district policy may require it, but there is no federal requirement for bilingual education. Bilingual education is not available at all schools. Some LEP students are not enrolled in any program designed to meet their special educational needs.

See Chapter 3 for additional information about district policies, and Chapter 5 for additional information about federal law.

Respondents
Bilingual education is also known as ESL; bilingual education is also known as immersion education.

Clarification
Various types of language immersion may be components of a bilingual program, but not all bilingual education programs include an immersion component. Bilingual education programs for language minority

students include ESL components. See Chapter 1 for additional information on the components of bilingual education.

Respondents
Bilingual education is considered to be special education; bilingual children are not necessarily less intelligent than students who are not enrolled in bilingual education.

Clarification
Some students (whether language majority or language minority) in bilingual education programs may also be eligible for special education services. These students are entitled to services that meet their special educational needs, just as they would be if they were in monolingual programs. Some students (whether language majority or language minority) in bilingual education programs may also be eligible to participate in programs for the gifted and talented. Some researchers, following the lead of Peal and Lambert (1962), have found metacognitive benefits associated with bilingualism.

Respondents
Students in bilingual education programs spend an equal amount of time studying each of two languages; bilingual education requires students to spend half a day learning with an English-speaking teacher and half a day learning with a Spanish-speaking teacher; bilingual education requires an alternate days approach: students study their own language one day and the second language the following day; instruction is given in two languages in a bilingual education classroom; it takes more time to teach less content; English-language-origin students resent it.

Clarification
Each of the five sentences in the preceding section may be an accurate description of some but not all bilingual programs. Overall, this set of responses demonstrates that even among those most knowledgeable about education (in-service and preservice teachers), there is a tendency to assume that the attributes and components of one specific example of a bilingual education program are also the attributes and components of all bilingual education programs.

Respondents' Comments Regarding Outcomes

Respondents
Bilingual education is not successful; it doesn't work; the school system should move away from ESL programs; the success rate is higher when

total immersion is used; I spoke only Greek when I started school; I was to-
tally immersed and learned the language well.

Clarification
Carefully conducted research studies have provided evidence that bilingual education is a useful and effective means for addressing language
learning needs of both language majority and minority students. For additional information on research findings regarding bilingual education, see the research summary presented in this chapter.

Many exceptional individuals have managed to acquire second
languages even under the worst of circumstances. For example, the
learning conditions in the 1940s and 1950s for language learning were
far from adequate. One indicator was that many LEP students dropped
out of school. As a partial solution to this problem, ESL programs were
initiated. In 1966, the professional organization for ESL teachers, Teachers of English to Speakers of Other Languages (TESOL), was organized
with the help of leaders of the National Council of Teachers of English
(NCTE). A decade later, bilingual education teachers organized the National Association for Bilingual Education (NABE), whose incorporation
in 1976 signaled the development of an additional tier of service in language education. The needs of English-language-origin students were
addressed by the National Defense Education Act of 1957, which provided funds for strengthening instruction in mathematics, science, and
foreign languages, areas deemed critically in need of improvement in
the flurry of reaction to the launching of Sputnik. More recently, the National Security Education Program was established in 1991 to help citizens of the United States understand foreign languages and cultures,
strengthen U.S. economic competitiveness, and enhance international
cooperation and security.

Respondents
Students need total immersion upon arriving in the country, the method
used in Israeli Absorption Centers; this method works for adults also.

Clarification
School and society in Israel and the United States are dissimilar in many
ways; nevertheless, it is useful to consider another country's approach.
Israel was established as a homeland and safe haven for Jews
after World War II. In 1950, the Israeli Knesset enacted the Law of Return; this law granted all Jews the right to immigrate to Israel. In 1970,
the Law of Return was amended to grant automatic citizenship not only

to Jews but also to their non-Jewish children, grandchildren, and spouses, and to the non-Jewish spouses of their children and grandchildren. The Minister of Immigration was directed to oversee the implementation of this law.

According to the Israeli Department of Immigration and Absorption, the Israeli Absorption Centers are part of a large-scale effort to invite immigrants to Israel and to be sure that every newcomer eligible under the provisions of the Law of Return finds housing, employment, access to instruction in the Hebrew language, and a support system. Aliyah representatives (resettlement counselors for those moving to the symbolic homeland) from the Israeli government are stationed in other countries to serve as conduits of information and assistance to those considering relocation to Israel.

Absorption Centers are managed by the Jewish Agency for Israel, whose function is to assist immigrants. The facilities at an Absorption Center for new arrivals include furnished apartments, clubrooms, recreation rooms or television lounges, and a synagogue. Some also have outdoor playing fields or garden areas and on-site day care. A cultural director in charge at the centers is in charge of planning social events, lectures, excursions, parties, and celebrations on holidays and national days. The Absorption Center staff also provides counseling on employment and other matters to help ease the new immigrant's integration into Israeli life. Grants and loan programs help immigrants to pay the fees for the Absorption Center's services. Residents in the facility are expected to enroll within eleven months of arrival in free language classes, typically offered at an Absorption Center. Students may be entitled to a modest living stipend while enrolled in those five-month-long classes. They are not expected to become fluent after one five-month course; additional courses are available on a sliding fee schedule. According to the 1995 *Israel Yearbook and Almanac,* fewer than half the students surveyed after completion of the course say they speak Hebrew at least "fairly well."

Both Hebrew and Arabic are official languages of Israel, though not co-equal in status. Arabic is the language of the major linguistic minority group in the country. Both are languages of instruction in the schools within their respective language zones, and both are required subjects in both zones.

According to Spolsky and Shohamy (n.d.), after consideration of the unfortunate loss of home-language resources of earlier immigrants, a new language education policy was established in 1996 to guide a shift from the previous primarily monolingual Hebrew-plus-English program to a policy that sanctions multilingualism and language maintenance. It may be that high dropout rates among immigrant students were also considered in developing a change in policy. A recent study by the Israeli Ministry of Education showed an extremely high dropout rate among immigrants. In the 1996–1997 school year, one-third of all seventeen-year-old immigrants were not in school (Hakuta 1998b).

Under the provisions of the new policy, new immigrants are encouraged to maintain their home languages while acquiring Hebrew, and students who have lived overseas for long periods may take high school exit examinations in languages other than the language of instruction. The new policy encourages the study of a third foreign language and the development of special language schools. English will continue to be a required subject as a first foreign language.

Under the terms of this "Three Plus" policy, it is compulsory for Jews to learn three languages (Hebrew, English, and Arabic) plus additional heritage, community, or world languages. Arabic, Hebrew, and English are also required for Arab students, who may choose to study any other additional language (Spolsky and Shohamy 1999).

Israel's prior monolingual language policy was not a representative case of efforts toward linguistic assimilation. The Arab minority (17 percent of Israel's population) was under no pressure to lose its mother tongue, nor was there an expectation of home-language replacement by Hebrew for other linguistic minority groups in that country. For immigrants who are Jews, however, the expectation is that such replacement will take place. "There is an ideology in Israel that people should natively speak a language associated with their own religion, not someone else's religion, and this is why Jews are pushed to switch to Hebrew while non-Jews are not" (Kheimets and Epstein 2000, n.d.).

Respondents' Comments Regarding Disadvantages of Bilingual Education

Respondents
Parents use bilingual education as a security blanket for their children; bilingual education can be used as an excuse to delay English proficiency.

Clarification
Students and parents feel more secure when their own language is used in the schools. These feelings of security and comfort are among the factors leading to the effectiveness of bilingual programs in teaching English, a goal highly sought by language minority parents for their children.

Evidence that immigrant students are learning English rapidly is provided by Rumbaut (1998) who reports that in 1995–1996, 79 percent of San Diego high school seniors who are immigrants or children of immigrants preferred to use English; the comparable figure for Miami was 95 percent.

Respondents' Comments Regarding Advantages of Bilingual Education

Respondents
If they have the advantage of participation in the bilingual education program, LEP students will succeed; English-language-origin students will acquire the language skills needed in today's society, giving them more opportunities in the future; it is the wave of the future.

Clarification
There are many reasons to share the optimism expressed in the preceding set of respondents' comments. At the same time, those expectations must be kept in check by the realization that schooling, by itself, has a limited effect on school outcomes. As Gallagher puts it (1998), education is a weak treatment, accounting for less than 25 percent of the total effect on any program outcome. A related observation is Glenn's (1997) admonition that bilingual education possesses no magic answer to the challenge of educating children at risk. With specific reference to language education, Fishman (1994) reminds us that schools only really succeed in teaching those things for which there is ample societal support. More specifically, DeVoretz and Werner (2000) identify the labor market as the primary determinant of language-learning outcomes. Zentella (1986) notes a cyclical expansion and retraction in the extent of foreign-language competence in the United States. The standing of the United States in language education in any given period is related to military or economic challenges facing the nation, our tendency to accept or reject the nations or ethnic groups associated with specific foreign languages, and the treatment accorded to language minority speakers. These admonitions are intended to shield the enthusiast from disappointment if the potential of bilingual education is not immediately realized, and to offer as modest solace the reminder that the pendulum has swung many times before in our history, and is likely to do so again. See Chapter 2 for a listing of key events in the history of language education in the United States.

Recap: The first two parts of this section included a review of research on bilingual education and an analysis of media coverage of language issues, both factors affecting the formation of public opinion about language matters. A review and response to currently popular myths, whose persistence is attributable at least in part to constricted access to information about bilingual education, was presented in the third part of this section.

LANGUAGE LEGISLATION IN THE UNITED STATES

Arguments for and against restrictive language legislation in the United States will be presented in this section, along with a brief report on the status of English Only laws. Predictions about the effects of selected language policies will be compared with reports on the outcomes of those policies as implemented in other countries.

English Only and English Plus

As Zentella (1986) noted about the recurrent expansion and retraction in the extent of foreign-language competence in the United States, public opinion and legislative support for restrictive or expansive language legislation are also cyclical. The alternating themes of hospitality and hostility are linked to changes in public opinion about immigration and national identity. Immigrants have fallen out of favor in line with changes in the proportion or composition of the immigrant population, during transitions to newcomers of an area's economic or political ascendancy, in times of major economic downturns, and with each new set of foreign enemies in times of war. Immigrants have been welcomed as potential "real Americans" when their labor was needed, in appreciation for their support in times of war, and when their admission and treatment had a favorable impact on world opinion about the United States. The phases in the cycle of attraction and repulsion coincident with the rejection of immigrants often included sporadic outbursts of bigotry. The historical evidence indicates, therefore, that legislation restricting immigration and linguistic diversity could be expected to enjoy popularity in any given area until the majority no longer considers its immigrant residents atypical, related to foreign enemies, or an economic or political threat.

Several characteristics of contemporary society support an expectation of expanded language rights, however. Chief among them is commitment to civil and human rights. Additional support for expansion of language rights and bilingual programs stems from:

➥ *School finance reform.* The evolution of the courts' positions on reforming school finance systems has resulted in increased funding for districts with language minority students. The most recent cases have linked standards reform to adequate funding. Both aspects of current school finance litigation seem likely to channel more resources to education programs for English-language learners.

↠ *Education reform.* Many school reform measures include requirements for the publication of information about the standing of schools and districts on statewide testing programs. Other measures require the disaggregation of scores for English-language learners. The cumulative effect of developments directing attention to the achievement levels of LEP students, coupled with the availability of funding as a result of school finance litigation, may be increased reliance on home-language support in instructional programs.

↠ *Globalization.* An additional factor that can be expected to limit the spread of nativist positions arises from their inherent conflict with achieving the economic goals of the United States. Achievement of these goals requires markets for goods in the global economy and a workforce both for highly skilled and for often-avoided jobs. Immigrants fill positions in both types of occupations. Commercial transactions between countries are eased by cordial relations with trading partners (a status affected by the treatment accorded each country's immigrants to the United States) and by bilingual intermediaries (stimulating demand for a biliterate workforce).

↠ *Demographic trends and political influence.* The influence of language minority group members (in solid majority opposed to English Only legislation and in favor of bilingual education) on the political process is bound to grow as their numbers increase. For the first time, for example, Spanish-language campaign materials were distributed by both major candidates in the 2000 presidential election campaign. The numbers of language minority voters and of language minority elected officials have both grown. According to the National Association of Latino Elected and Appointed Officials (NALEO), in June 1999, there were 4,966 Latino elected officials in the United States. Hispanics serve as members of Congress, state legislatures, city and county councils, and school boards. June 2001 saw several large cities with Hispanic mayors (Miami and San Antonio, for example), and two of the largest cities now have Hispanic candidates for mayor (Los Angeles and New York). Asian Americans serve on many levels of government, primarily in California and the northwest states. California has two Asian congressmen. In 1996, Gary Locke was elected governor of the state of Washington, becoming the first Asian American governor on the U.S. mainland. Minnesota elected a South Asian to the state senate. New York City has Chinese American representation. A Haitian American has been elected to the Florida legislature. Haitian Americans have been elected as mayors in two cities in south Florida (the village of El Portal and North Miami). American Indians have held office at several levels of government, including the United States Senate. Several hold office as state legislators in New Mexico. Also in New Mexico, an Indian rights activist has announced his intention to run for governor in 2002.

•➤ *Growth of coalitions.* Latino political solidarity in the 1990s was promoted by resistance to California's Propositions 187 and 227. As these measures made clear the connections between immigrant rights and social justice issues, the backlash also paved the way for renewed efforts at coalition-building among immigrant and minority groups, with labor unions, and with faith-based organizations.

Quiroz-Martinez's (2001) summary of successful multiethnic and multiracial grassroots coalitions includes examples from California, Georgia, Illinois, Kansas, Oregon, and Texas, where Latinos and African Americans jointly opposed guest-worker program expansion and supported immigrant amnesty, living-wage, and health care initiatives. In Oregon, Latinos and their allies from a wide spectrum of social justice groups prevailed in opposing efforts to replicate English Only measures. In ten states, campaigns for access to driver's licenses for undocumented immigrants were successful. An ongoing campaign is in progress for changes in state tuition rules to provide access to higher education for undocumented graduates of high schools in the United States. African American participation in demonstrations against continuation of naval bombing exercises at Vieques, Puerto Rico, is an example of high-profile coalition efforts also taking place.

Possible Responses to Diversity

Language policy in a country with immigrant or minority populations can be based on four types of majority responses to diversity (Inglis 1996). The policy goals associated with those responses may be:

1. The *expulsion or removal* of ethnic minorities. The Immigration Act of 1924 (whose quota system limited Italian and Jewish immigration to the United States), the forced relocation of the Georgia Cherokee (the journey known as the Trail of Tears), and the Chinese Exclusion Acts (barring immigration to the United States and eligibility for citizenship for Chinese and later other Asian groups) are examples of implementation of this policy goal.
2. The *elimination of contact* with ethnic minorities, and if needed, the establishment of parallel institutions to serve those excluded from access to mainstream services. Jim Crow laws (officially sanctioned discrimination against or segregation of African Americans during the period between the abolition of slavery and the civil rights movement, almost a century later) illustrate policy based on differentiation goals.
3. The *assimilation* of the immigrant or minority population contingent on their elimination of distinctive linguistic, cultural, and social characteristics. It is assumed that as individuals divest themselves of markers of their minority status, conflict based on ethnicity will cease to exist. Implementation of policies based on this goal requires no change in the practices of mainstream institutions. This is the position closest to that of advocates for English Only laws, and for English-only education for language minority students.
4. The *incorporation* into mainstream society of immigrant and minority populations who are enabled to keep (or lose, if they so choose) their cultural distinctiveness. This process of *adding* an additional set of cultural and linguistic skills, rather than *replacing* those first acquired, is referred to as acculturation. Multiculturalist policies derived from this goal are based on the assumption that the process of full participation is the key to eradicating ethnic conflict. Implementation of the option requires extensive changes in the practices of mainstream institutions to provide equally for those from different cultural and linguistic backgrounds. This is the position closest to those who advocate for English Plus legislation and for bilingual education.

Options 3 and 4 (assimilation or multicultural incorporation, English Only, or English Plus) are featured in most contemporary arguments in the United States on language legislation.

English Only

English Only is the term used to refer to legislation that establishes English as the official language of the United States or any of its jurisdictions, or as the only language government officials and agencies may use to carry out their work. The hyphenated term *English-only* is used in this chapter to refer to instructional options that employ the English language exclusively or almost exclusively.

U.S.ENGLISH, Inc., describes itself as the nation's oldest, largest citizens' action group dedicated to preserving the unifying role of the English language in the United States. It was founded in 1983 by the late Senator S. I. Hayakawa. On April 27, 1981, Senator Hayakawa introduced the first Official English measure (a proposed amendment to the Constitution of the United States) to be considered by Congress. The lobbying group's Web site, http://www.us-english.org/inc/default.asp, presents 1990 Census Bureau data reporting that 329 languages are spoken in the United States; it also reports that 97 percent of Americans speak English "well" or "very well." The nearly universal level of English-language proficiency does not support fears that English is a threatened language in the United States.

Assurance is provided in the organization's Web site materials that Official English legislation contains commonsense exceptions permitting the use of languages other than English for such things as public health and safety services, translations of judicial proceedings, foreign-language instruction, and the promotion of tourism. Chen (1995), however, comments that even if an Official English law were purely symbolic, its effect would be to exacerbate societal discord and ethnic tension because the message that underlies the symbolism is pejorative of immigrants.

As noted by Chen (1995), from 1980 to 1998, English-only laws have been interpreted to impose severe restrictions on the use of languages other than English by government employees and officials. In Dade County, Florida, he reminds us, passage of an Anti-Bilingualism Ordinance resulted in a prohibition on distributing bilingual materials on fire prevention, publishing Metrorail schedules in foreign languages, providing consumer information in Spanish, and giving prenatal advice in Haitian Creole at the county hospital.

Almost twenty years later, in *Ruiz v. Hull*, the Arizona Supreme Court ruled that the Official English amendment to the state constitution approved by voters in 1998 was unconstitutional. The amendment stated that English is the official language of the state of Arizona and that the state and its political subdivisions, including all government officials and employees performing government business, must "act" only in English.

The court held that the amendment violates the First Amendment to the United States Constitution because it adversely impacts the constitutional rights of non-English-speaking persons with regard to their obtaining access to their government and limits the political speech of elected officials and public employees. The court also held that the amendment violates the Equal Protection Clause of the Fourteenth Amendment to the United States Constitution because it unduly burdens core First Amendment rights of a specific class without materially advancing a legitimate state interest. The decision is available in full text online at http://www.supreme.state.az.us/opin/pdf98/cv960493.pdf.

CURRENT STATUS OF OFFICIAL LANGUAGE LEGISLATION

English First is a grassroots lobbying organization that supports official English legislation. According to the Issues and Legislation section of the organization's Web site at http://capwiz.com/ef/issues/?search.x=20&search.y=7, three Official English bills were pending in Congress on April 21, 2001:

1. (H.R. 280) The National Language Act of 2001 would repeal the Bilingual Education Act, make English the official language of the U.S. government, and require the government to conduct its official business in English, including publications, income tax forms, and informational materials.
2. H.J. RES. 16) An English Language Amendment Bill to the Constitution to make English the official language of the United States.
3. (H.R. 969) A bill to nullify Executive Order 13166 (Improving Access to Services for Persons with Limited English Proficiency).

According to U.S.ENGLISH, Inc., twenty-six states have enacted Official English laws. English First reports that although twenty-three states have passed such laws, only twenty are still in effect. English First does not include Hawaii, New Mexico, Oregon, and Rhode Island among the twenty-three states listed because Hawaii is officially bilingual and the other three states have passed English Plus resolutions. James Crawford's language policy Web site at http://ourworld.compuserve.com/homepages/JWCRAWFORD/langleg.htm includes reference to twenty-one states that have passed Official English legislation since 1981 and four that adopted such provisions prior to that year.

Crawford's site also identifies the states with pending language legislation. By April 21, 2001, language legislation had been introduced during 2000–2001 in four states:

- In Iowa, legislation declaring English the official language of government was pending.
- In Massachusetts, English Only legislation patterned after California's Proposition 227 and Arizona's Proposition 203 was pending.
- In New York, a bill proposing a constitutional amendment declaring English the official language of New York and a bill to establish English as the language of government in the state were pending.
- In Oregon, English Only legislation patterned after California's Proposition 227 and Arizona's Proposition 203 was pending.

Example of Official English Legislation

Utah's initiative petition for an official state language, titled Initiative A, was approved by the voters in 2000 and survived constitutional challenge in 2001. The Third District Court in Utah held that the law was a symbolic gesture of no constitutional consequence that would not discriminate against those who want to communicate with government officials or employees. The text of the proposition is available in the online version of the Utah Code at http://www.le.state.ut.us/~code/code.htm. The first four sections of the law follow.

> Official state language: (1) English is declared to be the official language of Utah. (2) As the official language of this State, the English language is the sole language of the government, except as otherwise provided in this section. (3) Except as provided in Subsection (4), all official documents, transactions, proceedings, meetings, or publications issued, conducted, or regulated by, on behalf of, or representing the state and its political subdivisions shall be in English. (4) Languages other than English may be used when: (1) required by the United States Constitu-

tion, the Utah State Constitution federal law, or federal regulation; (2) required by law enforcement or public health and safety needs; (3) required by public and higher-education systems according to rules made by the State Board of Education and the State Board of Regents to comply with Subsection (5); (4) required in judicial proceedings, when necessary to insure that justice is served; (5) required to promote and encourage tourism and economic development, including the hosting of international events such as the Olympics; and (6) required by libraries to: (1) collect and promote foreign-language materials; and (2) providing foreign-language services and activities.

Section 4 of Utah's measure contains many of the provisions U.S.ENGLISH calls "common sense exceptions" permitting government use of languages other than English for such things as public health and safety services. On March 5, 2001, U.S.ENGLISH. Chairman Mauro E. Mujica released a press release expressing delight at the court's decision to uphold Initiative A, interpreting that decision as recognition that the Official English measure respects the fundamental rights of all citizens of Utah. On March 15, Mr. Mujica released a press release in which he chided Utah's Attorney General Mark Shurtleff for making light of the Official English law by holding a session with members of the Hispanic community conducted almost entirely in Spanish. Mr. Shurtleff called that session a "pretend" meeting. According to Utah's Official English legislation, official meetings must be conducted in English. Both press releases are available in full text online at http://www.us-english.org/inc/news/preleases/.

The English Only groups seem to be caught on the horns of a dilemma. If they succeed in gaining passage of legislation that meets their goals, the courts may overturn it, as they did in the case of the constitutional amendment adopted by voter initiative in Arizona. If, however, they gain passage of legislation that is sufficiently riddled with exemptions to pass the scrutiny of the courts, as in the case of Utah's law, they gain very few of their objectives. Why bother? And why so much emphasis by U.S.ENGLISH and by English First on counting the number of states that have passed English Only legislation?

The first English Only measure considered by Congress was a proposed amendment to the Constitution of the United States. That bill failed. Few proposals for constitutional amendments succeed, perhaps because of the difficulty involved in meeting the requirements for the amendment process. Article V of the Constitution defines a two-phase amendment process. Proposed amendments must be approved with a two-thirds majority vote in each of the two houses of Congress, and must be ratified by three-fourths of the states. The more states that have adopted English Only legislation, the greater the encouragement provided to Congress to reconsider an English Only amendment to the Constitution, an amendment that could subsequently become the law of the land. It makes sense, therefore, for language restrictionists to celebrate the passage of any English Only law, no matter how weakened, and for English Plus advocates to resist even symbolic versions of those laws.

Position Statement

This review of the rationale for and current status of English Only legislation concludes with a summary of "Welcoming Immigrants to a Diverse America: English as Our Common Language of Mutual Understanding" issued June 5, 1996, by the House Republican Policy Committee. It presents the position of restrictive-language legislation campaigns and of its assimilationist philosophy, couched in terms appropriated from civil rights discourse. To preserve the flavor as well as the substance of the authors' key points, the summary is composed of selected text from the document, its sentences rearranged from the original to maintain the logic of the argument in the abridged version that follows.

Welcoming Immigrants to a Diverse America: English as Our Common Language of Mutual Understanding

The use of English is indispensable to immigrants and their children who wish to participate fully in American society and realize the American Dream.

The experience of two other immigrant nations—Canada and Israel—offers us clear lessons on just how powerful a force language can be in either uniting or dividing a people. Canada chose to make both English and French its official languages. The evidence is clear: That experiment is a horrid failure. Israel's insistence on Hebrew as the national language insures that the children of immigrants quickly become Hebrew speakers first, and speakers of their parents' language second. By stressing a single, unifying language, Israel has built a strong, cohesive society—despite the amazingly diverse composition of its people. Many people do not realize that, while English is our common language, government at all levels is actively undermining its unifying function. Today, American taxes are being spent so that people who cannot understand or communicate in English can nonetheless receive ballots to vote in Filipino, Vietnamese, or Chinese. Federal government job announcements frequently invite applications from people with limited English skills. Bilingual-education programs often require teaching children in their native language and discourage the learning of English. These programs are a shameful example of the damage to our society caused by official multilingualism. They are wasteful, discriminatory, and too often produce children who are illiterate in any language. The simple truth is that those who cannot function in our country's predominant language are less able to find jobs. As a result, they are cheated of the opportunity for improvement and happiness that America promises to millions.

The lesson for America should be clear. English is our common language, which has enabled us to become and remain the United States of America. We need only ensure that we do not lose it by neglect or inaction. English should be and remain the official language of our national government.

The document is available in full text on the English First Web site at http://www.englishfirst.org/english/goppol.htm.

Additional Arguments for Language Legislation

Syndicated columnist and radio commentator Phyllis Schlafly of the Eagle Forum tersely summarized the sentiments expressed above with this line: "You can't be an American if you don't speak English." For more on this, see the Web site at http://www.englishfirst.org/schafley.htm. This conclusion is similar to that of ProjectUSA, whose members believe that no human can be multicultural; see the Web site at http://www.projectusa.com/Arguments/argument4.html.

Arguments in support of language or immigration restriction sometimes focus directly on immigration rather than on language or culture. For example, the *Alamance Independent* (New York) observes that illegal immigration is not a victimless crime, and describes scuffles between Farmingville, New York, teens and undocumented day workers who have "infested the town" to make its point clear. Mixed reports of the incidents include claims of taunting insults by the teenagers countered by claims that the day workers stole their bicycles and sexually molested the girls. The conclusion of the *Independent* is that easygoing coexistence with a large illegal-alien population is impossible. See http://www.alamanceind.com/immig/immig_2.html for the full text of the article.

In Brimelow's *Alien Nation: Common Sense About America's Immigration Disaster,* the point is made that too many immigrants differ from the population norm in the United States, which is predominantly

European in origin. He expresses his fear that the immigrants' presence in the United States transforms and could ultimately destroy our national identity, economic preeminence, and social harmony. Among his recommendations for reform: Competency in the English language should be made a requirement for immigrants, and the Constitution should be amended so that the children of illegal immigrants born on U.S. soil do not automatically become citizens of the United States.

This same point of view was expressed over the Fourth of July weekend in 1998: Population projections appeared in the press that in two years, Whites would be the minority group in California, and in fifty years, in the country. Jonathan Tilgrove of the *Times* Washington Bureau observed that by the middle of the twenty-first century, a nation conceived by White people and for White people would be, according to the best estimates, less than half White; for more on this, see the Web site at http://bc.mlive.com/news/daytwo.htm. He questions the country's ability to maintain democratic traditions without the White majority from whose culture they sprang.

Another dimension of the discussion is expressed by language majority persons who are tired of dealing with sales clerks who assume that everyone understands the language of the minority language group in areas with large immigrant populations. They complain that hearing the minority language is exasperating and rude, a complaint that frequently surfaces in the workplace. The investigations conducted by the Equal Employment Opportunity Commission (EEOC) to determine whether workplace language incidents are violations of civil rights are also the object of criticism as unwarranted interference with private enterprise.

Although spokespersons for Official English organizations maintain that the only anti-immigrant attitudes are those created by opposition to Official English legislation and resistance to assimilation, some of the arguments presented in the preceding part of this section seem more representative of exclusion or elimination policy options than of assimilation goals.

English Plus

English Plus is a term used to signal opposition to English Only legislation and to English-only limitations to education programs. Opponents of those provisions support full access to instruction leading to English competence for everyone in this country, and also advocate for the development of skills in multiple languages and in content areas in addition to language. This emphasis on education is understandable, given the genesis of the expression.

The term was coined in Florida by Paul Cejas, then a member of the Dade County School Board. It was used as part of the recurring refrain (Not English Only, English *Plus!*) in a hastily authored and mimeographed position paper drafted in 1985 by the director of the University of Miami LAU Center under the auspices of the education committee of a Miami community-based organization. Intended as a primer for advocates, it was prepared in response to statements about bilingual education made by former secretary of education William Bennett (Bennett 1985). The paper (Education Committee 1985) was widely distributed by the Spanish American League Against Discrimination (SALAD) Education Committee to bilingual educators and community-based activists in several states. The quick popularity of the title phrase among the recipients is testament to their pent-up exasperation at a long series of provocations. According to Combs (1992), this document played a role in mobilizing resistance to restrictive language legislation and led to the establishment in 1987 of the English Plus Information Clearinghouse (EPIC), an organization sponsored by the Joint National Council on Languages (JNCL) and the National Immigration, Refugee, and Citizenship Forum, with the support of over fifty civil rights and education-association organizational members. Two sections from the SALAD document follow to illustrate the English Plus position on bilingual education (Section 3) and on language legislation (Section 15).

> Spanish-American League Against Discrimination (SALAD) Education Committee, October 15, 1985, Miami, Florida.
> NOT ENGLISH ONLY, ENGLISH *PLUS!*
> Bilingual Education Issue Analysis
> 3) Secretary of Education Bennett fears that "we have lost sight of the goal of learning *English* as key to equal educational opportunity" (Bennett 26 Sept. 1985, 6).
>
> We fear that Secretary Bennett has lost sight of the fact that English is *a* key to equal educational opportunity, necessary but not sufficient. English by itself is not enough. NOT ENGLISH ONLY, ENGLISH *PLUS!* Bennett is wrong. We won't accept English Only for our children. We want English plus. English plus math. Plus science. Plus social studies. Plus equal educational opportunities. English plus competence in the home language. Tell Bennett to enforce bilingual education and civil rights laws you enacted, or tell the President he cannot do his job. English *Plus!* for everyone!
> 15) "Our common forefathers speak to us through the ages in English."
> My forefathers did not speak English, nor did my *foremothers.* Neither did the ancestors of Native Americans, Puerto Ricans, Hispanics in the

Southwest and California territories, the French in the Louisiana Territory, the Germans in the Midwest, or the Asians, Italians, Poles, Greeks,
Arabs, or Afro-Americans throughout this nation. Linguistic chauvin-
ism has no place in today's interdependent world and receives no support from American patriots.

As the Honorable Baltazar Corrada, Resident Commissioner from
Puerto Rico noted, "America is great not because we speak one language or other but because we are united by the fundamental principles that bind our people together: freedom, justice, equal opportunity
for all, fairness, democracy." To say that we make our country stronger
because we make it "U.S. English" is like saying that we make it
stronger by making it "U.S. White." It is as insidious to base the strength
or unity of the United States in one language as it is to base that
strength or unity in one race. A Spanish-speaking American can be as
patriotic as an English-speaking American just like a black American
can be as patriotic as a white American. When *Jimmy Lopez* was held
hostage in Iran for more than one year together with other Americans,
he wrote an inscription in his cell: *Viva la Roja, Blanca y Azul [Long live
the Red, White, and Blue]*. Today, I repeat here: *Viva la Roja, Blanca y
Azul!* (remarks on Senate Joint Resolution 167, June 12, 1984, 8).
NOT ENGLISH ONLY, ENGLISH *PLUS!*

This account illustrates political roles played in language legislation controversies by government officials, members of community-
based and civil rights organizations, and educators.

Current Status of English Plus Legislation

James Crawford's Web site on language policy at http://ourworld.
compuserve.com/homepages/JWCRAWFORD/langleg.htm includes
reference to one bill pending in Congress in April 2001: (H. CON. RES. 9)
An English Plus Resolution in opposition to English Only initiatives and
in support of expanding opportunities for language proficiency in English and in other languages.

Example of English Plus Legislation

In 1989, the New Mexico legislature passed House Joint Memorial 16, a
nonbinding resolution. According to James Crawford, this was the first
state adoption of an English Plus resolution. Links to this measure, and
similar legislation from other states, are available in full text at the language policy section of his Web site at http://ourworld.compuserve.

com/homepages/JWCRAWFORD/LL.htm. The New Mexico resolution, as reprinted in *Language Loyalties* (1992), follows.

> Supporting Language Rights in the United States
>
> WHEREAS the people of New Mexico promote the spirit of diversity-with-harmony represented by the various cultures that make up the fabric of our state and American society; and
>
> WHEREAS the people of New Mexico acknowledge that "English Plus" best serves the national interest since it promotes the concept that all members of our society have full access to opportunities to effectively learn English plus develop proficiency in a second or multiple languages; and
>
> WHEREAS the people of New Mexico recognize that the position of English in the United States needs no official legislation to support it; and
>
> WHEREAS the people of New Mexico recognize that for survival in the twenty-first century our country needs both the preservation of the cultures and languages among us and the fostering of proficiency in other languages on the part of its citizens;
>
> NOW THEREFORE BE IT RESOLVED . . . that the First Session of the Thirty-Ninth Legislature of the State of New Mexico hereby reaffirms its advocacy of the teaching of other languages in the United States and its belief that the position of English is not threatened. Proficiency on the part of our citizens in more than one language is to the economic and cultural benefit of our state and the nation, whether that proficiency derives from second language study by English speakers or from home language maintenance plus English acquisition by speakers of other languages. Proficiency in English plus other languages should be encouraged throughout the State.

Position Statements

Three brief statements in support of English Plus positions are presented in this section. The first, from TESOL, addresses the role of native-language proficiency in acquiring a second language. The second, from the American Civil Liberties Union (ACLU), stresses civil rights aspects of language rights issues. The third, from the Council of Great City Schools (CGCS), speaks to the harmful and divisive effects of restricting program options available to local school systems that serve limited English proficient children.

TESOL

In December 1999, the Board of Directors of Teachers of English to Speakers of Other Languages (TESOL) approved a statement, adapted from TESOL's ESL Standards for Pre-K-12 Students (1997), declaring that full proficiency in the native language facilitates second-language development. TESOL' s statement is unequivocal:

> Use of ESOL students' native languages, especially if they are literate in that language, promotes learners' academic achievement while they are acquiring the English needed to benefit fully from instruction through English. . . . Native-language literacy skills—whether in English or another language—are necessary for successful second-language development.

The full text of the statement is available at http://www.tesol.org/assoc/statements/nativelangsupport.html.

ACLU

On December 5, 1995, Laura W. Murphy, director; Gregory T. Nojeim, legislative counsel; and Edward M. Chen, staff counsel of the American Civil Liberties Union of Northern California; sent a letter urging opposition to several pending English Only bills to the United States House of Representatives Committee on Economic and Educational Opportunities Subcommittee on Early Childhood, Youth, and Families. The following excerpts identify the civil liberties implications of "Official English" legislation.

> English Only bills would infringe upon important constitutional rights and legitimize and encourage discrimination against language-minority residents. Such bills could interfere with the right to vote by banning bilingual ballots, or with the education of the nation's children by restricting instruction in a language that immigrant children can understand. In addition, legislation that mandates court and administrative proceedings in English only would severely jeopardize the ability of non-English speakers to understand the proceedings. The impact on our elderly citizens, many of whom need not learn English as a condition of citizenship and for whom acquisition of English language proficiency is not a real possibility, cannot be overstated. We urge you to oppose English Only legislation.

The full text of the letter is available at http://www.aclu.org/congress/chen.html.

CGCS

The third and final position statement included in this section reflects the opinion of the Council of Great City Schools (CGCS), a coalition of fifty-six large city school districts. Its mission is to promote the cause of urban schools and to advocate for inner-city students through legislation, research, and media relations. The officers of the organization are school board members and superintendents of schools. This is not an association of bilingual educators, but of educational policymakers. They object to English Only legislation as an impediment to implementation of sound education programs and as policy that is divisive, exclusionary, and harmful to schools. The full text of the March 24, 1996, CGCS resolution is available at http://www.cgcs.org/services/onissues/resol11.htm.

> Resolution: English Only, March 24, 1996, Washington, D.C.,
> WHEREAS,
> the several bills have been introduced in the U.S. Congress to make English the official language of the United States; and WHEREAS, the issue of an official U.S. language is likely to be raised as an issue in the Presidential campaign and the political campaigns of candidates for Congress and Senate; and WHEREAS, the issue often has a divisive effect on the public and does not meet with the inclusive spirit and vision of a democratic and diverse society; and WHEREAS, the passage and implementation of such legislation could restrict the program options that local school systems have for limited English proficient children; and WHEREAS, such legislation could have a harmful effect on the ability of school systems to communicate with and involve parents who do not yet speak English; THEREFORE, LET IT BE RESOLVED THAT the Council of the Great City Schools opposes federal legislation that mandates that English is the official U.S. language; AND FURTHER THAT the Council of the Great City Schools opposes such legislation that may appear in state legislatures and on state ballots.

Implementation in Other Countries

The final part of this review of language legislation includes a summary of responses to diversity in several countries prepared by Inglis (1996) for the United Nations Educational, Scientific, and Cultural Organization (UNESCO). This chapter's summary of the effect of the implementation of multicultural policies in two countries may provide an additional perspective from which to examine the issues of language diversity. The two countries, Australia and Canada, like the United

States, are countries historically based on immigration and currently receiving immigrants. In all three countries, immigrants may become naturalized citizens.

Australia

The majority population of Australia, like that of the United States, is of European origin. Like the United States, assimilation was the goal of its diversity policies. The assimilation model came under increasing attack as a factor leading to the alienation and marginalization of ethnic minority group members. Shortly before the 1980s, integration goals began to predominate. This policy distinguished private from public life, assuming that cultural traditions might be retained in the private sphere but would have no place in the public institutions of Australia. In the 1980s, Australia began adopting a multiculturalist policy to manage ethnic diversity.

The policy's first phase reflected concerns about disadvantages faced by many non-English-speaking immigrants. During this phase, cultural and linguistic maintenance was fostered and the government concentrated on providing linguistically and culturally appropriate services and education. In the second phase, racism, community relations, and structurally based social disadvantage were the primary issues. This shift in emphasis coincided with efforts to overcome the inequities affecting the country's minorities, the disabled, and women, as well as those affecting immigrants with a non-English-speaking background. Policy changes intended to foster social justice were codified in the 1989 National Agenda for a Multicultural Australia.

The concept of economic efficiency is an important aspect of multiculturalism in Australia. Stress is placed on the ways cultural diversity contributes to the economic development of Australia and thereby benefits all Australians. General understanding of the competitive advantage afforded by using the professional, linguistic, and cultural talents of all Australians grew hand-in-hand with national acceptance of policies of multiculturalism. Inglis (1996) noted the absence of extensive intergroup conflict between majority and minority populations or among minority or immigrant populations resulting from a policy of multiculturalism in Australia.

Canada

In the United States, Canada is often used as an example of the divisive potential of multilingualism. Many scholars agree, however, that conflict between French and English speakers in Canada is a reaction to historic economic, political, and cultural inequalities (Chen 1995), alleviated, not exacerbated, by the recognition of French as a co-official language. Canadians seem satisfied with the results of their language policy because they did not choose to move from a 100-year-old bilingual and bicultural policy to a monolingual policy. Instead, in 1971, they adopted an official policy of multiculturalism (Inglis 1996) to supplement the provisions of their dual-language charters. As in the case of Australia, they were motivated to move to multiculturalism because preexisting assimilation models for those who were not members of the country's English- or French-speaking communities were failing.

The first phase of policy implementation was directed to preserve minority culture and ethnicity as part of Canadian national identity. In a subsequent phase, the emphasis shifted to resolution of issues of inequality, unity, and social disadvantage. Canada's policy of multiculturalism was supported by the 1982 Charter of Rights and Freedoms. This enactment prohibited discrimination on the basis of race, national or ethnic origin, color, or religion. In 1988, the Multiculturalism Act was passed. This measure included two main provisions (Inglis 1996):

1. All members of Canadian society are free to preserve and share their cultural heritages; their cultures and ancestral languages should be protected and enhanced.
2. All federal institutions should promote policies, programs, and practices that ensure that Canadians of all origins have an equal opportunity to obtain employment and advancement in those institutions. Such policies should also enhance the understanding of and respect for the diversity of the members of Canadian society.

In both Canada and Australia, programs have been established to ensure that children have opportunities to learn the national and home languages to a reasonable level of competence. Minority language initiatives were given importance as a means of cultural maintenance and as ways to provide access to mainstream society. In Australia, for example, the Translating and Interpreting Service (TIS) provides a nationwide telephone service, twenty-four hours a day, seven days a week, for both emergency and nonemergency access to interpreters. The multilingual Special Broadcasting Service (SBS) provides radio and television broadcasts in more than sixty languages.

Summary

Drawing on Inglis's (1996) assessment of the experience of Australia and Canada in implementation of multiculturalist policies to incorporate diverse groups into mainstream society, the following conclusions emerge:

- ⇥ In contradiction of those who hope that bilingual education will solve all problems (as do some advocates of English Plus policies in the United States), the experience in Australia and Canada was that neither education nor special language services alone ensure access to government services or eliminate structural disadvantage. Issues of racism and discrimination in areas such as employment and housing must also be addressed directly.
- ⇥ Multiculturalist management of diversity in Australia and Canada made clear the aim of providing meaningful choice. Immigrant and minority populations were neither forced to assimilate nor forced into ethnically separate sectors of society.
- ⇥ Both countries emphasized rights as well as obligations in their statements of diversity policies.
- ⇥ In contradiction of the critics of multiculturalist policies (such as English Only groups in the United States), implementation of those policies in Australia and Canada has resulted in limited evidence of interethnic conflict. On the contrary, opportunities for ethnic minority groups to participate fully in society without sacrificing their ethnic identity have been a factor instrumental in encouraging high commitment to their country. At the same time, majority group members, although in some instances contesting these policies, have generally accepted what has proved to be a durable model for managing diversity in light of its benefits for all members of society.
- ⇥ Institutionalization of diversity policies was aided by the private sector. Australia and Canada harnessed economic motivations to encourage the adoption of multiculturalism among business entities seeking advantages in gaining markets or in using the culturally based skills of their employees.
- ⇥ In contradiction of those who hold that a democratic majority is inherently opposed to the rights of minority groups, the experience of Australia and Canada in gaining consensus on diversity issues has demonstrated that although such a goal is challenging, it is certainly obtainable.

CONCLUSION

The overall purpose of this chapter has been to identify major political issues related to linguistic diversity and to summarize associated bodies of knowledge. The crux of the chapter is the consideration of two alternative policy goals for the incorporation of ethnic minority groups into mainstream society: assimilation and acculturation. Current policies in the United States, mostly based on an assimilationist model, have contributed to undesirable consequences, such as high dropout rates, low achievement, language loss, and economic marginalization among various language and other minority group members. The competing alternative model of acculturation (referred to as "multiculturalist" in the discussion of Canada and Australia) inspires fears that its implementation would cause divisiveness, entail unreasonable expense, or threaten the foundations of American democracy.

Although the point was made by Inglis that the advantages of multiculturalism affect everyone in the society, that conclusion equally applies to the consequences of assimilationist polices, which also affect all members of the society, whether positively or negatively. With each updated report of the 2000 Census, the urgency of reaching well-informed decisions in the United States on the best approach to the management of diversity grows. The nature of our society in the twenty-first century will be greatly affected by the outcome of processes resulting from that decision.

REFERENCES

Amnesty International. June 1996. United States of America: *Police brutality and excessive force in the New York City police department.* Report AMR 51/36/96. Author. [Online]. Available: *http://www.amnesty.it/AIlibtop/ 1996/AMR/25103696.htm.*

Anders, G. 2000a. Talking the talk. *American Journalism Review* (November) [Online]. Available: *http://ajr.newslink.org/ajrgiginov00.html.*

————. 2000b. The Little Saigon beat. *American Journalism Review* (November) [Online]. Available: *http://ajr.newslink.org/ajrgiginov00c.html.*

————. 2000c. The right translation. *American Journalism Review* (November) [Online]. Available: *http://ajr.newslink.org/ajrgiginov00b.html.*

Anti-Defamation League (ADL). 2000. *2000 Audit of anti-Semitic incidents.* New York: Author. [Online]. Available: *http://www.adl.org./2000audit/2000_ audit.pdf.*

August, D., and K. Hakuta, eds. 1997. *Improving schooling for language-minority children: A research agenda.* Washington, DC: National Academy Press. [Online]. Available: *http://lab.nap.edu/catalog/5286.html.*

Beaudin, M. 1998. The contribution of a minority to its region: The Acadians of southeast New Brunswick. In A. Breton, ed., *New Canadian perspectives: Economic approaches to language and bilingualism.* Ottawa: Official Languages Support Programs Branch, The Department of Canadian Heritage. [Online]. Available: *http://www.pch.gc.ca/offlangoff/perspectives/english/ economic/ch6_08.html.*

Bennett, William J. 1985. Address to the Association for a Better New York, 26 September 26. Washington, DC: U.S. Department of Education.

Bodi, M. 1994. The changing role of minority languages in Australia: The European and the Asia-Pacific nexus. *Journal of Multilingual and Multicultural Development* 15, nos. 2 and 3.

Boger, J. 1998. *Leandro v. State*: A new era in educational reform? *Popular Government* 63, no. 3 (spring).

Boswell, T. D. 1998. Implications of demographic changes in Florida's public school population. In S. H. Fradd and O. Lee, eds., *Creating Florida's multilingual global work force: Educational policies and practices for students learning English as a new language.* Tallahassee, FL: Florida Department of Education. [Online]. Available: *http://www.ncbe.gwu.edu/ websites/confla/boswell/demographic.htm.*

Brimelow, P. 1996. *Alien nation: Common sense about America's immigration disaster.* New York: Random House.

Carveth, R., and D. Alverio. 1998. *Network brownout 1998: The portrayal of Latinos in network television news.* Washington, DC: National Association of Hispanic Journalists and National Council of La Raza.

Chávez, L. 1995. What to do about immigration. *Commentary* 99, no. 3. [Online]. Available: *http://www.ceousa.org/.*

Chen, E. 1995. Statement of Edward M. Chen, Staff Counsel, American Civil Liberties Union of Northern California, on civil liberties implications of "Official English" legislation before the United States House of Representatives Committee on Economic and Educational Opportunities Subcommittee on Early Childhood, Youth and Families. American Civil Liberties Union. [Online]. Available: *http://www.aclu.org/congress/chen. html.*

Chorney, H. 1998. Bilingualism in employee recruitment and the role of symbolic analysts in leading export-oriented firms. In A. Breton, ed., *New Canadian perspectives: Economic approaches to language and bilingualism.* Ottawa: Official Languages Support Programs Branch, The Department of Canadian Heritage. [Online]. Available: *http://www.pch.gc.ca/ offlangoff/perspectives/english/economic/index.html.*

Clune, W. 1994. The shift from equity to adequacy in school finance. Special issue, Equity and Adequacy in Education: Issues for Policy and Finance. *Educational Policy* 8, no. 4 (December).

Comal Union School. 1999. *The handbook of Texas online.* [Online]. Available: *http://www.tsha.utexas.edu/handbook/online/articles/view/CC/kcc6. html.*

Combs, M. C. 1992. English Plus: Responding to English Only. In J. Crawford, ed., *Language Loyalties: A source book on the official English controversy.* Chicago: University of Chicago Press. [Online]. Available: *http://ourworld. compuserve.com/homepages/jwcrawford/combs.htm.*

Council of Great City Schools. 1999. Characteristics of member districts. Washington, DC: Author. [Online]. Available: *http://www.cgcs.org/about/about. htm.*

Crawford, J. 1998a. The bilingual education story: Why can't the news media get it right? Paper presented at the meeting of the National Association of Hispanic Journalists, June 26, Miami, Florida. [Online]. Available: *http:// ourworld.compuserve.com/homepages/JWCRAWFORD/NAHJ.htm.*

———. 1998b. *Ten common fallacies about bilingual education.* (ERIC Digest EDO-FL-98-10) (November). Washington, DC: ERIC Clearinghouse on Languages and Linguistics. [Online]. Available: *http://www.cal.org/ ericcll/digest/crawford01.html.*

———. 1999. *Hold your tongue: Bilingualism and the politics of English only.* Reading, MA: Addison-Wesley.

Croteau, D. 1998. *Examining the "liberal media" claim: Journalists' views on politics, economic policy and media coverage.* A FAIR Report Fairness and Accuracy in Reporting. (June). [Online]. Available: *http://www.fair.org/ reports/journalist-survey.html.*

Cummins, J. 1999. Alternative paradigms in bilingual education research: Does theory have a place? *Educational Researcher* 28, no. 7 (October).

Daniels, R. 1990. *Coming to America: A history of immigration and ethnicity in American life.* New York: HarperCollins.

DeVoretz, D., and C. Werner. February 2000. A theory of social forces and immigrant second-language acquisition. Discussion Paper No. 110, Institute for the Study of Labor IZA, Bonn, Germany. [Online]. Available: *http:// netec.mcc.ac.uk/WoPEc/data/Papers/izaizadpsdp110.html.*

Education Committee. October 15, 1985. Not English Only, English *Plus!* Miami, FL: Spanish American League Against Discrimination (SALAD).

Education Vital Signs 1998: Leadership. 1998. *American School Board Journal.* [Online]. Available: *http://www.asbj.com/evs/98/leadership.html.*

Education Week. Bilingual education traces its U.S. roots to the colonial era. 1987. *Education Week* 6, no. 27 (April 1). [Online]. Available: *http://www. edweek.org/ew/1987/27early.h06.*

Fishman, J. 1994. Interview with Joshua Fishman conducted by Dan Holt and

David Dolson, July 18. Sacramento CA: California Department of Education. [Online]. Available: *http://www.cde.ca.gov/iasa/fishman.html.*

Fradd, S., and T. Boswell. 1999. Income patterns of bilingual and English-only Hispanics in selected metropolitan areas. In S. H. Fradd, *Creating Florida's multilingual global work force: Educational policies and practices for students learning new languages.* Tallahassee, FL: Florida Department of Education. [Online]. Available: *http://www.ncbe.gwu.edu/miscpubs/florida/workforce99/income.htm.*

Gallagher, J. 1998. Education, alone, is a weak treatment. *Education Week* 17 (June 3). [Online]. Available: *http://www.edweek.org/ew/1998/4 2gallag.h17.*

Garcia, O., and R. Otheguy. 1994. The value of speaking a LOTE in U.S. business. *Annals of the American Academy* 532 (March).

Gibson, C., and E. Lennon. February 1999. Historical census statistics on the foreign-born population of the United States: 1850–1990. Division Working Paper No. 29. Washington, DC: U.S. Bureau of the Census, Population Division.

Ginsberg, T. 2000. A call for more immigrants. *Philadelphia Inquirer,* December 11. [Online]. Available: *http://inq.philly.com/content/inquirer/2000/12/11/national/IMMIG11.htm.*

Glenn, C. L. 1997. *What does the National Research Council study tell us about educating language minority children?* Washington, DC: The READ Institute. [Online]. Available: *http://www.ceousa.org/READ/nrc.html.*

Goodnough, A. 2001. New York City is shortchanged in school aid, state judge rules. *New York Times on the Web,* January 11. [Online]. Available: *http://www.nytimes.com/2001/01/11/nyregion/11SCHO.html?pagewanted=all.*

Greene, J. 1997. A meta-analysis of the Rossell and Baker review of bilingual education research. *Bilingual Research Journal* 21, nos. 2 and 3 (spring and summer). [Online]. Available: *http://brj.asu.edu/archives/23v21/indext.html.*

Grin, F. 1996. European research on the economics of language: Recent results and relevance to Canada. *New Canadian perspectives: Proceedings of the official languages and the economy colloquium.* Ottawa: Official Languages, Department of Canadian Heritage. [Online]. Available: *http://www.canadianheritage.gc.ca/offlangoff/perspectives/english/econo/part2b.htm.*

Grin, F., and F. Vaillancourt. 1999. *The economics of multilingualism: Overview of the literature and analytical framework.* Washington, DC: World Bank. [Online]. Available: *http://www-itsweb4.worldbank.org/wbiep/decentralization/Library12.htm.*

Hakuta, K. 1998a. Declarations prepared for a motion for preliminary injunction for Proposition 227 in *G. Valeria et al. v. Pete Wilson et al.,* U.S. District

Court in Northern California No. C-98-2252-CAL. [Online]. Available: *http://www.stanford.edu/~hakuta/EducationPolicy.htm.*

————. 1998b. Supplemental Declaration prepared for a Motion for Preliminary Injunction for Proposition 227 in *G. Valeria et al. v. Pete Wilson et al.,* U.S. District Court in Northern California No. C-98-2252-CAL. [Online]. Available: *http://www.stanford.edu/~hakuta/UnzSupplementalDeclaration.html.*

Helliwell, J. 2000. Language and trade. In A. Breton, ed., *New Canadian perspectives: Exploring the economics of language.* Ottawa: Official Languages Support Programs Branch, The Department of Canadian Heritage. [Online]. Available: *http://www.pch.gc.ca/OFFLANGOFF/perspectives/english/explorer/page_01.html.*

Hess, A., Jr. 1995. School-based finance: An equity solution for urban schools. EJ509 900. *School Business Affairs* 61, no. 8 (August).

Hy, R. J. 1995. Academics in service to the legislature: Legislative utilization of college and university faculty and staff. EJ511209. *Public Administration Review* 55, no. 5 (September/October).

Ibarra, I. 2000. INS inflames Cochise residents. *Arizona Daily Star,* November 16. [Online]. Available: *http://ranchrescue.com/news_articles/azstarnet_001116agentswarning.PDF.*

Intercultural Development Research Association (IDRA). 1996. Separating fact from fiction about education. *Class Notes* (October 28). [Online]. Available: *http://www.idra.org/Notes/Notes02.htm.*

Inglis, C. 1996. *Multiculturalism: New policy responses to diversity.* Paris: UNESCO. Management of Social Transformations MOST Clearinghouse. [Online]. Available: *http://www.unesco.org/most/pp4.htm#policy.*

Kheimets, N. G., and A. D. Epstein. August 2000. Between nation, state, and community: Dilemmas of socio-linguistic self-identification of the Russian Jewish intelligentsia in Israel. A lecture proposed for presentation at the First International Conference "People Across Borders." [Online]. Available: *http://www.mevic.org/papers/kheimets-epstein.html.*

Lambert, W. E., and G. R. Tucker. 1972. *Bilingual education of children: The St. Lambert experiment.* Rowley, MA: Newbury House.

Leonor, M. 1996. Americanization and the new immigrant, 1880–1924: A documentary history (Italian-Americans, Polish-Americans, Jewish-Americans). Ph.D. diss., Columbia University Teachers College. Abstract in *Dissertation Abstracts International* 57:07A.

Levine, D. U., and R. F. Levine. 1997. Cultural pluralism and minority education in the United States. In Miguel Angel Escotet, ed., *Cultural & social foundations of education: An interdisciplinary approach.* Needham Heights, MA: Simon & Schuster Education Group.

Lollock, L. January 2001. *The foreign-born population in the United States.* (Current Population Reports. Series P-20, Population Characteristics, 534). Washington, DC: U.S. Department of Commerce, Economics and Statistics Administration, U.S. Census Bureau. [Online]. Available: *http://www. census.gov/prod/2000pubs/p20–534.pdf.*

Long, D. August 1999. Introduction to school finance litigation. Washington, DC: National Center for Education Statistics (NCES). [Online]. Available: *http://nces.ed.gov/edfin/Litigation/Introduction.asp#NDD.*

McQuillan, J., and L. Tse. 1996. Does research matter? An analysis of media opinion on bilingual education, 1984–1994. *The Bilingual Research Journal* 20, no. 1 (winter).

Minorini, P., and S. Sugarman. 1999. School finance litigation in the name of educational equity: Its evolution, impact, and future. In H. Ladd, R. Chalk, and J. Hansen, eds., *Equity and adequacy in education finance: Issues and perspectives.* Committee on Education Finance, National Research Council. Washington, DC: National Academy Press.

National Asian and Pacific American (APA) Legal Consortium. 1997. *1997 Audit of violence against APAs.* Washington, DC: Author.

National Committee for Responsive Philanthropy (NCRP). September 1995. Conservative foundations and their activist grantees. *Foundations in the Newt era.* (A NCRP Special Report). Washington, DC: Author. [Online]. Available: *http://www.ncrp.org/articles/dap/13.htm.*

Pascucci, R. R. 1984. Electric city immigrants: Italians and Poles of Schenectady, New York, 1880–1930. Ph.D. diss., State University of New York at Albany, 1984. Abstract in *Dissertation Abstracts International* 45:09A.

Peal, E., and W. Lambert. 1962. The relation of bilingualism to intelligence. *Psychological Monographs: General and Applied* 76, no. 546.

Prince, C. D., and J. A. Hubert. 1994. Measuring the cost of bilingual education. *The Journal of Educational Issues of Language Minority Students* 13 (spring). [Online]. Available: *http://www.ncbe.gwu.edu/miscpubs/ jeilms/ vol13/measur13.htm.*

Quiroz-Martínez, J. 2001. A fair and just amnesty. *The Nation* (May 21). [Online]. Available: *http://www.thenation. com/doc.mhtml?i=20010521&s=quiroz-martinez.*

Ramírez, D., S. Yuen, D. Ramey, and D. Pasta. 1991. *Final report: Longitudinal study of structured immersion strategy, early-exit, and late-exit transitional bilingual education programs for language-minority children.* Vols. 1 and 2. San Mateo, CA: Aguire International.

Reutzel, D. R. 1996. Issues in reading instruction: U.S. state legislators' perceptions and knowledge. ED392999. *Research to Practice* (February).

Rossell, C. H., and K. Baker. 1996. The educational effectiveness of bilingual education. *Research in the Teaching of English* 30, no. 1.

Rothfarb, S. H., M. J. Ariza, and R. Urrutia. 1987. Evaluation of the Bilingual Curriculum Content BCC project: A three-year study, final report. Dade County Public Schools: Office of Educational Accountability.

Rothstein, R. 1998. Bilingual education: The controversy. *Phi Delta Kappan* (May).

Ruiz-de-Velasco, J., M. Fix, and B. Chu Clewell. December 2000. *Overlooked & underserved: Immigrant students in U.S. secondary schools.* Washington, DC: Urban Institute Press. [Online]. Available: *http://www.urban.org/ immig/overlooked2001.html.*

Rumbaut, R. 1998. Transformations: The post-immigrant generation in an age of diversity. Paper presented at the American Diversity: Past, Present, and Future meeting at the annual meeting of the Eastern Sociological Society, March 21, Philadelphia, Pennsylvania.

Rural Trust Policy Program (RTPP). June 21, 1999. School boards—leadership and leadership potential: Survey of executive directors of state school boards association. [Online]. Available: *http://www.ruraledu.org/sb_ survey3_99.html.*

Schnaiberg. L. 1994a. O.M.B. study puts price tag on educating illegal immigrants, *Education Week* (September 21). [Online]. Available: *http:// www.edweek. org/ew/ewstory.cfm?slug=03omb.h14&keywords=Schnaiberg.*

———. 1994 b. N.Y.C. bilingual-ed. Report spurs questions and complaints. *Education Week* (November 2). [Online]. Available: *http://www.edweek.org/ ew/ewstory.cfm?slug=03omb.h14&keywords=Schnaiberg.*

Schwartz, W. 1996. Immigrants and their educational attainment: Some facts and findings. EDO-UD-96-4 no. 116. ERIC Clearinghouse on Urban Education (November). [Online]. Available: *http://eric-web.tc.columbia. edu/ncbe/immigration/.*

Shipman, A. 1992. Talking the same languages. *International Management* (June).

Slayton, J. 1997. School finance in California and the consequences and implications for LAUSD. Los Angeles: University of California. [Online]. Available: *http://www.gseis.ucla.edu/gseisdoc/study/finance1.html.*

Smith, J. P., and B. Edmonston, eds. 1997. *The new Americans: Economic, demographic, and fiscal effects of immigration.* National Research Council, Commission on Behavioral and Social Sciences and Education, Panel on the Demographic and Economic Impacts of Immigration. Washington, DC: National Academy Press. [Online]. Available: *http://books.nap.edu/ books/0309063566/html/34.html#pagetop.*

Spolsky, B., and E. Shohamy. n.d. Language in Israeli society and education. Draft version of paper to appear in an issue of *International Journal of the Sociology of Language*. [Online]. Available: *http://www.biu.ac.il/ HU/lprc/ijslpap.htm.*

———. 1999. *Languages of Israel: Policy, ideology and practice.* Clevedon, England: Multilingual Matters.

Stepick, A. 1998. *Pride against prejudice: Haitians in the United States.* Boston: Allyn and Bacon.

Straight, H. S. 1998. Languages across the curriculum (ERIC Digest). Washington, DC: ERIC Clearinghouse on Languages and Linguistics. [Online]. Available: *http://www.cal.org/ericcll/digest/lacdigest.html.*

Study: Hispanic students more likely to quit school. 2000. *Education News* (March 31). [Online]. Available: *http://www.cnn.com/2000/fyi/teacher.resources/education.news/03/27/hispanic/#r.*

Teachers of English to Speakers of Other Languages, Inc. (TESOL). 1975. *Guidelines for the certification and preparation of teachers of English to speakers of other languages in the United States.* Alexandria, VA: Author.

———. 1997. *ESL Standards for Pre-K-12 students.* Alexandria, VA: Author.

———. 2001. *The ESL Standards for Pre-K-12 students: Table of contents.* Alexandria, VA: Author. [Online]. Available: *http://www.tesol.org/assoc/k12standards/it/01.html.*

Thomas, W., and V. Collier. 1997. *School effectiveness for language minority students.* (NCBE Resource Collection Series, No. 9). Washington, DC: National Clearinghouse for Bilingual Education. [Online]. Available: *http://www.ncbe.gwu.edu/ncbepubs/resource/effectiveness/index.htm.*

Tucker, G. R. 1999. A global perspective on bilingualism and bilingual education (August). (ERIC Digest EDO-FL-99-04). Washington, DC: ERIC Clearinghouse on Languages and Linguistics. [Online]. Available: *http://www.cal.org/ericcll/digest/digestglobal.html* .

Tyler, J. H., R. H. Murnane, and J. B. Willett. June 2000. Estimating the labor market signaling value of the GED (NCSALL Research Briefs). Cambridge, MA: Harvard Graduate School of Education, National Center for the Study of Adult Learning and Literacy. [Online]. Available: *http://gseweb.harvard.edu/~ncsall/research/report_extra.html.*

United Nations. March 21, 2000. *Replacement migration: Is it a solution to declining and aging populations?* New York: United Nations Secretariat, Population Division, Department of Economic and Social Affairs. [Online]. Available: *http://www.un.org/esa/population/unpop.htm.*

U.S. Immigration and Naturalization Service (INS). 1997. *Statistical yearbook of the immigration and naturalization service, 1996.* Washington, DC: U.S. Government Printing Office.

Unz, R. 1999. The right kind of outreach for the GOP. *Weekly Standard,* Monday, March 1. [Online]. Available: *http://www.onenation.org/9903/030199.html.*

Verstegen, D., and T. Whitney. 1997. From courthouses to schoolhouses: Emerging judicial theories of adequacy and equity. *Educational Policy* 11, no. 3 (September). [Online]. Available: *http://www.arts.mcgill.ca/programs/misc/white.htm.*

White. P. 2000. Non-territorial federalism: A new approach to identity politics or how Canadians can become born-again federalists and save the world (J. R. Mallory Annual Lecture, The McGill Institute for the Study of Canada, January 26). Québec: McGill University. [Online]. Available: *http://www.arts.mcgill.ca/programs/misc/white.htm.*

Willig, A. 1985. A meta-analysis of selected studies on the effectiveness of bilingual education. *Review of Educational Research* 55, no. 3.

Zentella, A. C. 1986. Language minorities and the national commitment to foreign language competency: Resolving the contradiction. *ADFL Bulletin* 17, no. 3 (April).

Zhou, M. 1997. Growing up American: The challenge confronting immigrant children and children of immigrants. *Annual Review of Sociology* 23.

Chapter Seven

➊➌ Directory of Agencies and Organizations Associated with Bilingual Education

The federal and state government agencies, professional associations, training and technical assistance centers, and university-based centers listed in this chapter are among the major sources of information on bilingual education.

FEDERAL GOVERNMENT AGENCIES

Among federal government agencies, the major source of information about bilingual education is the U.S. Department of Education and its divisions.

U.S. Department of Education
Richard W. Riley
U.S. Secretary of Education
400 Maryland Avenue, SW
Washington, DC 20202-0498
(800) USA-LEARN
http://www.ed.gov/

Principal duties of the U.S. Department of Education (USDE) include managing government-funded grants and contracts, collecting and disseminating statistical data, and enforcing civil rights laws and regulations.

Department of Education Office for Civil Rights (OCR)
Norma V. Cantú
Assistant Secretary for Civil Rights
U.S. Department of Education
Office for Civil Rights
Mary E. Switzer Building
330 C Street, SW

Washington, DC 20202
(202) 205-5413; (800) 421-3481
Fax: (202) 205-9862
TDD: (202) 205-5166
E-mail: OCR@ED.Gov
http://www.ed.gov/offices/OCR/

The Department of Education Office for Civil Rights (OCR) enforces five federal statutes that prohibit discrimination. It enforces federal civil rights laws prohibiting discrimination in education programs on the basis of race, color, national origin, sex, disability, and age. Language-related matters typically fall under the category of national origin, but may also involve other categories as well. All state education agencies, elementary and secondary school systems, colleges and universities, vocational schools, proprietary schools, state vocational rehabilitation agencies, libraries, and museums that receive U.S. Department of Education funds must comply with federal civil rights laws enforced by OCR. Among the major responsibilities of this agency are resolving complaints of discrimination and initiating compliance reviews on compliance problems that appear particularly acute. Complaints about civil rights violations should be directed to one of the twelve regional offices of OCR listed below.

Office for Civil Rights, Atlanta Office
U.S. Department of Education
61 Forsyth Street SW
Suite 19T70
Atlanta, GA 30303-3104
(404) 562-6350
Fax: (404) 562-6455
TDD: (404) 331-7236
E-mail: OCR_Atlanta@ed.gov

Serving Alabama, Florida, Georgia, South Carolina, Tennessee

Office for Civil Rights, Boston Office
U.S. Department of Education
J. W. McCormack Post Office and Courthouse
Room 707, 01-0061
Boston, MA 02109-4557
(617) 223-9662
Fax: (617) 223-9669
TDD: (617) 223-9695

E-mail: OCR_Boston@ed.gov

Serving Connecticut, Maine, Massachusetts, New Hampshire, Rhode Island, Vermont

Office for Civil Rights, Chicago Office
U.S. Department of Education
111 North Canal Street
Suite 1053
Chicago, IL 60606-7204
(312) 886-8434
Fax: (312) 353-4888
TDD: (312) 353-2540
E-mail: OCR_Chicago@ed.gov

Serving, Illinois, Indiana, Minnesota, Wisconsin

Office for Civil Rights, Cleveland Office
U.S. Department of Education
600 Superior Avenue East
Bank One Center
Room 750
Cleveland, OH 44114-2611
(216) 522-4970
Fax: (216) 522-2573
TDD: (216) 522-4944
OCR_Cleveland@ed.gov

Serving Michigan and Ohio

Office for Civil Rights, Dallas Office
U.S. Department of Education
1999 Bryan Street
Suite 2600
Dallas, TX 75201
(214) 880-2459
Fax: (214) 880-3082
TDD: (214) 880-2456
E-mail: OCR_Dallas@ed.gov

Serving Arkansas, Louisiana, Mississippi, Oklahoma, Texas

Office for Civil Rights, Denver Office
U.S. Department of Education
Federal Building

Suite 310, 08-7010
1244 Speer Boulevard
Denver, CO 80204-3582
(303) 844-5695
Fax: (303) 844-4303
TDD: (303) 844-3417
E-mail: OCR_Denver@ed.gov

Serving, Arizona, Colorado, Montana, New Mexico, Utah, Wyoming

Office for Civil Rights, District of Columbia Office
U.S. Department of Education
1100 Pennsylvania Avenue, NW
Room 316
P.O. Box 14620
Washington, DC 20044-4620
(202) 208-2545
Fax: (202) 208-7797
TDD: (202) 208-7741
E-mail: OCR_DC@ed.gov

Serving North Carolina, Virginia, Washington, DC

Office for Civil Rights, Kansas City Office
U.S. Department of Education
10220 North Executive Hills Boulevard
8th Floor, 07-6010
Kansas City, MO 64153-1367
(816) 880-4200
Fax: (816) 891-0644
TDD: (816) 891-0582
E-mail: OCR_KansasCity@ed.go

Serving Iowa, Kansas, Missouri, Nebraska, North Dakota, South Dakota

Office for Civil Rights, New York Office
U.S. Department of Education
75 Park Place, 14th Floor
New York, NY 10007-2146
(212) 637-6466
Fax: (212) 264-3803
TDD: (212) 637-0478
E-mail: OCR_NewYork@ed.gov

Serving New Jersey, New York, Puerto Rico, Virgin Islands

Office for Civil Rights, Philadelphia Office
U.S. Department of Education
Wanamaker Building
Suite 515
100 Penn Square East
Philadelphia, PA 19107
(215) 656-8541
Fax: (215) 656-8605
TDD: (215) 656-8604
E-mail: OCR_Philadelphia@ed.gov

Serving Delaware, Maryland, Kentucky, Pennsylvania, West Virginia

Office for Civil Rights, San Francisco Office
U.S. Department of Education
Old Federal Building, 09-8010
50 United Nations Plaza
Room 239
San Francisco, CA 94102-4102
(415) 556-4275
Fax: (415) 437-7786
TDD: (415) 437-7783
E-mail: OCR_SanFrancisco@ed.gov

Serving California

Office for Civil Rights, Seattle Office
U.S. Department of Education
915 Second Avenue
Room 3310, 10-9010
Seattle, WA 98174-1099
(206) 220-7900
Fax: (206) 220-7887
TDD: (206) 220-7907
E-mail: OCR_Seattle@ed.gov

Serving Alaska, Hawaii, Idaho, Nevada, Oregon, Washington, American
Samoa, Guam, Trust Territory of the Pacific Islands

National Center for Education Statistics (NCES)
1990 K Street, NW
Washington, DC 20006
(202) 502-7300
Fax: (202) 502-7466

http://nces.ed.gov/

The National Center for Education Statistics is responsible for collecting and analyzing education data. Program areas include vocational education, K–12 practitioners, education finance, and postsecondary education.

Office of Bilingual Education and Minority Languages (OBEMLA)
Art Love, Acting Director
600 Independence Avenue, SW
Washington, DC 20202-6510
(202) 205-5463
E-mail: art_love@ed.gov
http://www.ed.gov/offices/OBEMLA/

The federal agency in the Department of Education that manages bilingual education programs is the Office of Bilingual Education and Minority Language Affairs (OBEMLA). The duties of this office include administering Title VII (the Bilingual Education Act) of the Education Excellence for All Children Act (previously the Elementary and Secondary Education Act). The office conducts a discretionary grant program whose authorization level permits direct service to approximately 10 percent of the eligible English-language learners in the country and indirect service to all students in bilingual programs through support of teacher-training programs, research, and dissemination activities. This office also administers the Foreign Language Assistance Program (FLAP).

Office of Educational Research and Improvement (OERI)
Assistant Secretary Cyril Kent McGuire
U.S. Department of Education
Capital Place
Room 600D
555 New Jersey Avenue, NW
Washington, DC 20208-5500
(202) 219-1385
http://www.ed.gov/offices/OERI/

The Office of Educational Research and Improvement (OERI) is responsible for research and development in education, including the operation of the National Center for Education Statistics.

STATE EDUCATION AGENCIES

State departments of education are responsible for implementing legislative mandates and state board of education policies. Areas of responsibility typically include the approval of teacher-training programs, determination of standards for teacher certification, oversight of school district in-service training plans, elaboration of curriculum frameworks for each subject area, and development of procedures for setting standards and monitoring for compliance with state and federal civil rights laws. A state's body of school law may include provisions for educational reform and accountability, statewide testing programs, and minimum standards for high school graduation and grade-to-grade promotion, matters that affect English-language learners and programs serving them. This section lists directory information for the main offices of state departments of education to facilitate access to information on the wide range of state education activity related to language education and language minority students.

Alabama

Alabama Department of Education
Gordon Persons Office Building
50 North Ripley Street
P.O. Box 302102
Montgomery, AL 36130-2101
(334) 242-9700
Fax: (334) 242-9708
E-mail: dmurray@sdenet.alsde.edu
http://www.alsde.edu

Alaska

Alaska Department of Education and Early Development
801 West 10th Street
Suite 200
Juneau, AK 99801-1894
(907) 465-2800
Fax: (907) 465-4156
http://www.eed.state.ak.us

Arizona

Arizona Department of Education
1535 West Jefferson
Phoenix, AZ 85007
(602) 542-5460
Fax: (602) 542-5440
http://www.ade.state.az.us

Arkansas

Arkansas Department of Education
General Education Division
Four State Capitol Mall
Room 304 A
Little Rock, AR 72201-1071
(501) 682-4204
Fax: (501) 682-1079
http://arkedu.state.ar.us/

California

California Department of Education
721 Capitol Mall
Second Floor
Sacramento, CA 94244-2720
(916) 657-2577
Fax: (916) 657-2682
E-mail: dholt@cde.ca.gov
http://www.cde.ca.gov/iasa/

Colorado

Colorado Department of Education
201 East Colfax Avenue
Denver, CO 80203-1704
(303) 866-6600
Fax: (303) 830-0793
E-mail: Howerter_C@cde.state.co.us
http://www.cde.state.co.us/

Connecticut

Connecticut Department of Education
State Office Building
Room 305
165 Capitol Avenue
Hartford, CT 06106-1080
(860) 566-5061
Fax: (860) 566-8964
E-mail: ctsde@aol.com
http://www.state.ct.us/sde/

Delaware

Delaware Department of Education
John G. Townsend Building
Federal and Loockerman Streets
P.O. Box 1402
Dover, DE 19903-1402
(302) 739-4601
Fax: (302) 739-4654
http://www.doe.state.de.us

District of Columbia

District of Columbia Public Schools
The Presidential Building
825 North Capitol Street, NE
Washington, DC 20002
(202) 724-4222
Fax: (202) 442-5026
http://www.k12.dc.us

Florida

Florida Department of Education
Capitol Building
Room PL 08
Tallahassee, FL 32399-0400
(850) 487-1785
Fax: (850) 413-0378
http://www.firn.edu/doe/index.html

Georgia

Georgia Department of Education
2054 Twin Towers East
205 Butler Street
Atlanta, GA 30334-5001
(404) 656-2800
(800) 311-3627
Toll Free Restrictions: GA residents only
Fax: (404) 651-6867
E-mail: help.desk@doe.k12.ga.us
http://www.doe.k12.ga.us

Hawaii

Hawaii Department of Education
1390 Miller Street
Honolulu, HI 96813
(808) 586-3310
Fax: (808) 586-3320
E-mail: supt_doe@notes.k12.hi.us
http://www.k12.hi.us/

Idaho

Idaho Department of Education
Len B. Jordan Office Building
650 West State Street
P.O. Box 83720
Boise, ID 83720-0027
(208) 332-6800
(800) 432-4601
TTY: (800) 377-3529
Fax: (208) 334-2228
http://www.sde.state.id.us/Dept/

Illinois

Illinois State Board of Education
100 North First Street
Springfield, IL 62777
(217) 782-4321

TTY: (217) 782-1900
Fax: (217) 524-4928
http://www.isbe.state.il.us

Indiana

Indiana Department of Education
State House
Room 229
Indianapolis, IN 46204-2798
(317) 232-6665
Fax: (317) 232-8004
http://www.doe.state.in.us

Iowa

Iowa Department of Education
Grimes State Office Building
East 14th and Grand Streets
Des Moines, IA 50319-0146
(515) 281-3436
Fax: (515) 281-4122
http://www.state.ia.us/educate/

Kansas

Kansas Department of Education
120 South East 10th Avenue
Topeka, KS 66612-1182
(785) 296-3201
Fax: (785) 296-7933
E-mail: atompkins@ksbe.state.ks.us or lasnider@ksbe.state.ks.us
http://www.ksbe.state.ks.us

Kentucky

Kentucky Department of Education
1930 Capital Plaza Tower
500 Mero Street
Frankfort, KY 40601
(502) 564-3421
(800) 533-5372

Toll Free Restrictions: KY residents only
Fax: (502) 564-6470
E-mail: kwilborn@kde.state.ky.us
http://www.kde.state.ky.us

Louisiana

Louisiana Department of Education
626 North Fourth Street
P.O. Box 94064
Baton Rouge, LA 70704-9064
(225) 342-4411
Fax: (225) 342-7316
E-mail: webmaster@mail.doe.state.la.us
http://www.doe.state.la.us

Maine

Maine Department of Education
23 State House Station
Augusta, ME 04333-0023
(207) 287-5800
TTY: (207) 287-2550
Fax: (207) 287-5802
http://janus.state.me.us/education/homepage.htm

Maryland

Maryland Department of Education
200 West Baltimore Street
Baltimore, MD 21201
(410) 767-0462
Fax: (410) 333-6033
http://www.msde.state.md.us

Massachusetts

Massachusetts Department of Education
Educational Improvement Group
350 Main Street
Malden, MA 02148
(781) 388-3300

Fax: (781) 388-3396
E-mail: www@doe.mass.edu
http://www.doe.mass.edu

Michigan

Michigan Department of Education
Hannah Building
Fourth Floor
608 West Allegan Street
Lansing, MI 48933
(517) 373-3324
Fax: (517) 335-4565
http://www.mde.state.mi.us/

Minnesota

Minnesota Department of Children, Families, and Learning
1500 Highway 36 West
Roseville, MN 55113-4266
(651) 582-8200
E-mail: children@state.mn.us
http://cfl.state.mn.us

Mississippi

Mississippi State Department of Education
359 North West Street
Suite 365
Jackson, MS 39201
(601) 359-3513
Fax: (601) 359-3242
http://www.mde.k12.ms.us/

Missouri

Missouri Department of Elementary and Secondary Education
P.O. Box 480
Jefferson City, MO 65102-0480
(573) 751-4212
TTY: (800) 735-2966
Fax: (573) 751-8613

E-mail: pubinfo@mail.dese.state.mo.us
http://www.dese.state.mo.us

Montana

Montana Office of Public Instruction
P.O. Box 202501
Helena, MT 59620-2501
(406) 444-2082
Fax: (406) 444-3924
E-mail: cbergeron@opi.mt.gov
http://www.metnet.state.mt.us/MAIN.html

Nebraska

Nebraska Department of Education
301 Centennial Mall South
P.O. Box 94987
Lincoln, NE 68509-4987
(402) 471-2295
TTY: (402) 471-7295
Fax: (402) 471-0017
E-mail: eduneb@nde4.nde.state.ne.us
http://www.nde.state.ne.us

Nevada

Nevada State Department of Education
700 East Fifth Street
Carson City, NV 89701
(775) 687-9141
Fax: (775) 687-9101
E-mail: fsouth@nsn.K12.nv.us
http://www.nsn.k12.nv.us/nvdoe/

New Hampshire

New Hampshire Department of Education
101 Pleasant Street
State Office Park South
Concord, NH 03301
(603) 271-3144

(800) 339-9900
TTY: (800) 735-2964
Fax: (603) 271-1953
E-mail: ckilmister@ed.state.nh.us
http://www.state.nh.us/doe/

New Jersey

New Jersey Department of Education
P.O. Box 500
100 Riverview
Trenton, NJ 08625-0500
(609) 292-4469
Fax: (609) 777-4099
http://www.state.nj.us/education

New Mexico

New Mexico State Department of Education
Education Building
300 Don Gaspar
Santa Fe, NM 87501-2786
(505) 827-6516
TTY: (505) 827-6541
Fax: (505) 827-6696
http://sde.state.nm.us/

New York

New York Education Department
111 Education Building
Washington Avenue
Albany, NY 12234
(518) 474-5844
Fax: (518) 473-4909
E-mail: rmills@mail.nysed.gov
http://www.nysed.gov

North Carolina

North Carolina Department of Public Instruction
Education Building

301 North Wilmington Street
Raleigh, NC 27601-2825
(919) 715-1299
Fax: (919) 715-1278
http://www.dpi.state.nc.us

North Dakota

North Dakota Department of Public Instruction
600 East Boulevard Avenue
11th Floor
Department 201
Bismarck, ND 58505-0440
(701) 328-2260
Fax: (701) 328-2461
E-mail: wsanstea@mail.dpi.state.nd.us or tlalonde@mail.dpi.state.nd.us
http://www.dpi.state.nd.us/

Ohio

Ohio Department of Education
65 South Front Street
Room 1005
Columbus, OH 43215-4183
(877) 644-6338
Fax: (614) 644-5960
E-mail: ims_help@ode.state.oh.us
http://www.ode.state.oh.us/

Oklahoma

Oklahoma State Department of Education
2500 North Lincoln Boulevard
Oklahoma City, OK 73105-4599
(405) 521-3301
Fax: (405) 521-6205
E-mail: sandy_garrett@mail.sde.state.ok.us
http://sde.state.ok.us

Oregon

Oregon Department of Education
255 Capitol Street, NE
Salem, OR 97310-0203
(503) 378-3569
TTY: (503) 378-2892
Fax: (503) 373-7968
http://www.ode.state.or.us

Pennsylvania

Pennsylvania Department of Education
333 Market Street
10th Floor
Harrisburg, PA 17126-0333
(717) 787-5820
Fax: (717) 787-7222
http://www.pde.psu.edu/

Rhode Island

Rhode Island Department of Elementary and Secondary Education
255 Westminster Street
Providence, RI 02903-3400
(401) 222-4600
Fax: (401) 222-6033
E-mail: ride0015@ride.ri.net
http://www.ridoe.net/

South Carolina

South Carolina Department of Education
1006 Rutledge Building
1429 Senate Street
Columbia, SC 29201
(803) 734-8492
Fax: (803) 734-3389
http://www.state.sc.us/sde

South Dakota

South Dakota Department of Education and Cultural Affairs
700 Governors Drive
Pierre, SD 57501-2291
(605) 773-3134
TTY: (605) 773-6302
Fax: (605) 773-6139
E-mail: janelle.toman@state.sd.us or jolene.brakke@state.sd.us
http://www.state.sd.us/deca/

Tennessee

Tennessee State Department of Education
Andrew Johnson Tower
Sixth Floor
710 James Robertson Parkway
Nashville, TN 37243-0375
(615) 741-2731
Fax: (615) 741-6236
http://www.state.tn.us/education/

Texas

Texas Education Agency
William B. Travis Building
1701 North Congress Avenue
Austin, TX 78701-1494
(512) 463-8985
Fax: (512) 463-9008
http://www.tea.state.tx.us

Utah

Utah State Office of Education
250 East 500 South
Salt Lake City, UT 84111
(801) 538-7500
Fax: (801) 538-7521
E-mail: SLAING@usoe.k12.ut.us
http://www.usoe.k12.ut.us

Vermont

Vermont Department of Education
120 State Street
Montpelier, VT 05620-2501
(802) 828-3147
Fax: (802) 828-3140
http://www.state.vt.us/educ

Virginia

Virginia Department of Education
P.O. Box 2120
101 North 14th Street
Richmond, VA 23218-2120
(804) 225-2020
(800) 292-3820
Toll Free Restrictions: VA residents only
Fax: (804) 371-2455
E-mail: cmakela@pen.k12.va.us
http://www.pen.k12.va.us/go/VDOE

Washington

Office of Superintendent of Public Instruction (Washington)
Old Capitol Building
600 South Washington
P.O. Box 47200
Olympia, WA 98504-7200
(360) 586-6904
TTY: (360) 664-3631
Fax: (360) 753-6712
http://www.k12.wa.us

West Virginia

West Virginia Department of Education
1900 Kanawha Boulevard East
Building 6
Charleston, WV 25305-0330
(304) 558-0304
Fax: (304) 558-2584

E-mail: wvde@access.k12.wv.us
http://wvde.state.wv.us

Wisconsin

Wisconsin Department of Public Instruction
125 South Webster Street
P.O. Box 7841
Madison, WI 53707-7841
(608) 266-3108
(800) 441-4563
TTY: (608) 267-2427
Fax: (608) 267-1052
http://www.dpi.state.wi.us

Wyoming

Wyoming Department of Education
2300 Capitol Avenue
Second Floor
Cheyenne, WY 82002
(307) 777-7675
Fax: (307) 777-6234
E-mail: jcatch@educ.state.wy.us
http://www.k12.wy.us/wdehome.html

TERRITORIES

American Samoa

American Samoa Department of Education
Pago Pago, AS 96799
(684) 633-5237
Fax: (684) 633-4240
http://www.government.as/education.htm

Commonwealth of the Northern Mariana Islands

Commonwealth of the Northern Mariana Islands Public School System
P.O. Box 1370
Saipan, MP 96950
(670) 664-3720

Fax: (670) 664-3798
E-mail: coe@saipan.com
http://www.saipan.com/gov/branches/pss/index.htm

Guam

Guam Department of Education
P.O. Box DE
Agana, GM 96932
(671) 475-0457
http://www.doe.edu.gu/

Puerto Rico

Puerto Rico Department of Education
P.O. Box 190759
San Juan, PR 00919-0759
(787) 753-2062
Fax: (787) 250-0275
http://www.de.gobierno.pr/

Virgin Islands

Virgin Islands Department of Education
44-46 Kongens Gade
St. Thomas, VI 00802
(340) 774-0100
Fax: (340) 779-7153
E-mail: rsimmonds@sttj.k12.vi.us
http://www.usvi.org/education/

PROFESSIONAL ASSOCIATIONS

Three of the major national professional associations related to bilingual education are included in this section. Each offers a full range of services to its members, such as sponsorship of annual conferences, journals, and newsletters. These groups are also involved in activities designed to improve the quality of education offered to students. These activities include participation in educational reform networks; the development of student, program, and teacher preparation standards; and leadership in instructional innovations. Contact the national office of each organization for contact information for its state and regional affiliates and special-interest groups.

American Council on the Teaching of Foreign Languages (ACTFL)
Edward C. Scebold, Executive Director
6 Executive Plaza
Yonkers, NY 10701-6801
(914) 963-8830
Fax: (914) 963-1275
E-mail: headquarters@actfl.org
www.actfl.org

National Association for Bilingual Education (NABE)
Delia Pompa, Executive Director
1220 L Street, NW
Suite 605
Washington, DC 20005
(202) 898-1829
E-mail: d_pompa@nabe.org
http://www.nabe.org/

Teachers of English to Speakers of Other Languages (TESOL)
Charles Amorosino, Executive Director
700 South Washington Street
Suite 200
Alexandria, VA 22314
(703) 836-0774
Fax: (703) 836-7864 or (703) 836-6447
E-mail: info@tesol.org
http://www.tesol.org/index.html

TRAINING AND TECHNICAL ASSISTANCE CENTERS

Two sets of training and technical assistance sources are listed in this directory, the Comprehensive Center and the Equity Assistance networks.

Comprehensive Center Network

Fifteen national centers are funded by the United States Department of Education under Title XIII of the Improving America's Schools Act of 1994 (IASA). The Comprehensive Centers replace and integrate the functions of previously funded technical assistance centers providing services to districts with students in Title I, Migrant, Drug-Free Schools, Title VII (Bilingual Education), and Indian Education programs. These centers help states, school districts, and schools meet the needs of children, including children in high-poverty areas, migratory children, immigrant children, children with limited English proficiency, neglected or delinquent children, homeless children and youth, American Indian children, children with disabilities, and, where applicable, Native Alaskan and Hawaiian children.

Alaska Comprehensive Regional Assistance Center
210 Ferry Way
Suite 200
Juneau, AK 99801
(907) 586-6806
(888) 43-AKRAC
Fax: (907) 463-3811
E-mail: webmas@akrac.k12.ak.us or lindal@akrac.k12.ak.us
http://www.akrac.k12.ak.us

Serving Alaska

Comprehensive Regional Assistance Center Consortium–Region VI
University of Wisconsin–Madison
1025 West Johnson Street
Madison, WI 53706
(608) 263-4220
(888) 862-7763
Fax: (608) 263-3733
E-mail: ccvi@mail.wcer.wisc.edu
http://www.wcer.wisc.edu/ccvi/

Serving Iowa, Michigan, Minnesota, North Dakota, South Dakota, Wisconsin

New England Comprehensive Assistance Center
Education Development Center
55 Chapel Street
Newton, MA 02158
(617) 969-7100
(800) 332-0226
Fax: (617) 969-4902
E-mail: compcenter@edc.org

http://www.edc.org/NECAC/

Serving Connecticut, Massachusetts, Maine, New Hampshire, Rhode Island, Vermont

New York Technical Assistance Center
New York University, School of Education
82 Washington Square East
Suite 72
New York, NY 10003-6680
(212) 998-5100
(800) 4NYU-224 (469-8224)
Fax: (212) 995-4199
E-mail: lamar.miller@nyu.edu
http://www.nyu.edu/education/metrocenter/nytac/nytac.html

Serving New York

Northern California Comprehensive Assistance Center
WestEd
730 Harrison Street
San Francisco, CA 94107
(415) 565-3029
(800) 64LEARN (645-3276)
Fax: (415) 565-3012
E-mail: jcuevas@wested.org
http://www.wested.org/cc

Serving California

Northwest Regional Educational Laboratory's Comprehensive Center
Region X
Northwest Regional Educational Laboratory
101 Southwest Main Street
Suite 500
Portland, OR 97204-3297
(503) 275-9500
(800) 547-6339
Fax: (503) 275-9625
E-mail: nwrac@nwrel.org
http://www.nwrac.org

Serving Idaho, Montana, Oregon, Washington, Wyoming

Region III Comprehensive Center
The George Washington University
Center for Equity and Excellence in Education
1730 North Lynn Street
Suite 401
Arlington, VA 22209
(703) 528-3588
(800) 925-3223
Fax: (703) 528-5973
E-mail: r3cc@ceee.gwu.edu
http://r3cc.ceee.gwu.edu

Serving the District of Columbia, Delaware, Maryland, New Jersey, Ohio, Pennsylvania

Region IV Comprehensive Center
1700 North Moore Street
Suite 1275
Arlington, VA 22209-1903
(703) 276-0200
(800) 624-9120
Fax: (703) 276-0266
E-mail: aelinfo@ael.org
http://www.ael.org/cac/

Serving Kentucky, North Carolina, South Carolina, Tennessee, Virginia, West Virginia

Region VII Comprehensive Center
University of Oklahoma
555 East Constitution Street
Norman, OK 73072
(405) 325-1729
(800) 228-1766
Fax: (405) 325-1824
E-mail: regionvii@ou.edu or bpbiscoe@ou.edu
http://region7.ou.edu

Serving Illinois, Indiana, Kansas, Missouri, Nebraska, Oklahoma

Region IX Comprehensive Assistance Center
1700 Grande Court
Suite 101
Rio Rancho, NM 87124

(505) 891-6111
(800) 247-4269
Fax: (505) 891-5744
E-mail: swcc@cesdp.nmhu.edu
http://www.cesdp.nmhu.edu/swcc/

Serving Arizona, Colorado, New Mexico, Nevada, Utah

Region XIV Comprehensive Center
Educational Testing Service
1000 North Ashley Drive
Suite 312
Tampa, FL 33602
(800) 756-9003
Fax: (813) 228-0632
E-mail: thensley@ets.org
http://www.ets.org/ccxiv

Serving Florida, Puerto Rico, Virgin Islands

Region XV Comprehensive Assistance Center
Pacific Resources for Education and Learning
Alii Place
25th Floor
1099 Alakea Street
Honolulu, HI 96813-4513
(808) 441-1300
Fax: (808) 441-1385
E-mail: askprel@prel.org
http://www.prel.org

Serving American Samoa, Federated States of Micronesia, Guam, Hawaii, Republic of the Marshall Islands, Commonwealth of the Northern Mariana Islands, Republic of Palau

Southeast Comprehensive Technical Assistance Center
Southwest Educational Development Laboratory
3330 North Causeway Boulevard
Suite 430
Metairie, LA 70002
(504) 838-6861
(800) 644-8671
Fax: (504) 831-5242
E-mail: htran@sedl.org

http://www.sedl.org/secac/welcome.html

Serving Alabama, Arkansas, Georgia, Louisiana, Mississippi

Southern California Comprehensive Assistance Center
9300 East Imperial Highway
Downey, CA 90242-2890
(562) 922-6343
Fax: (562) 940-1798
E-mail: mothner_henry@lacoe.edu
http://sccac.lacoe.edu

Serving California

STAR Center—Region VIII Comprehensive Assistance Center
Intercultural Development Research Association
5835 Callaghan Road
Suite 350
San Antonio, TX 78228-1190
(210) 444-1710
Fax: (210) 444-1714
E-mail: contact@idra.org
http://www.starcenter.org/

Serving Texas

EQUITY ASSISTANCE CENTERS

Equity Assistance Centers, previously known as Desegregation Assistance Centers, offer services in the areas of race, gender, and national-origin equity. Their services are available to school districts and education agencies within each center's designated service areas.

Intercultural Development Research Association Desegregation
Assistance Center
5835 Callaghan Road
Suite 350
San Antonio, TX 78228-1190
(210) 444-1710
Fax: (210) 444-1714
E-mail: bscott@idra.org
http://www.idra.org

Serving Arkansas, Louisiana, New Mexico, Oklahoma, Texas

Interwest Equity Assistance Center
Colorado State University
School of Education
110 16th Street
Suite 600
Denver, CO 80202
(303) 623-9384
Fax: (303) 623-9023
E-mail: villarreal@cahs.colostate.edu
http://www.colostate.edu/programs/EAC/index.html

Serving Colorado, Montana, North Dakota, South Dakota, Utah, Wyoming

Mid-Atlantic Equity Consortium, Inc.
5454 Wisconsin Avenue
Suite 655
Chevy Chase, MD 20815
(301) 657-7741
Fax: (301) 657-8782
E-mail: equity@maec.org or publications@maec.org
http://www.maec.org

Serving District of Columbia, Delaware, Maryland, Pennsylvania, Virginia, West Virginia

Midwest Desegregation Assistance Center
Kansas State University, College of Education
401 Bluemont Hall
1100 Midcampus Drive
Manhattan, KS 66506-5327
(785) 532-6408
(800) 232-0133, Ext. 6408
Fax: (785) 532-5548
E-mail: ronna@ksu.edu
http://mdac.educ.ksu.edu

Serving Iowa, Kansas, Missouri, Nebraska

New England Equity Assistance Center
Education Alliance
Brown University
222 Richmond Street
Suite 300

Providence, RI 02903
(401) 351-7577
Fax: (401) 351-9594
E-mail: maria_pacheco@brown.edu
http://www.brown.edu/Research/The_Education_Alliance

Serving Connecticut, Massachusetts, Maine, New Hampshire, Rhode Island, Vermont

New York University Equity Assistance Center
82 Washington Square East
Suite 72
New York, NY 10003-6644
(212) 998-5100
(800) 469-8224
Fax: (212) 995-4199
E-mail: laruth.gray@nyu.edu
http://www.nyu.edu/education/metrocenter

Serving New Jersey, New York, Puerto Rico, Virgin Islands

Northwest Regional Educational Laboratory Equity Center
101 Southwest Main Street
Suite 500
Portland, OR 97204
(503) 275-9603
Fax: (503) 275-0452
E-mail: harrisj@nwrel.org
http://www.nwrel.org/cnorse

Serving Alaska, American Samoa, Guam, Hawaii, Idaho, Commonwealth of the Northern Mariana Islands, Oregon, Republic of Palau, Washington

Programs for Educational Opportunity
University of Michigan
1005 School of Education
610 East University
Ann Arbor, MI 48109-1259
(313) 763-9910
Fax: (313) 763-2137
E-mail: peo@umich.edu
http://www.umich.edu/~eqtynet

Serving Illinois, Indiana, Michigan, Minnesota, Ohio, Wisconsin

Southeastern Equity Center
Miami Equity Associates, Inc.
8603 South Dixie Highway
Suite 304
Miami, FL 33143
(305) 669-0114
Fax: (305) 669-9809
E-mail: SEDAC@aol.com
http://www.southeastequity.org/

Serving Alabama, Florida, Georgia, Kentucky, Mississippi, North Carolina, South Carolina, Tennessee

WestEd Center for Educational Equity
4665 Lampson Avenue
Los Alamitos, CA 90720
(562) 598-7661
Fax: (562) 985-9635
E-mail: asancho@wested.org
http://www.wested.org/deseg/welcome.html

Serving Arizona, California, Nevada

NATIONAL FOREIGN LANGUAGE RESOURCE CENTERS

Nine Language Resource Centers are funded by the U.S. Department of Education. Their mission is to improve and strengthen the nation's capacity to teach and learn foreign languages. These centers serve as national resources through their teacher training, research, materials development, and dissemination projects.

Center for Advanced Research on Language Acquisition (CARLA)
Andrew D. Cohen, Director
University of Minnesota
619 Heller Hall
271 19th Avenue South
Minneapolis, MN 55455
(612) 626-8600
Fax: (612) 624-7514
E-mail: carla@tc.umn.edu
http://carla.acad.umn.edu

Center for Language Education and Research (CLEAR)
Susan M. Gass and Patricia R. Paulsell, Codirectors
Michigan State University
A712 Wells Hall
East Lansing, MI 48824
(517) 432-2286
E-mail: gass@msu.edu, paulsell@msu.edu, clear@msu.edu
http://clear.msu.edu/index.asp

Center for Slavic and East European Language Resource Center (SEELRC)
Professor Edna Andrews, Director (Department of Slavic Languages and Literatures)
Duke University & University of North Carolina
Duke University
Box 90260
Durham, NC 27708-0260
(919) 660-3157
Fax: (919) 660-3188
E-mail: cseees@acpub.duke.edu
http://www.duke.edu/web/CSEEES/index.html

Georgetown University
Center for Applied Linguistics and
The George Washington University
James E. Alatis, Director
2600 Virginia Avenue, NW
Suite 105
Washington, DC 20037-1905
(202) 739-0607
Fax: (202) 739-0609
E-mail: nclrc@gwu.edu
http://www.cal.org/nclrc/

National African Languages Resource Center (NALRC)
Antonia Schleicher, Director
University of Wisconsin
4231A Humanities Building
455 N. Park Street
Madison, WI 53706
Tel: (608) 265-7906
Fax: (608) 265-7904

E-mail: ayschlei@facstaff.wisc.edu
http://african.lss.wisc.edu/nalrc/org/index.html

National East Asian Languages Resource Center (NEALRC)
Galal Walker, Director
The Ohio State University
276 Cunz Hall
1841 Millikin Road
Columbus, OH 43210
(614) 292-4361
Fax (614) 292-2682
E-mail: walker.17@osu.edu
http://flc.ohio-state.edu/nflrc/

The National Foreign Language Resource Center
at the University of Hawaii at Manoa
Richard Schmidt, Director
1859 East-West Road #106
Honolulu, HI 96822
(808) 956-9424
Fax: (808) 956-5983
E-mail: schmidt@hawaii.edu
http://www.lll.hawaii.edu/nflrc/

National K–12 Foreign Language Resource Center
Marcia Rosenbusch, Director
Iowa State University and the Center for Applied Linguistics in
Washington, DC
Iowa State University
N131 Lagomarcino Hall
Ames, IA 50011
(515) 294-6699
E-mail: mrosenbu@iastate.edu
http://www.educ.iastate.edu/nflrc/

National Language Resource Center
Mary Ann Lyman-Hager, Director
San Diego State University
5500 Campanile Drive, BAM 424
San Diego, CA 92182-7703
(619) 594-6177
Fax: (619) 594-0511

E-mail: nlrcsd@mail.sdsu.edu
http://ssrl.sdsu.edu/larcnet/home.html

UNIVERSITY-BASED CENTERS

The following university-based centers are among those that generate, analyze, and disseminate knowledge on bilingual education.

Center for Bilingual Education and Research (CBER)
Josué M. González, Director
College of Education, Arizona State University
P.O. Box 871511
Tempe, AZ 85287-1511
(480) 965-7134
Fax: (480) 965-5164
E-mail: josue@asu.edu
http://www.asu.edu/educ/cber/index.htm

This center undertakes policy analysis and scholarship on issues and opportunities related to language, race, and ethnicity. It applies its expertise to contextualizing bilingual and dual-language education in a broader framework of school restructuring and modernization to better serve all children. Among its goals is the development of a binational pedagogy uniquely suited to education in the Mexico/U.S. border area, fast becoming one of the most important binational regions in the hemisphere.

Center for Language Minority Education and Research (CLMER)
J. David Ramirez, Executive Director
College of Education, California State University, Long Beach
1250 Bellflower Boulevard
ED1, Room 18
Long Beach, CA 90840
(562) 985-5806
E-mail: clmer@csulb.edu
http://www.clmer.csulb.edu

The center initiates comprehensive service projects for linguistically, culturally, and ethnically diverse students, families, and communities. These projects address school reform through application of research derived from community learning, critical pedagogy, language acquisition, antiracist education, standards, and technology research.

Center for Multilingual Multicultural Research
Michael Genzuk, Director

Rossier School of Education University of Southern California
Waite Phillips Hall
Los Angeles, CA 90089-0031
E-mail: genzuk@rcf.usc.edu
http://www.usc.edu/dept/education/CMMR/

The center conducts research in multilingual education, English as a Second Language, and foreign-language instruction, multicultural education, and related areas. Among its specialties are teacher and paraprofessional recruitment, preparation, and induction; language policy and language rights; and technology applied to education.

Center for Research on Education, Diversity and Excellence (CREDE)
Roland Tharp, Director

University of California, Santa Cruz
1156 High Street
Santa Cruz, CA 95064
(831) 459-3500
Fax: (831) 459-3502
http://www.crede.ucsc.edu/ and http://www.cal.org/crede/
OERI Contact: Gilbert N. Garcia (202) 219-2144

The purpose of CREDE's research is to identify and develop effective educational practices for linguistic and cultural minority students placed at risk by factors associated with race, poverty, and geographic location. CREDE is one of twelve national research and development centers funded by the U.S. Department of Education, Office of Educational Research and Improvement, National Institute on the Education of At-Risk Students. Links are provided to the other eleven centers. CREDE's mission is carried out in collaboration with its partner universities, centers, and nonprofit organizations across the country. Included in the set of partners are the following organizations:

ARC Southern California

13006 E. Philadelphia Street
Suite 411
Whittier, CA 90601-9408
(562) 907-9408
Fax: (562) 907-6809

Arc's projects assist schools to better serve diverse learners, improve ethnic and race relations, create opportunities for youth and community empowerment, and promote effective use of technology for the twenty-first century.

Art, Research, and Curriculum (ARC) Associates
1212 Broadway
Suite 400
Oakland, CA 94611
(510) 834-9455
Fax: (510) 763-1490
E-mail: arc@arcassociates.org
http://www.arcassociates.org/

Center for Applied Linguistics (CAL)
Donna Christian, President
4646 40th Street, NW
Washington, DC 20016-1859
(202) 362-0700
Fax: (202) 362-3740
E-mail: info@cal.org
http://www.cal.org/

CAL Sunbelt Office
Allene Grognet, Director
630 South Orange Avenue
Suite 103
Sarasota, FL 34236
(941) 953-5387
Fax: (941) 364-9000

The Center for Applied Linguistics is one of the world's premier research and dissemination centers on issues of language, language learning, and culture. The center's current projects address dialects in the classroom, content ESOL, teacher observation guides for second-language teachers, foreign-language education in the early grades, international assessment of second-language education, heritage language, and adult literacy issues. Linguists and educators who staff the center are engaged in research, policy analysis, training activities, conference management, and technical assistance activities.

National Clearinghouse on Bilingual Education (NCBE)
The George Washington University
Center for the Study of Language & Education

2011 Eye Street NW
Suite 200
Washington, DC 20006
(202) 467-0867
(800) 531-9347
(202) 467-4283 (within DC area)
E-mail: askncbe@ncbe.gwu.edu
http://www.ncbe.gwu.edu

The National Clearinghouse on Bilingual Education (NCBE) is a federally funded searchable database with extensive holdings. The function of NCBE is to collect, analyze, and disseminate information relating to the effective education of linguistically and culturally diverse learners in the United States. Center services include mailing lists, publications, electronic newsletters, and Web-site presentations.

School of Education
University of Colorado
UCB 247 Boulder
Colorado 80309-0249
(303) 492-5416
E-mail: Leonard.Baca@colorado.edu
http://www.colorado.edu/education/BUENO/index2.html

The Center promotes high-quality education with an emphasis on cultural pluralism and equal educational opportunities for cultural and language minority students. An annual bilingual-, multicultural-, and special-education institute is hosted by the center each summer.

TERC
Barbara C. Sampson, President and CEO
2067 Massachusetts Avenue
Cambridge, MA 02140
(617) 547-0430
Fax: (617) 349-3535
communications@terc.edu www.terc.edu

TERC is a not-for-profit education research and development organization located in Cambridge, Massachusetts. Its mission is to improve mathematics, science, and technology teaching and learning. TERC's Chèche Konnen ("search for knowledge" in Haitian Creole) Center explores innovative ways to teach science to students whose first language was not English.

The University of California Linguistic Minority Research Institute (UC LMRI)
Russell Rumberger, Director
University of California–Santa Barbara
South Hall
Room 4722
Santa Barbara, CA 93106
(805) 893-2250
Fax: (805) 893-8673
E-mail: infodesk@lmri.ucsb.edu
http://lmri.ucsb.edu/

This center is a multicampus research unit established in 1984 in response to the California legislature's request that the University of California pursue knowledge applicable to educational policy and practice in the area of language minority students' academic achievement and knowledge. Center activities include funding research of UC faculty and graduate students; providing research training for predoctoral and postdoctoral students; and disseminating research findings to researchers, practitioners, and policymakers. Center-sponsored newsletters and other publications, conferences, and mailing lists provide updated information on issues of language, education, and public policy, especially as they relate to linguistic minorities.

Chapter Eight

❧ Print and Nonprint Resources

PRINT RESOURCES

The works listed in this chapter are a sampling of the variety of sources and perspectives available in the literature on bilingual education. The items in this annotated bibliography of print resources are selected from three categories: books, papers, and articles; government publications; and reports from nonprofit organizations and think tanks.

Books, Papers, and Articles

Andersson, T., and M. Boyer. 1978. ***Bilingual schooling in the United States.*** 2d ed. Austin, TX: National Educational Laboratory Publishers.

The first edition of this work provided guidance to those developing programs supported by funds from the Office of Bilingual Education. The second edition, published ten years after passage of the Bilingual Education Act, documents the changes affecting implementation of bilingual programs during the prior decade, describes programs first funded by the Bilingual Education Act, and identifies contextual and historical factors affecting the success of those programs. Of particular relevance to current policy discussions is the chapter on the potential of home-language literacy instruction for preschool children.

Beebe, V. N., and W. F. Mackey. 1990. ***Bilingual schooling and the Miami experience.*** Coral Gables, FL: University of Miami, Institute of Interamerican Studies, Graduate School of International Studies.

This work is an account of Miami's pioneering experience with bilingual education and with the development of the two-way model in the Dade County Public Schools. Beebe is a principal in the Miami-Dade public school system.

Bernal, E. M. April 1994. **Finding and cultivating minority gifted/talented students.** Paper presented at the National Conference on Alternative Teacher Certification. ED391345.

This paper focuses on the selection of students and curricular programming in gifted education. The characteristics of a good teacher of gifted or talented children are also briefly considered.

Bernal, J. J. 1998. **An historic perspective of bilingual education in Texas.** *The Journal of the Texas Association for Bilingual Education* 4, no. 1.

This chronicle by a former state senator of the evolution of bilingual education legislation in Texas includes a description of the major factors supporting its enactment in 1969.

Christian, D., and F. Genesee. 2001. *Bilingual education.* Alexandria, VA: TESOL.

This volume includes descriptions of eleven programs at primary and secondary levels. Recommendations on how to teach bilingually are presented for implementers of programs for (1) learning a majority language, (2) maintaining an indigenous language, and (3) learning an international language.

Crawford, J. October 2000. *At war with diversity: U.S. language policy in an age of anxiety.* Clevedon, England: Multilingual Matters.

Crawford's latest book is a collection of essays on issues surrounding multiculturalism and bilingual education in the United States. He probes the sources and prominence of the antibilingual political movement, its changing directions, and its impact on education policy. Descriptions of efforts to resist the English-only trend, including projects to revitalize Native American languages, are also included in this volume.

Davies Samway, K., and D. McKeon. March 1999. *Myths and realities: Best practices for language minority students.* Portsmouth, NH: Heinemann.

The authors provide background information on forty-five issues in the education of language minority students in a format useful to mainstream teachers, administrators, and policymakers.

Echevaria, J., M. E. Vogt, and D. J. Short. 2000. *Making content compre-hensible for English language learners: The SIOP model.* Boston: Allyn and Bacon.

The authors define a field-tested model for sheltered instruction, present vignettes of classroom lessons to illustrate each of the thirty components of the model, and provide lesson-planning guides and rating forms. These resources for observing and quantifying sheltered teaching are useful tools for teachers, parents, administrators, and researchers.

Freeman, D., and Y. Freeman. 1999. **Checklist for effective practices with English Learners.** *TESOL Matters* (December/January).

This eight-question checklist helps teachers (and parents) determine if key factors leading to school success are included in the school curricu-lum and promoted in classroom instructional practices.

García, D., ed. 1996. *Family centered learning: A project guide for lin-guistically & culturally diverse populations.* Miami, FL: College of Ed-ucation, Florida International University.

The guide provides step-by-step instruction to workshop facilitators on how to train individuals interested in establishing family literacy pro-grams. A training video, a set of overheads, suggested handouts, training forms, and suggested procedures for designing and carrying out train-ing programs are provided. Topics addressed include methodological is-sues in ESL, guidelines for paraprofessionals and volunteers, and legal provisions related to language and culture that affect families from di-verse populations.

Hodgkinson, H. 2001. **Educational demographics: What teachers should know.** *Educational Leadership* 58, no. 4.

Hodgkinson describes the impact of shifting demographics on the stu-dent population in the United States, and how those changes affect teachers and students.

Jenks, F. L. 1997. **The quest for academic legitimacy: Building for lan-guage program entry into institutional and community infrastruc-tures.** In M. A. Christison and F. L. Stoller, eds., *A handbook for lan-guage program administrators.* Burlingame, CA: Alta Book Center Publishers.

Jenks argues that Intensive English Programs must act as full partners in education if they hope to be treated as such, and suggests ways to reach that goal.

Johnson, R. K., and M. Swain, eds. 1997. *Immersion education: International perspectives.* Cambridge: Cambridge University Press.

The authors define immersion education as a category within bilingual education, identify eight core features that distinguish it from other types of second-language programs, define ten variable features that distinguish immersion programs from each other, and describe eleven immersion models that illustrate combinations of the core and variable features.

Krashen, S. January 1999. *Condemned without a trial: Bogus arguments against bilingual education.* Portsmouth, NH: Heinemann.

Krashen presents an analysis and refutation of five myths surrounding bilingual education. His emphasis is on major issues of the debate prior to passage of California's Proposition 227, among them the relationship between bilingual education and the Hispanic dropout rate, immigrants who succeeded without bilingual education, and language policy in other countries.

Lee, S. K. 1999. **The relationship between cultural identity and academic achievement of Asian-American students.** *APA Perspectives* (March).

This article examines the issue of educational attainment from the perspectives of individual Asian American students. The importance of recognizing the educational significance of cultural diversity within the Asian American population is stressed.

Lemberger, N. 1997. *Bilingual education: Teachers' narratives.* Mahwah, NJ: Lawrence Erlbaum Associates.

Lemberger presents narratives from eight experienced bilingual and English as a Second Language (ESL) teachers in New York, California, and Illinois that illustrate what it's like to be a bilingual teacher on a day-to-day basis. The teachers' language backgrounds include Russian, Haitian-Creole, Cantonese/Mandarin, Vietnamese, and Spanish.

Lidman, W. 1999. **Solita: An invisible bilingual education miracle: An ombudsman speaks.** *NJ TESOL/NJ Bilingual Educators Voices* 28, no. 4.
A New Jersey secondary school bilingual educator tells the story of one of his students in a narrative that projects the voices of both teacher and pupil.

Padilla, R. 1998. **Title VII: The ambivalence of language policy in the United States.** *Bilingual Research Journal* 22, no. 1.

Padilla introduces this special issue of the *Bilingual Research Journal* (BRJ) devoted to retrospective analysis of three decades of experience with Title VII by focusing on the negative value attached to individual binguality at the same time that societal bilingualism is positively valued. That inconsistency has characterized language policy during the past thirty years and is reflected in programs that prohibit those for whom a foreign language is not foreign from mastering it.

Pousada, A. 1996. **Puerto Rico: On the horns of a language planning dilemma.** *TESOL Quarterly* 30, no. 3.

Pousada reviews the historical, political, socioeconomic, and educational consequences of language policies in Puerto Rico. Language planning is described and recommended as a means of dealing with language issues.

Reitzel, A. C. 1999. **Service learning, real experiences, and teacher training in intercultural communication.** *TESOL Matters* (June/July).

Preservice teachers' reflection and active self-assessment on service learning are described as one of the best means of learning the principles and practices of intercultural communication. A set of working principles for intercultural communication is presented.

Santiago Santiago, I. 1986. ***Aspira v. Board of Education* revisited (special issue on the education of Hispanic Americans: A challenge for the future).** *American Journal of Education* 95, no. 1.

The Aspira Consent Decree required the implementation of a transitional bilingual-education program in New York City. Santiago argues, however, that the board failed to provide the program to large numbers of children, to systematically monitor implementation, and to evaluate the educational outcomes of the consent-decree program for LEP children. This analysis provides background information useful in understanding contemporary discussions about revisions in bilingual education in New York City.

Skutnabb-Kangas, T. 2000. ***Linguistic genocide in education—or worldwide diversity and human rights?*** Mahwah, NJ: Lawrence Erlbaum Associates.

The author explains that it is normal and desirable for people, groups, countries, and schools to be multilingual and multicultural. A synthesis of theories and information from the areas of linguistic human rights, minority and multilingual education, language ecology, and threatened languages is marshaled to make that point, in support of linguistic human rights.

Sosa, A. 2001. **Through the years: NABE looks back at its history.** *NABE News* 24, no. 3.

The *NABE News* editor presents a description of the organization's goals and leaders and a timeline of major events in the history of bilingual education on the occasion of NABE's twenty-fifth anniversary.

Stepick, A. 1998 *Pride against prejudice: Haitians in the United States.* Needham Heights, MA: Allyn and Bacon.

Stepick illuminates important aspects of the realities of Haitian life in south Florida, thereby giving voice to members of that community and helping to dispel negative stereotypes about them.

Wong Fillmore, L. 2000. **Loss of family languages: Should educators be concerned?** (Children and Languages at School). *Theory into Practice* 39, no. 4.

The phenomenon of language loss is described in terms of its effect on family interaction and socialization processes. In support of additive bilingualism, Wong Fillmore maintains that the family provides children what is most fundamental to success in life. The family's ability to impart the curriculum of the home is seriously compromised when children and adults no longer speak the same language.

Government Publications

de Cos, P. June 1999. *Educating California's immigrant children: An overview of bilingual education.* Technical Report Number CRB 99-009. Sacramento, CA: California Research Bureau, California State Library.

This report includes an examination of the driving forces behind Proposition 227, the context for and history of language policy in California, and the ways parents and districts have sought waivers to its implementation from the state board of education. A review of the literature on instructional programs for English-language learners and an explanation of the relationship between brain development and second-language acquisition and learning are also presented.

Figueroa, R. A., and S. Hernández. May 2000. *Testing Hispanic students in the United States: Technical and policy issues.* Washington, DC: Commission Assessment Committee, President's Advisory Commission on Educational Excellence for Hispanic Americans.

This document presents a rationale for the following thesis: In implementing standards-based reform supported by systems of accountability in the public schools, the educational future of Hispanic students has been compromised by high-stakes decisions based on inaccurate and inadequate testing information. The resulting data are often used to hold accountable only the students, rather than the educators or the public school systems charged with educating them.

Hakuta, K., and A. Beatty, eds. 2000. *Testing English-language learners in U.S. schools: Report and workshop summary.* Committee on Educational Excellence and Testing Equity, Board on Testing and Assessment, Center for Education, National Research Council. Washington, DC: National Academy Press.

The editors summarize problems involved in developing fair testing procedures for English-language learners. They suggest as a partial solution the inclusion of LEP students in testing programs for district accountability purposes, without use of their scores to make promotion or graduation decisions about them when it is inappropriate to do so.

Llanes, J. R. 1996. *Executive summary: Transformation to quality study.* Roma Independent School District and Center for Applied Research in Education (CARE). Edinburg, TX: University of Texas-Pan-American.

Llanes describes efforts to integrate a continuous improvement process as part of school reform in a linguistically isolated community on the border of the United States with Mexico.

New York City Board of Education. December 19, 2000. *Chancellor's report on the education of English language learners.* Brooklyn, NY: Author.

This document is a status report on the progress of English-language learners in New York's public schools. It includes a brief review of related research, a history of the district's Division of Assessment and Accountability (DAA) reports, and a set of recommendations for program revision.

Official Languages Support Programs. 1999. *Official languages: Myths and realities.* Ottawa, Ontario: The Department of Canadian Heritage.

This booklet provides information on the Canadian government's official languages policy and addresses myths such as "bilingualism services cost billions of dollars each year" and "bilingualism is a failure, Canadians don't want it."

U.S. Department of Education. January 1999. *Meeting the needs of migrant students in schoolwide programs: Technical report.* Congressionally Mandated Study of Migrant Student Participation in Schoolwide Programs. Washington, DC: Author.

Using data from a survey and case study analysis of Title I schools, the report examines how effectively migrant students are served within school-wide programs. Results from the study indicate that schools with larger numbers of migrant students, or a more mobile migrant student population, are more likely to address the needs of their migrant students and to integrate them into their school's instructional program.

U.S. General Accounting Office (GAO). 1994. *Limited-English proficiency: A growing and costly educational challenge facing many school districts.* Letter Report, 01/28/94, GAO/HEHS-94-38. Washington, DC: Author.

The GAO finds that the nation's ability to achieve the national education goals is increasingly dependent on its ability to educate LEP students, yet many districts are still struggling to meet this challenge. The report highlights the need to develop a teaching force prepared to educate English-language learners and the instructional and assessment tools they need to increase their effectiveness.

U.S. General Accounting Office. *Public education: Meeting the needs of students with limited English proficiency.* Letter Report, 02/23/2001, GAO/GAO-01-226. Washington, DC: Author.

This report presents a summary of findings on the amount of time needed by English-language learners to meet various standards of English proficiency. The GAO concludes that school district administrators found that officials from the Office for Civil Rights have been helpful in improving programs for LEP students, and were mindful of the effect of different circumstances on the types of programs selected by the districts.

Reports from Nonprofit Organizations and Think Tanks

Adams, W. P. 1990. *The German Americans: An ethnic experience.* Translated by L. J. Rippley and E. Reichmann. Indianapolis, IN: Indiana University, Max Kade German-American Center.

According to the 1990 Census, more Americans claimed German ancestry or ethnic origin than any other. Adams describes the German immigrant experience and the lengthy process leading to their incorporation into the American mainstream. Chapters 6 and 7 of this book describe German-language schools from colonial times to the early nineteenth century. Chapter 7 concludes with a quotation from Kurt Vonnegut's *Palm Sunday* describing the effect of World War I on the use of German in the United States.

Council of Chief School Officers, State Education Assessment Center. December 1998. *Key state education policies on K–12 education: Standards, graduation, assessment, teacher licensure, time and attendance: A 50-state report.* Washington: Author.

This publication provides a wealth of information on the status of educational reform in each of the states.

Dickson, P., and A. Cumming, eds. 1996. *Profiles of language education in 25 countries.* (Language education study of the International Association for the Evaluation of Educational Achievement). Berkshire, England: National Foundation for Educational Research.

This report draws on information gathered in 1995, under the auspices of the International Association for the Evaluation of Educational Achievement, to provide an international overview of the state of language teaching and learning. A profile for each of twenty-five countries is presented.

Epstein, N. 1977. *Language, ethnicity, and the schools: Policy alternatives for bilingual-bicultural education.* Washington, DC: Institute for Educational Leadership, George Washington University.

In this highly influential and equally controversial analysis, Epstein frames the issues surrounding bilingual education, which he equates with assigning to the federal government responsibility for financing and promoting student attachments to their ethnic languages and cultures. The reactions of Drs. José Cárdenas and Gary Orfield to Epstein's synthesis of policy alternatives are part of the volume.

Hajnal, Z., and M. Baldassare. March 2001. *Finding common ground: Racial and ethnic attitudes in California.* San Francisco: Public Policy Institute of California.

This report provides answers to various questions about California's racial and ethnic groups through an analysis of social, political, and economic attitudes in California. Ten statewide surveys of a total of 20,000 adults between April 1998 and May 2000 included a question on bilingual education. When the respondents were asked whether they thought local school districts should be able to decide whether to keep their bilingual education programs, 65 percent of Latinos, 69 percent of Asians, and 71 percent of Blacks said yes.

McLaughlin, B. 1992. *Myths and misconceptions about second language learning: What every teacher needs to unlearn.* Educational Practice Report 5. Santa Cruz: University of California, National Center for Research on Cultural Diversity and Second Language Learning.

The purpose of this report is to clarify commonly held myths or misconceptions in the area of second-language learning, and to show the implications of research in this area for classroom teachers. Topics addressed include the ease and rapidity with which children learn a second language, the optimal age at which to begin instruction in a second language, the importance of the extent of exposure to the second language, the relationship between oral communication skills and academic language skills, and cultural and individual differences in language learning styles.

National Education Association (NEA). 1996. *Official English/English Only: More than meets the eye.* Washington, DC: Author.

The purpose of this update on official English activity since 1988 is to clarify the debate on language issues and encourage the members of NEA to oppose English Only legislation.

Rice, R. *School-To-Work Opportunities Act programs and limited English proficient students: An initial overview.* Somerville, MA: META.

Based on a review of key issues in School-To-Work programs funded by the United States Departments of Education and Labor in 1994 and 1995, Rice finds that schools need to make certain adaptations to ensure full participation and inclusion of LEP students. He recommends that future school-to-work grant-making processes should include a rigorous examination of how applicants propose to achieve equity.

Richman, S. June 1997. ***Bilingual education: A failed experiment on the children.*** Independence Issue Paper. Golden, CO: Independence Institute.

This paper is an examination of bilingual education in Colorado and other public schools, from the point of view of a writer for a conservative, libertarian think tank.

Rossell, C., and K. Baker. 1996. ***Bilingual education in Massachusetts: The emperor has no clothes.*** Boston: Pioneer Institute.

The authors of this Pioneer Institute report conclude that there is no proof that transitional bilingual education in Massachusetts works better than other approaches, such as intensive English instruction.

Rumberger, R. W., K. A. Larson, G. J. Palardy, R. K. Ream, and N. C. Schleicher. 1998. ***The hazards of changing schools for California Latino adolescents.*** *Chicano/Latino Policy Project Brief* 10, no. 7. Berkeley: University of California, California Policy Research Center.

This examination of student mobility among California Latino adolescents describes the causes and educational consequences of non-promotional school change. The report includes recommendations for policy and practice.

Tharp, R. G., and L. A. Yamauchi. 1994. ***Effective instructional conversation in Native American classrooms.*** Educational Practice Report No. 10. Santa Cruz, CA, and Washington, DC: National Center for Research on Cultural Diversity and Second Language Learning.

The instructional conversation (IC) is a dialogue between teacher and learners in which prior knowledge and experiences are woven together with new material to build higher understanding. It contrasts with the "recitation script" often used in the public schools that is characterized by questions from the teacher directed to individual students. When factors related to students' cultural background and the social organization of their school and community are taken into account, and joint productive activity among students and adults is incorporated into the curriculum, IC can be an effective method for raising the academic achievement levels of various groups of Native American and other students.

NONPRINT RESOURCES

The Internet offers a wealth of online resources about bilingual education. Descriptions of selected Web sites and mailing lists are presented in this chapter.

Although locations of Web sites were identified for organizations listed in Chapter 7, those listed in the following section provide extensive information links. Both the general reader and the serious scholar, for example, will find that the National Clearinghouse for Bilingual Education (NCBE) is an impressive resource. Its searchable data banks, full-text articles library, and links sections should be the first stops on the bilingual education information highway. Teachers, parents, administrators, and university students or faculty members looking for information on programs, funding opportunities, and requirements would do well to review the online resources from the Office for Bilingual Education and Minority Language Affairs in the Department of Education, regional comprehensive technical assistance centers, and state education agencies. Links to each of these agencies are maintained by NCBE, its main page highlighting a section on bilingual education offices in state departments of education and teacher-training programs.

Similar services are offered by organizations such as the Center for Applied Linguistics (CAL), the Center for Research on Excellence and Diversity in Education (CREDE), the Center for Advanced Research on Language Acquisition (CARLA), and the Educational Resources Information Center for Languages and Linguistics (ERIC-LL). These organizations present findings from research projects and interpretation of the findings provided by scholars in learned organizations, providing a basis for policy development and program design. Searchable data banks, links to related agencies, and descriptions of recent publications add to the usefulness of their sites.

Advocates for children concerned about possible civil rights violations will find helpful information at the sites maintained by the Office for Civil Rights (OCR), its regional offices, and the Equity Assistance Centers. Educators in search of solutions to problems of daily practice may access the resources offered by professional associations for language teachers, such as the American Council on the Teaching of Foreign Languages (ACTFL), the National Association for Bilingual Education (NABE), and Teachers of English to Speakers of Other Languages (TESOL). Similarly, school administrators and policymakers will find use for the online documents provided by think tanks and policy centers such as the Tomas River Policy Center (TRPI) and the Linguistic Minority Research Institute (LMRI); children's advocacy centers such as Aspira;

and educational governance organizations such as the Council of Chief State School Officers (CCSSO) and the Education Council of the States (ECS).

Education is a value-laden enterprise. Public education depends on the allocation of public resources. For both reasons, education is a highly political activity. Expressions of conflicting value orientations and political preferences related to the politics of bilingual education can be reviewed in the resources available from ethnic group advocacy organizations such as the National Council of La Raza, and from language and immigration restrictionists such as U.S. English.

The last section of this chapter identifies electronic mailing lists related to bilingual education. These resources provide access to online discussions about current issues. The discussions (often archived) and the experts and practitioners who participate in them help translate information into knowledge.

These and additional resources listed in alphabetical order facilitate exploration of the large and growing body of information related to bilingual education.

Web Sites

American Association of University Supervisors and Coordinators and Directors of Foreign Language Programs (AAUSC)
http://www.aausc.org/

This site includes a section with course and program administration materials, and conference and publications announcements. The organization sponsors an electronic mailing list. Online access to the organization's newsletter will be available in the future.

American Council of the Teaching of Foreign Languages (ACTFL)
http://www.actfl.org/

ACTFL is a national organization dedicated to the improvement and expansion of the teaching and learning of all languages at all levels of instruction. See this site for news about the organization, conference announcements, links to resources, national foreign-language proficiency standards, and related information.

Aspira
http://www.aspira.org/

Aspira's mission is empowering the Latino community through the development of its youth. It is the only national nonprofit organization devoted solely to the education and leadership development of Puerto Rican, other Latino, and other minority youth. Aspira takes its name from the Spanish verb *aspirar*, which means "to aspire." Aspira has chapters in Connecticut, Florida, Illinois, New Jersey, New York, Pennsylvania, and Puerto Rico, with 500 staff members who work with over 25,000 youth and their families each year. Its national offices are in Washington, D.C.

Aspira's Web site includes organizational news and history, key documents, and sections for parents, students, educators, and policymakers. The links section includes an excellent set of financial aid resources, and links to each state chapter's Web site.

Association of Departments of Foreign Languages (ADFL)
http://www.ade.org/adfl/index.htm

This is the organizational home for departments of foreign languages and literatures and divisions of humanities at two- and four-year colleges. The ADFL Web site provides access to ADFL statements, reports, enrollment surveys, position announcements, and the current issue of the searchable *ADFL Bulletin*. Members of the organization may search the password-protected archives.

Center for Advanced Research on Language Acquisition (CARLA) at the University of Minnesota
http://carla.acad.umn.edu/CARLA.html

This center is one of nine National Language Resource Centers, whose role is to improve the nation's capacity to teach and learn foreign languages effectively. The site provides an extensive set of links to resources in immersion education (the delivery of the curriculum in a second language to students who share the same first language). It also features links to each of the other national foreign-language centers in the country. The online holdings of all these centers may be accessed from the Language Resource Centers search page at http://nflrc.msu.edu/.

Center for Applied Linguistics (CAL)
http://www.cal.org/

CAL is a research and dissemination center whose specialty in applied linguistics is brought to bear on research, training, technical assistance, policy analysis, and materials development activities. Access is provided to research centers, descriptions of ongoing research, conference announcements, and research reports. Publications from the Center for Research on Education, Diversity, and Excellence (CREDE), and from two

CAL-sponsored clearinghouses (the ERIC Clearinghouse on Languages and Linguistics [ERIC-LL] and the National Clearinghouse for ESL Literacy Education) are also available at the CAL site. It also provides access and links to additional resources on topics such as sheltered instruction, heritage-language education, early foreign-language learning, adult ESL literacy, refugee concerns, and immigrant education.

The site's searchable data banks include: Foreign Language Assessment Database for Grades 9–12; Materials for the Study of the Less Commonly Taught Languages; ESL Standards Implementation Database; Secondary Newcomer Programs in the U.S.; Two-Way Bilingual Immersion Programs in the U.S.

Center for Bilingual Education and Research
http://www.asu.edu/educ/cber/index.html

The *Bilingual Research Journal, Numbers and Needs,* and the archives of Biling, the electronic mailing list of the Bilingual Education Research Special Interest Group (SIG) of the American Educational Research Association (AERA), are available at this Arizona State University site.

Center for Multilingual, Multicultural Research
http://www-rcf.usc.edu/~cmmr/

This University of Southern California site features an excellent clipping collection, especially on California's Proposition 227. The site includes multiple links to resources on language rights, language policy, research, training programs for paraprofessionals, and teacher-training sites.

Center for Research on Education, Diversity, and Excellence (CREDE)
http://www.crede.ucsc.edu/

CREDE is one of twelve national research and development centers funded by the U.S. Department of Education, Office of Educational Research and Improvement (OERI), National Institute on the Education of At-Risk Students. Links are provided on CREDE's site to the other eleven centers, and to its partner organizations. The purpose of CREDE's research is to identify and develop effective educational practices for linguistic and cultural minority students, such as those placed at risk by factors of race, poverty, and geographic location. Summaries of its thirty-project research program are featured on this site, along with online access to Educational Practice Reports, the *Talking Leaves* newsletter, and project documents. A description of center training, evaluation, and technical assistance services is provided.

Civil Rights Organizations

Each of the following nonprofit organizations specializes in aspects of civil rights law affecting language minority students and populations. These groups have brought litigation on behalf of their language minority and other clients on issues such as access to services, school reform, high-stakes testing, education finance, language rights, and immigrant rights.

American Civil Liberties Union (ACLU)
http://www.aclu.org/

The ACLU works to protect the rights guaranteed by the constitution and laws to all persons in the United States. Its Web site includes summaries of pending immigration, language, and education legislation and of court decisions. It includes a search engine to locate items within the site. Links are provided to an archive of materials presented to Congress via correspondence or in-person testimony.

Asian Law Caucus (ALC)
http://www.asianlawcaucus.org/

The Asian Law Caucus is committed to the pursuit of equality and justice for all sectors of our society with a specific focus on addressing the needs of the low-income Asian and Pacific Islanders. The ALC site includes summaries of developments in its areas, such as affirmative action, immigrant rights, civil rights, hate violence, and language rights. The caucus is affiliated with the Asian American Legal Defense and Education Fund in New York and the Asian Pacific American Legal Center in Los Angeles. The caucus is also a founding member of the National Asian Pacific American Legal Consortium in Washington, D.C., which is involved in setting national policies and direction through national legislative advocacy. The site's Community Pages include links to these organizations and to other Asian resources.

Center for Law and Education (CLE)
http://www.cleweb.org/

The Center for Law and Education (CLE) strives to make the right of all students to high-quality education a reality, with an emphasis on assistance to low-income students and communities. Its key education programs and initiatives include Title I, vocational education programs, and school-to-work systems, parent and community involvement, programming for limited English proficient students, education of homeless children, access to higher education, and special education for students with disabilities. The CLE site includes action alerts and links to other advocacy and education organizations related to its areas of emphasis.

Clearinghouse for Immigrant Education (CHIME)
http://www.igc.org/ncas/chime.htm

CHIME, an affiliate of the National Coalition of Advocates for Students, is an interactive database and networking service that facilitates public access to literature, research, and Internet resources that promote the effective education of immigrant students. CHIME offers customized searches of its database to those who call its toll-free number (1-800-441-7192).

Comprehensive Center Network
http://www.ncbe.gwu.edu/tan/ccregions.htm

This site provides links to the fifteen national centers funded by USDE under Title XIII of Improving America's Schools Act of 1994 (IASA). The Comprehensive Centers replace and integrate the functions of previous technical assistance centers serving districts with students in Title I, Migrant, Drug-Free Schools, Title VII, and Indian Education. On the first page of this site, links are provided to current Title VII (Bilingual Education)–funded projects within each state or jurisdiction, and to other federally funded resources within each area.

Cross Site Index: Technical Assistance Centers
http://search.ed.gov/csi/index.html

This search engine can be used to find information from all of the following USDE-funded centers: Educational Resources Information Center (ERIC), Eisenhower Math/Science Regional Consortia and National Clearinghouse, Equity Assistance Centers, Foreign Language Resource Centers, National Research and Development Centers, Regional Educational Laboratories, Regional Resource and Federal Centers Network for Special Education, Regional Technology in Education Consortia, Special Education and Rehabilitation Services, Star Schools Program, Technology Innovation Challenge Grant Sites, Vocational and Adult Education and Literacy, other ED-supported sites, and Federal Resources for Educational Excellence (FREE).

The Eastern Stream Center on Resources and Training (ESCORT)
http://webserver1.oneonta.edu/faculty/thomasrl/

The ESCORT site consists of a list of programs serving migrant students in New York and other states. The list is organized into three areas: Electronic Mailing Lists and News Sources, State Migrant Programs, and Migrant Education Programs Listed by State.

Mexican American Legal Defense and Educational Fund (MALDEF)
http://www.maldef.org/

MALDEF's mission is to protect and promote the civil rights of the more than 35 million Latinos living in the United States. It emphasizes education, testing programs, immigrant rights, language rights, and public resource equity. A summary of policy recommendations presented to the George W. Bush administration, copies of briefs, press releases, action alerts, and a directory of regional offices are available on the MALDEF site.

Multicultural Education Training and Advocacy (META)
http://www.mindspring.com/~allumete/metapages/index.htm

META advocates for equal educational opportunity for low-income, immigrant, and language minority children. META attorneys have been involved in virtually every major legal initiative on behalf of immigrant students and language and other minority communities in the past two decades. Its site provides an overview of its current and prior projects and a useful set of links to book reviews and other resources for bilingual and multicultural education. META's *Handbook for Immigrant Parents* is available in full text on this site. It alerts parents to common problems that immigrant children encounter in U.S. schools, describes the rights of immigrant children, and identifies sources of direct legal assistance.

Native American Rights Fund
http://www.narf.org/

The Native American Rights Fund (NARF) provides legal representation and technical assistance to Indian tribes, organizations, and individuals. Language rights and language education are part of NARF's agenda. The site provides case updates, action alerts, press releases, general information about Indian nations, and access to full-text newsletter articles and to an online library of nearly 12,000 resource materials that relate to federal Indian and tribal law.

Puerto Rican Legal Defense and Education Fund (PRLDEF)
http://www.igc.org/IPR/

The Puerto Rican Legal Defense and Education Fund (PRLDEF) works to secure, promote, and protect the civil and human rights of the Puerto

Rican and wider Latino community through litigation, policy analysis, and education. PRLDEF's current legal work includes cases on language rights and education rights. Its Web site, currently under revision, will soon feature access to the Institute for Puerto Rican Policy (IPR) Publications Library.

Educational Governance and Management Associations

From time to time, these organizations address bilingual and second-language education issues.

American Association of School Administrators (AASA)
http://www.aasa.org/

Access to full-text articles related to bilingual education from the organization's publications is available on this site.

Association of Governing Boards of Universities and Colleges
http://www.agb.org/

Among their top ten policy issues are improving teacher education and increasing diversity on the campus.

Council of Chief State School Officers (CCSSO)
http://www.ccsso.org/

The CCSSO site is a good source of current data from member boards of education in each of the states; its ongoing emphasis is on school reform.

Council of Great City Schools (CGCS)
http://www.cgcs.org/

This is the organizational home for large urban school districts. The organization's policy documents and other information on bilingual education is periodically updated. See their statement on Proposition 227 for an example of their holdings.

Education Council of the States (ECS)
http://www.ecs.org/ecs/ecsweb.nsf

The council membership includes educational leaders from forty-nine states and four additional jurisdictions. Many of the members are elected officials. The council mission is to serve as an interstate planning commission on education. The Web site provides access to many of the documents prepared by council staff to provide guidance to its elected members.

Education Week on the Web
http://www.edweek.org/

This online version of *Education Week* provides excellent coverage of bilingual education issues. A compilation of background information on bilingual education is included in the Hot Topics section of the site.

Educational Resources Information Clearinghouse on Languages and Linguistics (ERIC-LL)
http://www.cal.org/ericcll/

This is one of sixteen federally funded Educational Resources Information Centers that specialize in language and linguistics. ERIC-CLL collects and disseminates information on current developments in multiple aspects of language education, source academic disciplines, and related theory and practice. ERIC-CLL prepares ERIC Digests that provide an overview of what is known about a particular language field and highlight sources of additional information on the topic. The site offers access to full-text copies of *The ERIC Review: K–12 Foreign Language Education,* and to *ERIC/CLL Language Link.* Personalized responses to information requests are provided by ASK ERIC. Questions will be answered within forty-eight hours (in the author's experience, within twenty-four hours, with subsequent follow-up services) by skilled researchers on staff at the center.

Searchable data banks include the National Directory of Early Foreign Language Program; Directory of Total and Partial Immersion Language Programs in U.S. Schools; Directory of Resources for Foreign Language Programs; and Directory of K–12 Foreign Language Assessment Instruments and Resources.

Equity Assistance Centers
http://www.maec.org/daclist.html

Previously known as Desegregation Assistance Centers, this network of technical assistance providers offers services in the areas of race, gender, and national-origin equity. Each center provides a set of links and resources related to equity issues within its service area.

National Conference of State Legislatures (NCSL)
http://www.ncsl.org/login.htm?returnpage=http://www.ncsl.org/

An information service on recurring legislative issues, including education, primarily for elected officials and their staff members. Provides online access to its monthly magazine, *State Legislatures.*

National School Boards Association
http://www.nsba.org/

Links to the Council of Urban Boards of Education, to the annual Education Vital Signs reports, and access to the current issue of the *American School Board Journal* are among the features of this site.

Ethnic Group History and Organizations

**American Memory: Historical Collections from the
Library of Congress**
http://lcweb2.loc.gov/ammem/

Access to more than 7 million digital items from more than 100 historical collections is offered on this site. A search of the site using the term *immigration* resulted in 217 hits.

Divining America: Religion and the National Culture
http://ipmwww.ncsu.edu:8080/tserve/divam.htm

This site is sponsored by TeacherServe, from the National Humanities Center. Access to essays by leading scholars on religion, immigration, and the national culture is available on this site. Essays are presented on topics such as the Jewish and Catholic immigrant experiences, Islam in America, early African religion, and Native American religions.

The National Congress of American Indians
http://www.ncai.org/index.htm

This organization serves the needs of a broad membership of American Indian and Alaska Native governments. The site includes links to tribal governments and Indian nations. Current issues affecting the protection of treaty and sovereign rights are identified.

National Council of La Raza
http://www.nclr.org/

This organization and its many affiliates represent the interests of Hispanic Americans. A policy briefing on affirmative action, an analysis of the 2001 federal budget, and a status report on economic progress for Hispanics are among the reports featured on this site. Issue analyses and action alerts on a broad range of issues affecting Hispanics are accessible from this site.

National Puerto Rican Coalition (NPRC)
http://www.bateylink.org/index.htm

The organization aims to improve the well-being of Puerto Ricans and other Hispanics on the mainland and in Puerto Rico. A directory of elected Puerto Rican officials, historic and current policy documents, and the organization's legislative agenda for the 107th Congress are available on the NPRC site. Education matters are presented in the site's Priority Issues section.

Organization of Chinese Americans (OCA)
http://www.ocanatl.org/

Issues and events of concern to the Chinese community are described on the OCA site.

Race, Ethnicity, and Politics
http://www.providence.edu/polisci/rep/

This site is the online home of the Section on Race, Ethnicity, and Politics of the American Political Science Association. A complete resource page on Asian and Pacific American issues is available online. Similar resources for other ethnic groups are under construction.

Language and Immigration Restrictionist Organizations

American Patrol
http://www.americanpatrol.com/

This site presents a large and current collection of clippings and reports on two basic themes: (1) Immigration is straining the bonds of our union, and (2) the *reconquista* (reconquest of territory now in the United States previously owned by Mexico) conspiracy is under way as part of a demographic war waged by Mexicans.

Center for Equal Opportunity (CEO)
http://www.ceousa.org/

CEO is opposed to multicultural and bilingual education and to affirmative action. The center supports litigation and distributes publications to advance its goals. The Web site is home to the READ Institute, which focuses on bilingual education. The READ site provides access to "campaign notes" from the Proposition 227 campaign in California, and news about the English-only initiatives in Arizona and Colorado. One Nation Indivisible (ONI) also shares space on the CEO site and concentrates on the same goals. ONI, a think tank and lobbying organization, was the official Web site for the Colorado English for the Children Initiative patterned after California's Proposition 227.

English First
http://www.englishfirst.org/

English First goals include making English America's official language and eliminating bilingual education and bilingual ballots. The site is a source of information on the status of Official English legislation, and provides resources in opposition to statehood for Puerto Rico, census forms in languages other than English, bilingual education, and election materials in languages other than English. Tips and techniques for lobbying efforts are suggested.

English Language Advocates (ELA), now named ProEnglish
http://www.elausa.org/index.html

This organization supports Official English legislation and is opposed to bilingual education and the admission of territories as states unless they have adopted Official English laws. The site offers access to news clippings on immigration and language issues and to the organization's newsletter.

English Language Political Action Committee (ELPAC)
http://www.workings.com/elpac.htm

ELPAC was established in 1986 to provide direct support to candidates for political office who support the goals of the organization. Those goals include passage of Official English legislation, teaching children English quickly without attempting to maintain other languages, eliminating multilingual voting materials, setting Official English requirements as a condition for statehood for Puerto Rico, and opposition to federal protection of language rights in the workplace. The ELPAC site provides action alerts and access to a congressional scorecard and a newsletter.

Federation for American Immigration Reform (FAIR)
http://www.fairus.org/

Along with information and tips on lobbying techniques supporting the organization's goals of restricting immigration, resources are available on this site on a number of related issues, including education. A collection of links is provided to census reports at the national, county, metropolitan, and city levels.

Town Hall
http://www.townhall.com

News of research reports and publications from many conservative organizations is available online through the Town Hall Web site. Their affiliated organizations that address bilingual education and language legislation issues include the Heritage Foundation, the Center for Equal Opportunity, and the Pacific Research Institute for Public Policy.

U.S. English
http://www.us-english.org/

This organization lobbies for passage of Official English legislation. Information on the organization's position on issues such as immigration, bilingual education, and statehood for Puerto Rico is available online at this site.

Policy and Information Dissemination Organizations

Joint National Committee for Languages (JNCL)
http://www.languagepolicy.org/jncl.html

The JNCL site includes news on language policies and congressional developments. It identifies and communicates national needs for sixty organizations representing all areas of the language-teaching profession.

Language Policy Research Center
http://www.biu.ac.il/HU/lprc

This center, based at Bar-Ilan University in Israel, carries out basic and applied research on how societies deal with the demands and benefits of multilingualism. Summaries of studies completed by the center are available online.

Language Policy Web Site & Emporium
http://ourworld.compuserve.com/homepages/JWCRAWFORD/

James Crawford, a former *Education Week* editor, maintains this site. It specializes in research on historical and contemporary politics of language, reporting on the English Only movement, English Plus developments, language policy, bilingual education, efforts to save endangered languages, and language rights. Several chapters from his books on these topics are available for viewing online, along with his recent papers and speeches.

Languages Across the Curriculum (L.A.C.) Internet Clearinghouse
http://www.language.brown.edu/LAC/Home_Page.html

Sponsored by the Brown University Language Resource Center, this clearinghouse makes available information on L.A.C. initiatives and procedures.

Linguistic Minority Research Institute (LMRI)
http://lmri.ucsb.edu/

The LMRI research area is educational policy and practice related to language minority students' academic achievement. The LMRI site includes links to ethnic studies and research centers, online newsletters, summaries of research, and a directory of electronic mailing lists.

Migrant Education Technology and Curriculum Resources
http://lone-eagles.com/migrant.htm

This site is a self-styled work in progress, funded by the U.S. Department of Education. It includes Spanish-language translators, search engines, curriculum units, links to federal and state migrant resources, and descriptions of technology-based programs for migrant students.

National Association for Bilingual Education (NABE)
http://www.nabe.org/

NABE is the only national organization exclusively concerned with the education of language minority students in the United States. NABE's Web site, currently under revision, includes news on pending legislation, an archive of news clippings on language minority Americans, Portraits of Success (descriptions of successful programs), and conference program overviews for current and previous annual conferences. The site provides a complete set of conference registration materials.

National Association for Multicultural Education (NAME)
http://www.nameorg.org/

NAME's concerns are diversity and equity, including but not limited to issues related to language and culture. The NAME site includes conference and publication announcements, a list of films shown at the NAME annual film festival, information about the organization and its state chapters, access to full-text articles, and links to resources. The Reference Library section includes a News Song Library along with suggestions for its use in multicultural education activities.

National Clearinghouse for Bilingual Education (NCBE)
http://www.ncbe.gwu.ed

The National Clearinghouse for Bilingual Education (NCBE) is funded by the U.S. Department of Education's Office of Bilingual Education and Minority Languages Affairs (OBEMLA) to collect, analyze, and disseminate information relating to the education of linguistically and culturally diverse learners in the United States. NCBE provides information through its publications and through its Web site, which includes the NCBE Online Library (a well-catalogued collection of full-text articles), Newsline (a biweekly e-mail news bulletin), and the NCBE Roundtable (an electronic discussion group). Census 2000 data are available on its State Pages. Its Bibliographic Database provides access to over 20,000 citations and abstracts from a variety of sources. Descriptions of effective programs and practices are available in a large and frequently updated collection on NCBE's Success Stories page. Another entry point to the holdings of this clearinghouse is the Language and Education page, which includes links to sources of information on aspects of the overall topic, and to resources for finding funding opportunities, jobs, and instructional material.

National Clearinghouse for ESL Literacy Education (NCLE)
http://www.cal.org/ncle/

This clearinghouse, sponsored by ERIC-CLL and CAL, provides access to articles about teaching English as a Second Language to adults in the United States, online newsletters, annotated bibliographies, and conference announcements.

National Clearinghouse for Multicultural/Bilingual Education
http://www.weber.edu/mbe/htmls/mbe.html#index

This site provides a directory of commercial and noncommercial sources of materials for multicultural and bilingual/ESL programs.

National Council of State Supervisors of Foreign Languages (NCSSFL)
http://www.ncssfl.org/

The NCSSFL site provides access to annual state reports on the status of foreign-language education. The site includes links to every state's foreign-language association, department of education, statement of curriculum standards, and graduation requirements.

National Foreign Language Resource Centers
http://polyglot.cal.msu.edu/nflrc/

Search the Web pages of all nine centers from this page. See especially CARLA for information on content teaching through the target language, and for immersion education information.

National Network for Early Language Learning (NNELL)
http://www.educ.iastate.edu/nnell/

The mission of the organization is to promote opportunities for all children to develop a high level of competence in at least one language in addition to their own. See the Political Action section for current issues and directory information for congresspersons, and the Journal section for sample articles.

Office for Civil Rights
http://www.ed.gov/offices/OCR/

The Office for Civil Rights enforces five federal statutes that prohibit discrimination in education programs and activities that receive federal financial assistance. Discrimination on the basis of race, color, and national origin is prohibited by Title VI of the Civil Rights Act of 1964. Policy statements, instructions for filing a complaint, and answers to frequently asked questions are available on this site.

Office of Bilingual Education and Minority Language Affairs (OBEMLA)
http://www.ed.gov/offices/OBEMLA/

News of funding opportunities, copies of proposal application guidelines, conference announcements, and links to sources of technical assistance are available at this site.

Teachers of English to Speakers of Other Languages (TESOL)
http://www.tesol.edu/index.html

The term *TESOL* refers both to the field and to the professional organization. This is the site for the professional organization. TESOL membership is international; it includes the spectrum of educators involved with the education of English-language Learners. TESOL differs from English instruction for native speakers in that its primary foci are language and cultural practices in English-speaking countries, as opposed to English literature. The program for the next annual conference, as well as abstracts from the previous year's conference, sample articles from publi-

LIM-A

LIM-A is a mailing list for discussions about language immersion programs. Teachers, administrators, and parents are welcome to join. To subscribe, send the following message: subscribe lim-a yourfirstname yourlastname

Send the message to:
LISTSERV@tc.umn.edu

NAME-MCE

This is the only official mailing list of the National Association for Multicultural Education (NAME). This is a moderated e-mail discussion group focusing on classroom and institutional practices. One of its goals is to nurture those new to multicultural education who seek a supportive environment for the exchange of ideas and best practices. To subscribe, send the following message: subscribe NAME-MCE your first and last name

Send the message to:
listserv@umdd.umd.edu

Ñandu

Ñandu is a mailing list devoted to discussion of foreign-language learning in grades K–8. To subscribe, send the following message: subscribe your firstname your lastname

Send the message to:
nandu-request@caltalk.cal.org

NIFL-ESL

NCLE moderates this electronic discussion forum sponsored by the National Institute for Literacy (NIFL) on ESL literacy instruction and policy issues. To subscribe, send this message: Subscribe NIFL-ESL your firstname lastname

Send the message to:
listproc@literacy.nifl.gov

TESOL-Advo

The TESOL advocacy listserv for language and language learning issues in the USA is open to all TESOL members. To subscribe, send this message: subscribe tesol-advo "your name"
Send the message to:
lyris@lyris.tesol.edu

TESOL-L

The purpose of this listserv is discussion of classroom issues for Teachers of English to Speakers of Other Languages. Messages and documents may be retrieved from the archives. To subscribe to the list, send this message: subscribe tesl-l your firstname lastname

Send the message to:
listserv@cunyvm.cuny.edu

◆◆ Index

✎ About the Author

Rosa Castro Feinberg is an associate professor of education in the Department of Educational Foundations and Professional Studies at Florida International University.